GLOBALIZATION
AND CULTURE

GLOBALIZATION

Series Editors

Manfred B. Steger

*Royal Melbourne Institute of Technology
and University of Hawai'i–Mānoa*

and

Terrell Carver

University of Bristol

"Globalization" has become *the* buzzword of our time. But what does it mean? Rather than forcing a complicated social phenomenon into a single analytical framework, this series seeks to present globalization as a multidimensional process constituted by complex, often contradictory interactions of global, regional, and local aspects of social life. Since conventional disciplinary borders and lines of demarcation are losing their old rationales in a globalizing world, authors in this series apply an interdisciplinary framework to the study of globalization. In short, the main purpose and objective of this series is to support subject-specific inquiries into the dynamics and effects of contemporary globalization and its varying impacts across, between, and within societies.

 Supported by the Globalization Research Center at the University of Hawai'i, Mānoa

GLOBALIZATION AND CULTURE

GLOBAL MÉLANGE

THIRD EDITION

JAN NEDERVEEN PIETERSE

ROWMAN & LITTLEFIELD
Lanham • Boulder • New York • London

Published by Rowman & Littlefield
A wholly owned subsidiary of The Rowman & Littlefield Publishing Group, Inc.
4501 Forbes Boulevard, Suite 200, Lanham, Maryland 20706
www.rowman.com

Unit A, Whitacre Mews, 26-34 Stannary Street, London SE11 4AB, United Kingdom

Copyright © 2015 by Rowman & Littlefield
First edition 2003. Second edition 2009.

British Library Cataloguing in Publication Information Available

Library of Congress Cataloging-in-Publication Data

Nederveen Pieterse, Jan.
  Globalization and culture : global mélange / Jan Nederveen Pieterse. — Third edition.
    pages cm. — (Globalization)
  Includes bibliographical references and index.
  ISBN 978-1-4422-2254-0 (cloth : alk. paper) — ISBN 978-1-4422-2255-7 (pbk. : alk. paper) — ISBN 978-1-4422-2256-4 (electronic) 1. Globalization. 2. Globalization—Moral and ethical aspects. 3. Globalization—Political aspects. 4. Acculturation. 5. Popular culture. I. Title.
  JZ1318.N43 2015
  303.48'2—dc23

                                                          2014042272

∞™ The paper used in this publication meets the minimum requirements of American National Standard for Information Sciences—Permanence of Paper for Printed Library Materials, ANSI/NISO Z39.48-1992.

Printed in the United States of America

CONTENTS

PREFACE TO THE THIRD EDITION

Major changes in this edition are an overhaul of chapter 1, an additional chapter on hybrid China, and many refinements. Chapter 1 needed revision because discussions of globalization have moved on and the profile of agreements and disagreements on globalization has changed. Throughout the book I have made the usual refinements and updates. Codas that were added in the second edition have been integrated into the chapter texts. Work I have done in the meantime has affected my approach to globalization. From 2007 I co-organized seven Global Studies conferences (in Chicago, Dubai, Busan, Rio de Janeiro, Moscow, New Delhi, and Shanghai), which meant engagement with many regional discussions on globalization (and several co-edited volumes on regional developments). Work on emerging economies and on histories of globalization and ancient Rome has also affected my approach. The chapter on hybrid China focuses on the key issue of agency and power in hybridization, which is important in emerging economies generally, with China as a particularly momentous case. This chapter draws a key distinction between passive and active forms of globalization (globalized and globalizing) and hybridity (being hybridized and hybridizing).

PREFACE TO THE SECOND EDITION

Globalization and culture is a live-wire theme in constant flux—in lifestyles, cross-cultural encounters, migration, global-local relations, music, media, movies, marketing, fashion, cuisine, and so forth. As the dynamics of globalization change—and in the twenty-first century they are changing markedly, even dramatically—so do not just the tides but the shorelines of culture. Probably the most significant change since this book was first published has been the rise of the global South as a driver of the world economy and global change. This dynamic isn't new but its pace has quickened and its scope widened, with changes in international trade policy (such as the World Trade Organization), the rise of industries and multinationals from the South, the impact of sovereign wealth funds from the South in finance and investing, the growing demand for commodities, and growing South-South and East-South relations. Over time this sea change in globalization will show its imprint in cultural styles and flows. For some two hundred years, since 1800, globalization was shaped and determined by North-South relations with a clear, often overwhelming dominance of the North in economic, political and cultural spheres. Eurocentrism, cultural imperialism, and Orientalism in knowledge and cultural styles, and the palette of western images and prejudices about the Orient and the global South have been familiar testimonies of this hegemony.

Most globalization literature took shape during the 1980–2000 phase of globalization when neoliberalism and American hegemony were the overriding trends. So keynotes of globalization literature have been critiques of neoliberalism and of structural adjustment policies that Washington institutions prescribed for developing countries, along with critiques of American hegemony. During the past two decades, these features have gradually weakened. Neoliberalism and American hegemony have not left the stage, of course, but they are past their peak and face mounting problems. A new phase of globalization has begun in which emerging societies play a greater role. I discuss these changes in the closing section of chapter 1 (and in chapter 7).

The major thrust of this book is that globalization in cultural terms tends toward a global mélange. This is essentially a book about globalization as hybridization. Chapter 3 introduces this perspective as one of three major paradigms of globalization and culture. Chapter 4 sets forth the hybridization argument in detail. Chapter 5 responds to critics of hybridity or the anti-hybridity backlash. Chapter 6 develops it in East-West relations.

When some of the material of this book was first written (one article was originally published in 1995) it was pioneering. At the time hybridity was mainly argued in postcolonial studies; in social science generally the other two paradigms—cultural homogenization and differentialism—were more prominent. Over the last ten years or so this has changed radically. Hybridity has become a regular, almost ordinary fixture in popular and mainstream culture—widely recognized as "The Trend to Blend." The Tiger Woods and Barack Obama aesthetic and sensibility—pardon the shorthand—have become standard fixtures in media and marketing. In social science and cultural studies, hybridity is inching up to become the leading paradigm with a steadily growing literature. Cultural studies take hybridity as a point of departure; region and country studies use hybridity perspectives as analytics. Criticisms of hybridity arguments, of the kind discussed in chapter 5 persist, but the thrust and appeal of everyday and experiential hybridity is unstoppable and outflanks the criticisms. The point of most discussion now is not to argue for or against hybridity but to explore finer points and meanings of hybridity. Since "everything is hybrid," hybridity is an avalanche and discussing examples of hybridity is like drinking from a fire hydrant. It follows that only those forms of hybridity are worth discussing that illuminate the variety, spread, depth, and meaning of hybridity, or shed light on history, past or future.

Since the first edition appeared, additional material under each of the book's headings has piled up higher than I could do justice to while keeping this a reasonably tight volume. I find there are reasons to fine-tune and update perspectives but not to fundamentally revise the core argument. In this edition I have made additions to the text as codas to chapters 1, 3, and 4 (and some minor changes in the text). The codas point to wider arguments and present *faits divers* that fine-tune or illustrate trends and debates. The major new addition is a chapter on *East-West Osmosis*, which develops the idea of globalization as braiding or interlacing influences and applies this with historical perspective on a particularly sensitive zone of cultural encounters, in a section devoted to Islam and Europe (chapter 6).

This book probably owes much of its appeal and bite to its combination of traits. I am originally an anthropologist, and anthropology is a savvy perspective on "culture." I have done extensive work in history, and globalization is a deeply historical theme. I have also worked on visual cultural studies, which is an appealing sensibility. I have done work on global political economy and development studies, which lends the treatment an edge beyond culture for culture's sake and embeds globalization and culture alongside political economy. Let me briefly refer to work I have done since this book came out. A sequel to this book focuses on ethnicity, migration, and multiculturalism and introduces a new perspective, global multiculture (Nederveen Pieterse 2007). I have also done work on the political economy of globalization and hegemony (2004), on the United States and globalization (2008a), and on new trends in twenty-first-century globalization (2008b, Nederveen Pieterse and Rehbein 2009).

I have kept the character of this book as a tight and fluent treatment, concise and focused rather than sprawling and cumbersome, so it serves not merely scholarly purposes as a critical, probing treatment of a vital and salient domain of globalization, but educational purposes as well.

ACKNOWLEDGMENTS

Early versions of several chapters appeared in journals or books. I gratefully acknowledge the permission of Sage Publications to reuse chapter 5 here. The material of several chapters has been discussed in seminars and I thank participants in all these occasions for sharing their reflections, in particular Durre Ahmed in Lahore, Mike Featherstone, the late Marian Kempny, Brigitte Kossek, Kobena Mercer, Everlyn Nicodemus, and Kazuhiko Okuda. I thank Emin Adas for references. I appreciate Manfred Steger and Terrell Carver's invitation to contribute the inaugural volume to their book series *Globalization*.

Versions of the first chapter were presented at seminars at Bergen University, Erasmus University in Rotterdam, CERFE in Rome, and other places; it appeared in an Italian translation. Chapter 2 appeared in *Futures* (32, no. 5 [2000]); I thank Ivan Light for references. The material of chapter 3 has been discussed at Meiji Gakuin University in Yokohama, the International University of Japan in Niigata, a counter-racisms conference in Vienna, the Polish Academy of Sciences in Warsaw, the Jan van Eyck Akademie in Maastricht, the Centre for Cultural Research at Aarhus University, and the Society for the Humanities of Cornell University. It was published in *Economic and Political Weekly* (31, no. 23 [1996]), in a volume published in Japan, and in Russian and German translations. Chapter 4 appeared in *International Sociology* (9, no. 2 [1994]) and in Mike Featherstone, Scott Lash, and Roland Robertson's volume *Global Modernities* (1995). It appeared in several other collections and in German and Chinese translations. Chapter 5 was originally prepared for the panel "Whatever Happened to Hybridity?" organized by Kobena Mercer at the New School for Social Research, New York, 2000. I thank Alev Cinar for commenting on an earlier version. It was discussed at the National College of Arts in Lahore and appeared in *Theory, Culture and Society* (18, nos. 2–3 [2001]) and in Scott Lash and Mike Featherstone's *Recognition and Difference* (2002). It has since been translated into Spanish.

Nezar AlSayyad dedicates his volume on *Hybrid Urbanism* "To the peoples of hybrid persuasions." I simply dedicate this book to everyone, on the assumption that everyone is hybrid.

ACKNOWLEDGMENTS TO THE SECOND EDITION

In response to the first edition friends and colleagues approached me with comments and advice, among others Daniel Araya, Sergio Costa, Vittorio Cotesta, Jeroen Dewulf, Jacob Hickman, Sang-Dawn Lee, Bhikhu Parekh, Andy Pickering, Amit Prasad, Gerhard Preyer, Fazal Rizvi, Livio Sansone, and Gerhard Wagner. Gernot Saalmann invited me to contribute to a volume on hybridity that was published in Germany; an early version of chapter 6 was a contribution to this volume (edited by Dominique Schirmer, Gernot Saalmann, and Christl Kessler, 2006). Claudio Baraldi in Modena prepared an Italian translation (Rome: Carocci, 2005). Many students made insightful critical comments and excellent enlightening papers, among others Hannah Cohen, Kristina Filippello, Steven Friberg, I-Chung Ke, Jongtae Kim, Jong-Young Kim, Kareem Muhammad, Reem Rahman, Rebecca Rohloff, and Christine Varghese. I thank them all.

ACKNOWLEDGMENTS TO THE THIRD EDITION

At Maastricht University I held a part-time chair on globalization and culture (2008–2011, and honorary professor 2011–2014), and I appreciate the contributions of many colleagues, including Ulrike Brunotte, Veronica Davidov, Rene Gabriels, Wiebe Nauta, and Ihab Saloul. I have benefited from many more encounters than I can credit here, but I single out Chan Kwok-bun in Hong Kong and his work on hybridity in Asia, Daniel Vukovich in Hong Kong, Surichai Wungaeo at Chulalongkorn University in Bangkok, and Changgang Guo at Shanghai University. At National University of Malaysia (UKM), I now hold the Pok Rafaeh research chair (2014–2015).

INTRODUCTION

Globalization and culture is a well-established theme. It has first come up in the work of Roland Robertson (1992) with considerable finesse. Robertson originally came to globalization as a sociologist of religion, so culture is fundamental to his perspective. In globalization studies, culture is prominent in the work of anthropologists, many sociologists, and in comparative literature, media, and cultural studies.

A common thesis in media and cultural studies is global cultural homogenization. Another recurrent theme, particularly in the context of political science and political journalism, is ethnic politics (ethnic cleansing and new nationalisms) and religious fundamentalism, suggesting a link between globalization and local identity politics and a combination of integration and fragmentation. Consequently much literature is polarized in diagnosing either growing global cultural uniformity (in the trail of commodification, consumerism) or, on the other hand, increasing cultural differentiation, a kind of global "Lebanonization" or cultural fragmentation. While culture figures in many treatments, it often does so as the annex of another paradigm or problematic. A trend in sociology is to revisit, through globalization, the discussion on modernity, and a trend in political economy is to revisit, through globalization, debates on capitalism. The career of globalization coincides then with the career of modernity (1800 plus) or with that of (modern) capitalism (1500 plus). Other approaches focus on the relations between late capitalism and culture. Both modernity and capitalism are quite pertinent, but if discussing globalization is another way to continue the conversation on modernity, there is a risk of carrying on an Atlantic conversation extrapolated to planetary scope. Would it make sense to expect treatments of globalization to be global in spirit?

Distinctive about this book is that it takes a historically deep approach, problematizes culture, and develops the perspective of global mélange or hybridization. Hybridity, a theme that is both well established and controversial, is the leitmotif in this work. I develop this in several chapters and try to make this a comprehensive treatment. In developing this perspective, I take a distinctive position in the analysis of globalization, one that is historically deep and geographically wide. Most globalization studies tend to be confined to a narrow time frame. Most economists view globalization as a matter of the past decades. For social movements and organizations such as the World Social Forum the key issue is neoliberal capitalism, so engagement with globalization becomes a polemic with neoliberalism. I share this concern (and discuss it in several publications), but I also find that globalization refers to a much wider and deeper human rendezvous. This is particularly relevant in relation to culture. As pressing or momentous as current issues are, there is more to globalization than its current form. A deep historical perspective on globalization is a view held by several anthropologists, historians, archeologists, and paleontologists. Taking a long view has profound consequences for one's understanding of globalization. Usually one's choice of discipline and, within a discipline, one's choice of outlook and problematics are shaped by one's biography and reflect existential dispositions. This certainly applies in my case.

While most of my work has been in sociology, development studies, political economy, and intercultural studies, I'm an anthropologist by training. At the University of Amsterdam at the time, cultural anthropology was synonymous with "nonwestern sociology," so the line between anthropology and sociology was thin. My family background also shapes my outlook. I am from a Dutch East Indies colonial family. One ancestor allegedly came to Java in the 1600s as a "noble-merchant" with the Dutch East Indies Company (VOC). The family remained in Java and the archipelago over three hundred years, mixed with Javanese, Sulawesi, Portuguese, French, Germans, and others, and steeped in Indo-Dutch mestizo culture (known as "tempo doeloe"). My father's line goes back to the East Indies from the early 1800s. The family came to the Netherlands only after the Second World War. I was born in Amsterdam eleven days after their arrival, the only member of the family born outside Indonesia for many generations. We are therefore Eurasians and hybrid in a genealogical and existential sense. This is not a matter of choice or preference but a just so circumstance. That it happens to be a matter of reflection is because my work is social science. My family history then is steeped in the history of western expansion, colonialism, and intercontinental migration. And this is only the known, recorded history. I don't mention this because I think it is unusual but rather because I think it is common; one way or another, we are all migrants. I feel affinity with the world's migrants and am inclined to view human history in a global setting, not merely since the past fifty years or so but for thousands of years. My choice of studying anthropology reflects this background. My personal history includes several intercontinental migrations: to West Africa to teach sociology in Ghana; to the United States to study global sociology, which at the time meant world-system theory; to the Netherlands, where I taught at an international graduate school of development studies; again to the United States to work on global sociology and global studies; and to Southeast Asia for a one-year research chair at National University of Malaysia.

These themes run through several chapters. Chapter 1 discusses the perspectives of different social science disciplines on globalization and their widely divergent time frames. Chapter 2 sets forth outlines of a deep historical approach to globalization. Globalization and modernity are discussed in chapters 2, 4, and 8. Chapter 5 discusses global mélange in the *longue durée*. And chapter 6 does so with respect to the interlacing of East and West influences. Chapter 7 takes up hybridity in China.

A brief guide to the chapters is as follows. The first chapter sets forth the general problematic of globalization by presenting areas of agreement and dispute in the literature. Globalization invites more controversy than consensus, and different disciplines hold widely diverse views on the fundamentals of globalization. Late-twentieth-century globalization comes in a package together with informatization and flexibilization in production and labor, while neoliberal globalization adds deregulation, financialization, and marketization. Twenty-first-century trends include the rise of emerging economies.

Chapter 2 asks whether globalization involves a trend toward human integration and develops a historical perspective on globalization. Visions of human unity are part of our legacy, but have been confronted with steep and growing inequality. Globalization is a long-term, uneven, and paradoxical process in which widening social cooperation and deepening inequality go together. This perspective is examined from the point of view of migration and diasporas, whose role has long been underestimated.

Chapter 3 takes us directly into the globalization and culture debate. This chapter finds that there are three fundamentally different paradigms of cultural difference: differences are lasting; they yield to growing homogenization; and they mix, generating new differences in the process. Thus, according to the "clash of civilizations" view, cultural difference is enduring and generates rivalry and conflict. In the second view, global interconnectedness leads to increasing cultural convergence, as in the global sweep of consumerism, in short, "McDonaldization." The third position holds that what have been taking place are processes of mixing or hybridization across locations and identities. This approach is elaborated in two chapters on global mélange.

Chapter 4 sets forth the thesis of globalization as hybridization. Globalization is often interpreted as a process of homogenization, but does this make sense considering there are multiple globalization processes at work? Globalization is also often tied up with modernity, but this amounts to a theory of westernization, which is geographically narrow and historically shallow. This chapter argues for viewing globalization as hybridization—structural and institutional hybridization or the emergence of new, mixed forms of social cooperation, and cultural hybridization, or the development of translocal mélange cultures. Theorizing hybridity and examining the politics of hybridity shows the variety of hybridities, on a spectrum from mimicry to coun-terhegemony. Two distinct concepts of culture are in use—territorial and translocal, inward and outward looking—which produce divergent views on cultural relations and globalization. Hybridization refers to the closed concept of culture and to its opening up, in the process ush-ering in post-hybridity.

Chapter 5 develops this perspective further in response to criti-cisms of hybridity. According to anti-hybridity arguments, hybridity is inauthentic and "multiculturalism lite." Examining these arguments provides an opportunity to deepen and fine-tune perspectives. What is missing in the anti-hybridity arguments is historical depth; this treat-ment deals with the *longue durée* and suggests multiple historical *layers of hybridity*. The chapter next turns to the politics of boundaries for the real problem is not hybridity, which is commonplace throughout history, but boundaries and the social proclivity to boundary fetishism. Hybridity is a problem only from the point of view of essentializing boundaries. What hybridity means varies not only over time but also in different cultures, and this informs different *patterns of hybridity*. In the end, the importance of hybridity is that it problematizes boundaries.

Chapter 6 deals with the braiding and interlacing of East-West and Islam-Europe influences and offers historical elaborations of mélange perspectives. Chapter 7 deals with hybridity in the momentous case of China and discusses the role of agency and power in hybridization, which offers a perspective on hybridity that is markedly different from most literature. Chapter 8 rounds off with a brief coda.

CHAPTER 1

GLOBALIZATION: CONSENSUS AND CONTROVERSIES

"Globalization" is both an historical fact and a political football.

—Stephen Toulmin (1999)

Globalization is like a prism in which major disputes over the collective human condition are now refracted: questions of capitalism, inequality, power, development, ecology, culture, gender, identity, population, all come back in a landscape where "globalization did it." Like a flag word, globalization sparks conflict. Globalization crosses boundaries of government and business, media and social movements, general and academic interest. As a political challenge, it crosses the ideological spectrum and engages social movements and politics at all levels. It involves a paradigm shift from the era of the nation state and international politics to politics of planetary scope.

This chapter gives an overview of globalization debates to situate questions of globalization and culture in a wider context and to show that major issues come up in other debates as well. Now some decades into the sprawling globalization debate, the literature is advanced enough to begin to identify areas of consensus and controversy. This bird's-eye overview focuses on the major debates; within each terrain there are numerous subsidiary debates, but that kind of treatment would require a book in itself.

Among analysts and policy makers, North and South, there is an emerging consensus on several features of globalization: globalization is being shaped by technological changes, involves the reconfiguration of states, goes together with regionalization, and is uneven. Another common understanding, that globalization means time-space compression, may be vague enough not to cause much stir. It means that globalization involves more intensive interaction across wider space and in shorter time than before, in other words, the experience of a shrinking world; yet this may also be too simple and flat an account. There is ample controversy about what these features mean, so it's not easy to draw a line between the consensus and controversies on globalization. Globalization invites more controversy than consensus, and the areas of consensus are narrow by comparison to the controversies. Controversies in relation to globalization are, in brief: Is globalization a recent or a long-term phenomenon? What is the definition of globalization? The use and abuse of the global. Is globalization neoliberal capitalism? And is globalization manageable? Older controversies, going back to the 1990s, are whether globalization is multidimensional or essentially economic, and whether globalization actually exists or is globaloney. These have now faded, but I will review the arguments.

A précis of areas of agreement and dispute is in table 1.1. Questions of globalization and culture are taken up in other chapters. The treatment follows this agenda with vignettes under each of these headings.

CONSENSUS

GLOBALIZATION IS BEING
SHAPED BY TECHNOLOGICAL CHANGE

A thread that runs through all globalization episodes and discourses is increasing connectivity. The boom in information and communications technologies (ICT) forms part of the infrastructure of globalization in

Table 1.1. Consensus and Controversies in Relation to Globalization

Consensus
- Globalization is being shaped by technological change
- Involves the reconfiguration of states
- Goes together with regionalization
- Is uneven

Controversies
- Is globalization multidimensional?
- Does globalization exist?
- Is globalization a recent or long-term historical process?
- What is "globalization"?
- Use and abuse of the global
- Is globalization neoliberal capitalism?
- Is globalization manageable?

finance, capital mobility and export-oriented business activity, transnational communication, migration, travel, and civil society interactions.

Information and microelectronics-based computer and telecommunications technologies since the early 1980s provide the technical means for *financial globalization*, such as twenty-four-hour electronic trading. They create the conditions for global product information and thus for the *globalization of demand*. Global marketing and the attempt to establish global brand names has made for an increase in global advertising expenditures from $39 billion in 1950 to $256 billion in 1990, growing three times faster than trade. By facilitating communications within and between firms, information technologies further enable the *globalization of supply*. For firms, the shortening life cycle of products leads to pressure to expand market shares to amortize growing research and development (R&D) costs. This prompts the *globalization of competition* and corporate tie-ups, mergers, and acquisitions to handle the cost and risks of R&D and global marketing.

Together the globalization of finance, demand, supply, and competition forms a series of interlocking flows of global circulation of information, which is wired in turn to the flexibilization of production. At issue are not simply the growth of international trade and the role of transnational corporations, but a new system of industrial organization, which is variously termed flexible specialization, flexible accumulation, lean manufacturing, just-in-time capitalism, or Toyotism. The shift from standardized mass production to flexible production systems, from Fordism to post-Fordism (D. Harvey 1989), involves greater flexibility in the organization of production, labor and enterprises, location, and marketing. These changes ramify throughout the international division of labor. Neoliberal trends since the 1980s result in deregulation of economies and informalization. Further developments include the new economy, e-commerce, dot-com, and mobile technologies.

At times this is interpreted in the sense that globalization is *driven* by technological change. But technology itself is socially embedded and shaped; technological determinism is not appropriate. What matters is not technology per se but the way it is harnessed by economic, political, and social forces. Technological changes and their ramifications contribute to the impression that globalization is "inevitable," "unstoppable." A reality underlying this is that globalization is a *macroeconomic phenomenon that is also driven by micro-economic forces*, that is, on the level of firms. The opportunities that new technologies provide apply not merely to transnational corporations but also to small and medium-size firms. Globalization is not merely driven by major corporations, international institutions, and governments but also by social forces, including consumers and social movements.

Globalization involves major changes in the economic landscape that are all intertwined: accelerated globalization comes in a *package* together with informatization, flexibilization, and deregulation. This package effect contributes to the dramatic character of the changes associated with globalization. In effect, globalization serves as the shorthand description of these changes. Since "globalization" per se refers to a spatial process, that is, world-scale effects (precisely of what is not determined), the term itself is inadequate but serves as a stand-in for or flag word signaling wider changes.

GLOBALIZATION INVOLVES THE RECONFIGURATION OF STATES

Earlier analyses claimed that globalization leads to the retreat and erosion of states (Strange 1996). According to a radical view, globalization means the onset of a borderless world (Ohmae 1992), the end of the nation state and the formation of region states (Ohmae 1995). Stephen Kobrin notes, "A critical issue raised by globalization is the lack of meaning of geographically rooted jurisdictions when markets are constructed in electronic space" (1998: 362). Thus, a general account of the political implications of globalization is the erosion of boundaries and the growth of crossborder and supraterritorial relations (Scholte 2000). These arguments now come with more nuanced views about the role of states.

According to sociological perspectives on globalization, the *form* of globalization from the nineteenth century onward was the growing predominance of nation states (Roland Robertson 1992). Between 1840 and 1960, nation states were the leading format of political organization worldwide (Harris 1990). From the 1960s, regionalization has come into the picture as a significant dynamic; the European Union is the leading example. Over time, state authority has been leaking upward—in international and supranational forms of pooling of sovereignty, a process that is also referred to as the internationalization of states—and leaking downward. If the latter happens in a controlled fashion, it is referred to as decentralization; if it happens in an uncontrolled fashion, it is termed ethnic or regional conflict, resulting in fragmentation and possibly state disintegration and collapse. The internationalization of the state refers to the blurring of the boundaries between international and domestic politics (producing "intermestic" politics).

What is the scope for state authority in contemporary globalization? States are not merely on the receiving end of globalization but are strategic actors (Boyer and Drache 1996, Mann 1997, Weiss 1998). States may now be leaner but also more active, and in some areas assume greater responsibility (Griffin and Khan 1992, Adams et al. 1999). This unpacks differently for different kinds of states—large or small, central or peripheral, advanced or developing. The question is not so much whether states are more or less important, but rather what *kind* of state; hence the importance of public sector reform. The fiscal crises of states in the wake of recessions and the neoliberal turn of the 1980s have led to cutbacks in government spending. The accompanying growth of market forces has led governments from local to national levels to attract foreign investment, and since they tend to follow similar strategies of fiscal concessions, infrastructure development, and "place marketing," they have been characterized as "hostile brothers." In the changing architecture of the state (Cerny 1990), the form of states has changed as they are increasingly involved in international arrangements; the basis of states has changed as they face fiscal crises; and the function of states has changed as they become competitor states. Connectivity and ICT infrastructure as a strategic area inspires the idea that those cities, countries, or regions that have been able to position themselves most successfully in relation to globalization are those that have stressed the development of information and communication infrastructure, such as Singapore, Malaysia, parts of India (Bangalore, Hyderabad), and the Dominican Republic. This is termed the "race to the intelligent state" (Connors 1997).

Does globalization foster democratization through transnational demonstration effects, growing human rights awareness, and civic activism across borders, or do the economic effects of globalization, by fostering social inequality, outweigh these democratic trends? Since the package deal of globalization coincides with growing social and political inequality *and* with trends toward democratization, the outcome is uneven and volatile.

Probably what meager consensus exists could be formulated in the twin processes of the *pooling of sovereignty* at different levels (regional, international, supranational) in combination with the shift from government to *multilevel governance*, from local and municipal, national and regional, to supranational levels. Table 1.2 is a précis of political processes associated with contemporary globalization.

GLOBALIZATION GOES TOGETHER WITH REGIONALIZATION

If between 1840 and 1960 the main *political* form of globalization was the nation state, presently the leading political form of globalization is regionalization. This takes forms ranging from regional customs unions (such

Table 1.2. Globalization and the State (from late twentieth century)

- Leaking of state authority, above:
  - Formation of international public sector
  - Pooling of sovereignty—regional, international, supranational
  - Postinternational politics (the entry of nonstate actors)
- Leaking of state authority, below:
  - Decentralization, or fragmentation
- State leaner but more active; public sector reform
- Democratization (participatory decision making, human rights, crossborder civic activism)

as AFTA), common market zones (such as NAFTA, ASEAN, APEC, Mercosur, SARC, and many others), and security alliances (NATO, SEATO, SCO) to the deep institutionalization of the European Union (Oman 1994). Beyond this factual account, the consensus unravels.

According to one view, what is happening is not globalization but regionalization, or the formation of regional free trade or investment zones (Ruigrok and van Tulder 1995), regional trade blocs along with regional neomercantilism, or the "regionalization of competition" (Morrison et al. 1991). As a general scenario, this does not seem likely because trade and capital flows and technological and market interdependence on the whole run *across* regional zones, which is only logical if a large share of world trade occurs within and between transnational corporations.

Can regional integration strengthen the bargaining position of developing countries in relation to transnational corporations and international institutions, or does it strengthen the orientation toward the market and toward liberalization and deregulation? A more precise question is under what political and international conditions is regional integration enabling for development? Regional formations may be viewed as anchors around which peripheries align—with China and Japan as centers in East and Southeast Asia; North America with Latin America and the Caribbean; and the EU and eastern Europe, the southern Mediterranean, and Africa (Stallings 1995). This is a political-spatial perspective on regional organization; a temporal perspective is to view regionalism as a stepping-stone toward growing multilateralism and eventually global governance (e.g., Group of Lisbon 1995).

GLOBALIZATION IS UNEVEN

Like predecessor notions such as internationalization and interdependence, globalization does not refer to a global level playing field or to symmetric or equal international relations. Twentieth-century globalization has been largely concentrated in the Triad of North America, Europe, and East Asia. Income and wealth are extremely unequal in distribution: in the period 1980–1991, 14 percent of the world's population accounted for 80 percent of investment flows, and in 1992, for 70 percent of the world's trade (Hirst and Thompson 1996: 15). The ratio of income of the top 20 percent of the population to the income of the bottom 20 percent has jumped from 30:1 in 1960 to 78:1 in 1994. The personal assets of 385 billionaires in the world now exceed the annual income of countries representing 45 percent of the world population (UNDP 1999). This circumstance is captured under headings such as "truncated" or "selective globalization." The idea of globalization as "Triadization," confined to the "interlinked economies" of Europe, North America, and Japan, is being overtaken by the rise of China, India, and East Asian economies. The closing section of this chapter on twenty-first-century globalization develops this further.

This prompts the idea that the "Third World" is excluded from globalization, but this overlooks the numerous ways the majority world is being affected by global dynamics. It would be too simple to describe these relations as exclusion; they are more accurately described as relations of asymmetric inclusion or hierarchical integration (see chapter 2).

While during the past decades the North-South development gap has widened in several respects, the development gap between advanced economies and new industrial countries has narrowed, but the gap between these and the least developed countries has been widening. Since the late 1970s, inequalities within and between societies have been growing steeply (Sutcliffe 2001, Nederveen Pieterse 2004). Paraphrasing the earlier terminology of uneven development, the present situation may be referred to as combined and uneven globalization.

CONTROVERSIES

Controversies over globalization range from fundamentals—what is globalization and how important is it?—to downstream questions about the politics and direction of globalization. Disputes over fundamentals are intertwined with everyday globalization issues. I first briefly review two older controversies.

IS GLOBALIZATION MULTIDIMENSIONAL?

A widespread but also rather vague understanding is that globalization refers to complex, multidimensional processes. Attempts are made to distinguish and combine different dimensions of and approaches to globalization (Roland Robertson 1992), but this often happens in too add-on a fashion (as in M. Waters 1995) to meaningfully change the understanding of globalization. Economic, political, cultural, and social dynamics are not simply different facets of a single globalization; rather, they are each prisms through which globalization takes shape and is experienced and mapped differently, yet they all mingle and interpenetrate as well. Thus, as each of the social sciences holds a different perspective on globalization, even a multidisciplinary approach to globalization still resembles eating soup with a fork.

Economic globalization is at times referred to as "corporate globalism," while globalization in the sphere of values is termed "global humanism" (Gurtov 1994). Globalization in politics is viewed as an extension of multilateralism, but also as "postinternational politics," or the entry of nonstate actors into international politics (Rosenau 1990). Globalization "from above" differs from globalization "from below" (Falk 1994). While none of these terms is particularly precise, what matters is the general awareness of globalization as a multidimensional process. An implication is that actual representations of globalization would match a post-cubist painting rather than the international trade statistics of economists or gung-ho accounts in business magazines.

Another controversy runs between quantitative and qualitative perspectives on globalization. Many economists view globalization essentially as an economic phenomenon that can be proven or disproved by statistical measures. Until recently the dominant thinking in economics has been to reduce globalization to trade, investment, and financial statistics, which constitute "objective" or "real" globalization, and all the rest is myth or fantasy (e.g., Sachs 1998). This approach can serve to circumscribe globalization or to deny its occurrence or significance. I don't dispute the validity of this empirical approach, but I consider it a partial account, if only considering dimensions of globalization such as global consciousness and global projects. More complex assessments of globalization prevail in global political economy (e.g., Palan 2000, Woods 2000). Globalization by its nature requires a multi-perspective and holistic approach. While there are textbooks, introductions, and handbooks on globalization (such as M. Waters 1995, Held et al. 1999, Scholte 2000), there is no textbook consensus on globalization, and many textbooks tend to confine themselves to disciplinary domains and perspectives.

Given the dispersion of social science disciplines, each social science claims globalization, privileges its disciplinary angle, and treats its debates as authoritative, usually without acknowledgment of their partial status. On the whole, sociology, anthropology, geography, and cultural studies perspectives on globalization tend to be more inclusive and complex than treatments in economics, political science, and international relations. The various disciplinary perspectives on globalization typically involve different globalizing actors and domains

Table 1.3. Globalization According to Social Science Disciplines

Disciplines	Period	Agency, domain	Keywords
Economics	1970s>	MNCs, banks, technologies	Global corporation, world product, global capitalism
	2000s>	Hedge funds, sovereign wealth funds	Knowledge economy, dot-com
Cultural and media studies	1970s>	Media, ICT, marketing, consumption	Global village, CNN world, McDonaldization, Disneyfication, hybridization, media capitals
Political science, international relations	1980s>	Internationalization of the state. Social movements, INGOs	Competitor states, post-international politics, global civil society
Geography	1900s>	Space and place, relativization of distance	Global-local dialectics, global cities, nodal cities
Sociology	1800s>	Modernity	Capitalism, nation states, industrialization, etc.
Philosophy	1700s>	Global reflexivity	Planetary ethics, universal morality, cosmopolitanism
Political economy	1500s>	Capitalism	World market
History, anthropology	5000 BCE>	Cross-cultural trade, technologies, world religions. Evolution	Global flows, global ecumene. Widening scale of cooperation
Ecology		Global ecology, integration of ecosystems	Spaceship earth, global risk

Table 1.4. Definitions of Globalization

Discipline	Definitions	Source
Economics	"Similarity of economic conditions and policies across national boundaries"	Gray (1993: 38)
	"Accelerated movement across national and regional barriers of economic 'goods,' i.e. people, products, capital, especially intangible forms of capital (technology, control of assets)"	Oman (1994: 56)
Sociology	"refers both to the compression of the world and the intensification of consciousness of the world as a whole"	Roland Robertson (1992: 8)
	"A social process in which the constraints of geography on social and cultural arrangements recede and in which people are increasingly aware that they are receding"	M. Waters (1995: 3)
History, anthropology	"Globalization is a long-term historical process of growing worldwide interconnectedness."	Nederveen Pieterse (1995: 45)

in which globalization unfolds, different periodizations, and different themes (table 1.3). These various diagnostics of globalization involve, of course, profoundly different definitions of globalization; a sample of definitions is in table 1.4.

Does Globalization Exist?

Does globalization actually exist or is it a myth or exaggerated rhetoric? Paul Hirst and Grahame Thompson (1996) criticized "globalization rhetoric" or "globaloney" on several grounds. Their key argument is that before 1914 the world economy was more internationalized than in the 1990s. The trade and investment statistics that are amply documented in their work appear to prove their point. But what is the explanation? The period of the new imperialism and belle époque (1870–1914) was shaped by territorial imperialism. Western countries then controlled as much as 96 percent of the earth's surface: no wonder that economies at the time seemed highly internationalized and open. What happened since then was the Depression, the Second World War, and decolonization, and this is what contemporary globalization should also be measured against. In taking 1870–1914 as a yardstick, one is in effect measuring how internationalized the British Empire was. This conceals what is distinctive about contemporary globalization: that it is *not* territorial and imperialist in the classic sense. Hirst and Thompson further argued that the number of genuine transnational corporations (as against multinational corporations as essentially national corporations with international reach) is small. A rejoinder is that they are trendsetters in global value networks; besides, this does not settle the location of foreign direct investments. Hirst and Thompson were concerned with economic globalization, but obviously there is much more to globalization: technological, political, social, and cultural dimensions and configurations such as global civil society. Their argument entirely passed over noneconomic literatures on globalization and technology. Before and since 1914 there have been several technological changes, in particular transport and communication revolutions, that make higher levels of economic internationalization both possible and necessary (Henderson 1993).

Is Globalization a Recent or a Long-Term Historical Process?

With different understandings of globalization come widely different views on the timing of globalization. Is globalization a recent process of the last thirty years or so, as most economists have it, or a long-term historical process? Table 1.5 is an overview of perspectives on the timing and the character of "globalization" (in quotes because this terminology is not used by all; further discussion is in chapter 4 and in Nederveen Pieterse 2012b). Short of a common definition of glo-

Table 1.5. Major Views on the Nature and Timing of Globalization

Time frame	Units of globalization	Disciplines
Short-term (post-1970s)	Firms, production technologies, marketing; media, Internet	Economics, cultural studies
Midterm (sixteenth to eighteenth century)	Capitalism. Modernity	Political economy, sociology
Long-term	Crosscultural trade. Forms of social cooperation	History, historical sociology, anthropology

balization, which is just not available, this question cannot be really settled. A compromise position, simply to bracket the issue, is to speak of *contemporary accelerated globalization* to characterize globalization processes since the 1970s.

WHAT IS GLOBALIZATION?

Globalization is an objective, *empirical process* of increasing economic and political connectivity, a subjective process unfolding in consciousness as the social *awareness* of growing global interconnectedness, and a host of specific globalizing *projects* that seek to shape global conditions. It isn't always clear *which* globalization is being talked about. Does globalization refer to a general, open-ended trend, or does it refer to specific economic and political projects? Does it have a systemic character? Globalization is diverse in itself, and there are wide discrepancies in the basic understandings of globalization. A précis of several distinctive views is in table 1.6.

Diagnostics and definitions of globalization correlate with globalization politics. We can distinguish a broad continuum of normative and policy positions in relation to globalization, which are usually interrelated. Table 1.7 outlines the analytic, evaluative, and policy views on globalization of various authors.

Table 1.6. **Perspectives on Globalization**

Perspectives	Keywords	Sources
As process (trend)	Growing worldwide interconnectedness	Robbie Robertson, etc.
As project	Washington consensus, MNCs, geopolitics, etc.	Ohmae, McMichael, Korten, Seabrook, Chomsky, Pentagon, etc.
As process and projects	See above	Dessouki
As system	Golden Arches and US hegemony	Thomas Friedman, Wallerstein
As discourse	Global babble, global capitalism, etc.	Media; Steger

Table 1.7.   Policy Perspectives on Globalization

Analysis	Evaluation	Policy	Sources
Does not exist	n.a.	National and regional policy	Hirst and Thompson
Powerful trend	Positive	Liberalization, deregulation	Ohmae, Washington consensus, *Economist, Wall Street Journal*
	Negative	Localism, new protectionism, decentralization	Vandana Shiva, José Bové, Hines, radical ecology
		Control capitalism and finance; capital controls	Soros, Stiglitz, Samir Amin, World Social Forum
Powerful system	Both	Golden Arches and US hegemony	Thomas Friedman
Dialectical	Both	Strategic, flexible engagement; smart globalization	Griffin and Khan, alter-globalization movements

USE AND ABUSE OF THE GLOBAL

Global culture, global capitalism, global economy, global market, global competition, global finance, global neoliberalism, global crisis, global modernity, global marketing, global power, global age, global food, global logistics, global energy, global design, global art, global fashion, global cities, global media, global news, global imaginaries, global icons, global celebrities, global terrorism, global crime, global security, global social movements, global social policy, global studies, global political economy, global history, global civil society, global events, global risk, and so on—the proliferating use of the global is surely a sign of the times. "Global" has become a substitute for what used to be "international." The problem is that "global" carries meanings and nuances across a wide spectrum, and in several if not most cases it involves rhetorical overdrive, analytical overstretch, or marketing ploys. Global news is a claim rather than a reality; regional or national bias prevails. In a similar way, we can dismantle and trim most of these notions. In some cases, the use of the global is empirically descriptive—the global economy, global market, and global finance do exist in a viable enough fashion—but in most cases the use of the global is homogenizing, suggests far greater standardization and uniformity than exists, and conceals variation.

Arguably, global culture, global capitalism, and global modernity exist, but they exist only in a thin, shallow, or limited sense. Global culture exists in the sense of a "global supermarket" of symbols and images, snippets and confetti of notions that are accessible worldwide, but does not exist in the sense of globally shared values and meanings. Global capitalism exists, but by the sweeping use of the global makes invisible the institutional varieties in how market economies are coordinated (as in the varieties of capitalism and comparative capitalisms literature), which matter at least as much as the overlap (Nederveen Pieterse 2014). Global crises do not exist, but regional crises can have global spillover. Global modernity possibly exists, but again only in a thin sense; institutional varieties in how modernity, or modernities, is organized matter but are obscured by the "global" heading. Global history exists, in contrast to world history (Mazlish and Buultjens 1993). Global political economy and global studies exist as fields of study. Global cities exist with a specific meaning (Sassen 1991), but "nodal cities" is a smarter category. Broadcasters such as BBC and Al Jazeera claim to provide "global news," but this refers to the aspired scope of broadcasting, not to the content of news, which invariably has a regional bias (Ginneken 1998). Global architecture probably does not exist. Global art exists in a specific meaning, which is contentious (Belting 2009). Global fruit and global wildlife don't exist for they are regional or local by nature. Thus we must assess on a case-by-case basis (a) whether the phenomenon empirically exists at a global scale, (b) what degree of relevance it refers to, and (c) how meaningful it is. Overuse and uncritical use of *global* as adjective indicates underlying rifts of perspective, notably in relation to culture, capitalism, and modernity (Nederveen Pieterse 2009, 2010b).

Is Globalization Neoliberal Capitalism?

In 1998, in response to the Asian crisis that began in Thailand, Alan Greenspan, chairman of the Federal Reserve, commented, "My sense is that one consequence of this Asian crisis is an increasing awareness in the region that market capitalism, as practiced in the west, especially in the US, is the superior model; that is, it provides greater promise of producing rising standards of living and continuous growth." Citing this, the *Financial Times* editorialized:

> The chairman is right. The combination of the stagnation of Japan with the crisis that has engulfed Thailand, Indonesia and South Korea has largely destroyed the glamour of Asian managed capitalism. The high unemployment of continental Europe has done almost as much damage to its traditional social democracy. What is left is Anglo-Saxon capitalism. It is becoming a "global standard." (18 April 1998)

This attempt to capture all the world's variations under a single heading is a familiar refrain of hegemony in action, featuring US capitalism as the end of history. Brief rejoinders are as follows. First, "American exceptionalism" (Lipset 1996) sheds light on American capitalism. It is only since the 1980s era of neoliberalism that it has been upheld as the norm of capitalism, as "real capitalism." Second, should we leave the definition of terminology to the global headlines? What prevails in the headlines is analysis squeeze: "globalization" is squeezed to fit the knowledge and decision-making frameworks of US policy makers, New York boardrooms, and the pages of the *Wall Street Journal* and the *Economist*. Third, the United States should not be essentialized or treated as a single unit. While from the outside the US appears as a superpower steering globalization and manipulating the IMF, World Bank, and WTO, within the US many, such as the labor movement, regard the US as being constrained by globalization (Milner 1998) and regions such as the Midwest as squeezed by globalization (Longworth 2008). Fourth, neoliberalism is by no means a homogeneous or coherent project, economically, politically, or culturally (Pratt 1998). Fifth, the American imperial turn in the wake of the September 11 attacks introduces very different logics. Sixth, the Washington consensus has unraveled. In the wake of the Enron episode and the 2008 crisis, the mood, from Wall Street to the World Economic Forum in Davos, has changed markedly. It follows that neoliberal capitalism cannot be taken at face value.

While neoliberal globalization is a matter of concern the world over, neoliberalism does not exhaust the varieties of capitalism, and capitalism does not exhaust globalization. At an early stage, social movements such as the International Forum on Globalization identified themselves as anti-globalization movements; later they fine-tuned their position as seeking alternative, democratic, or inclusive globalization (Nederveen Pieterse 2001, Held 2002). This comes with a wider understanding that globalization, taken in a broad sense, is here to stay and that what matters is the character and direction of globalization. The current *form* of globalization can be negotiated on the basis of the *trend* of globalization, which is the point of the democratization of globalization.

Is Globalization Manageable?

The inequalities of wealth and power are vast and growing. The status quo powers showed a greater proclivity to warfare, at least in the early twenty-first century, than to multilateralism and democratic reform. Nevertheless, a growing consensus favors some form of managing, steering, or shaping globalization. Global laissez-faire may involve greater risks than even the privileged few can afford (Soros 1998, 2002). The advanced nations ponder new global rules on investment, banking, and trade. "Planning globalization," a position at the other end of the spectrum, has takers only among adherents of world socialism. A broad middle ground favors managing globalization, but right away dispute takes over. Should global reform be implemented within the existing structures or through new institutions?

A case in point is the architecture of the international financial system and whether it requires modest adjustments or a new shape. Within the broad reform consensus, a minimum position held by the IMF, World Bank, WTO, and US Treasury is in favor of "transparency" and the standardization of accounting systems. This is a conservative position that matches the Washington consensus on the alignment of capitalisms. A midway position, held by the World Bank and OECD, considers imposing restrictions such as higher reserve requirements, higher thresholds of access to offshore banks, and modest reforms of international institutions. A stronger reform position held by UN agencies and global social movements favors new international institutions such as a global central bank that should impose restrictions on "hot money" and international taxes (UNDP 1999). Further progressive agendas include "double democratization," simultaneously within societies and in international relations, and "cosmopolitan democracy," including substantive UN reform and the formation of regional parliaments (Held 1995). The ongoing interregnum has been described as complex multilateralism (O'Brien et al. 2000).

This review of major debates on globalization shows that different social science disciplines hold quite diverse views on the scope, character, and timing of globalization. The questions of globalization and culture that this book focuses on are part of much wider controversies. This discussion provides a context to the perspective on globalization that I adopt in the following chapters—in brief, a critical, multidimensional, and long-term approach to globalization that is closer to historical sociology, anthropology, history, and global political economy than to mainstream sociology or other disciplines.

TWENTY-FIRST-CENTURY GLOBALIZATION

If globalization during the second half of the twentieth century coincided with the "American Century" and the period 1980–2000 coincided with the dominance of Anglo-American capitalism and American hegemony, twenty-first-century globalization shows markedly different dynamics. American hegemony has weakened; the US economy is import dependent, deeply indebted, and mired in financial crises. "Free enterprise" as a model has lost credibility because it has led to permissive capitalism, from Enron to the subprime mortgage crisis and the collapse of Bear Stearns, Lehman Brothers, and so forth. Financial crises were supposed to take place in the global South, but when financial crisis came to the United States, the picture changed. The twenty-first century is the era of what Fareed Zakaria calls, following the rise of the West, the "rise of the rest" (2008).

The new trends of twenty-first-century globalization are the centers of the world economy shifting to the global South, to the newly industrialized countries, and to the energy exporters. This rise unfolds, first, in economic spheres—with newly industrializing countries acting as drivers of world economic growth and their demand pushing commodity prices. Second, it unfolds in financial spheres. The sovereign wealth funds of the industrial exporters in Asia and Latin America, and of the energy exporters, from the Persian Gulf to Norway, have become financial insiders and market makers. Third, it unfolds in international institutions. Emerging economies repaying their debt to the IMF early changes the equation for Washington financial institutions. WTO talks have bogged down. Fourth, their social impact and appeal is gradually beginning to be felt, notably in changing patterns of migration. Thus,

China has become increasingly attractive to migrants. In international politics and culture, the influence of emerging societies still lags behind. The winners of the Second World War continue to rule international institutions such as the UN Security Council. The cultural influence of emerging societies may be slowest to take shape.

The unquestioned cultural hegemony of the West is past. New patterns, fashions, confluences, and mixtures are taking shape. In the emerging configurations, the BRICS (Brazil, Russia, India, China, South Africa) and formations such as "Chime" (China, India, Middle East) will be increasingly important. Regional cultural trends are changing markedly and affect global trends. An example is the "Korean wave" in East Asia—the popularity of Korean soap operas, movies, and music—which has already peaked. The turn to the East has cultural ripple effects. Since major new markets or opportunities for market expansion are the emerging economies in the global South, producers, marketing, and media across the world will tune in to their cultural horizon. Prosecco producers in Italy who seek to expand their global market share now look at how they can find favor with trendy club audiences in Beijing and Busan (Wildt 2008). At a time when advertising budgets in the UK and US are shrinking, western advertising agencies register their biggest growth in emerging markets. European luxury brands such as Louis Vuitton find new buyers in Asia.

The emerging societies owe their rise, to a large extent, to their exports to advanced countries; hence, tuning in to markets and sensibilities in the West is part of their makeup, even as domestic and regional demand becomes increasingly important. To cater to western and international buyers, East Asian automakers give their models American Sunbelt or Mediterranean-sounding names, such as Kia's Sedona, Hyundai's Santa Fe, and Toyota's Sienna. Another major relationship is taking shape between emerging societies and their growing appetite for raw materials, from iron ore to rubber, and commodities-exporting countries and regions. These two relationships—between emerging societies and the West and between emerging societies and commodity exporting economies in the global South—are shaping global political economy. They also represent major vortices of hybridization and interlacing South-South or East-South or South-North (rather than, as in the past, North-South). These trends are taken up further in chapters 6 and 7.

Chapter 2

Globalization and Human Integration: We Are All Migrants

Does globalization involve a trend toward human integration? Growing worldwide interconnectedness or the "shrinking world" and the trend toward the overall widening scale of human cooperation would point in this direction. However, contemporary globalization also comes with polarizing effects that deepen uneven development and inequality on a world scale. Widening cooperation and deepening inequality are not a novel combination in history. Thus, taking a long-term and evolutionary perspective on globalization might overcome this problem. But this would in turn generate a different problem: teleological thinking, or attributing a direction to evolutionary change. Experiences with teleologies have not been fortunate; they have usually been steeped in cultural and ideological bias and have been associated with discourses of domination. Familiar instances are religious prophecies (such as the Second

Coming in Christianity), Marxism (world socialism), developmentalism and progress western style (modernization = westernization), and the end of history (à la Hegel, Kojève, Fukuyama). If globalization can be taken to involve human integration, these problems need to be addressed. I will argue that globalization involves a trend toward human integration based on the following provisos:

- That globalization is viewed as a long-term historical process
- That the trend toward human integration is viewed not as a straightforward but as a dialectical process
- That this perspective is combined with analysis of power and hierarchy
- That utopian visions of human unity are possibly taken as pointers but not as shortcuts
- That since globalization involves complex multidimensional processes (concrete processes, changing subjectivities, and specific globalizing projects), movement toward human integration unfolds unevenly across many different fields and dimensions
- That diasporas and migration are part of the trend toward human integration
- That from this assessment follows a commitment to policy intervention toward global equity, for without it the idea of human integration would become manipulative or meaningless, hypocritical or rhetorical.

This chapter first addresses long-term trends and perspectives on globalization, contrasting them to Eurocentric views. Taken up next are utopian and prophetic visions of human unity, alongside the question of uneven globalization. The second part probes the question of how migration and diasporas fit into this general picture.

GLOBALIZATION AS A DEEP HISTORICAL PROCESS

That globalization is a long-term historical process is not the common assessment of globalization among economists, political scientists, or sociologists, as discussed in the previous chapter, but it is among several historians and anthropologists. Taking a long view, dimensions and components of globalization include the following:

- The ancient population movements across and between continents
- Long-distance cross-cultural trade
- The world religions—the wanderings that have gone into the making, spread, and varieties of Buddhism, Hinduism, Christianity, and Islam
- The diffusion of technologies including Stone Age obsidian, neolithic agricultural know-how, military technologies, numeracy, literacy, sciences and philosophies, and the development of new technologies due to intercultural contact.

These dimensions have been studied under various headings well before the terminology of globalization. Paleontologists and philologists have studied ancient population movements. Cross-cultural trade has been dealt with extensively (Curtin 1984). The philosopher Karl Jaspers has thematized the role of the world religions in the "axial age" (500 BCE). Goonatilake (1999) has taken up the intercultural history of science. The historian William McNeill studied the early diffusion of military and other technologies (1982). Andre Gunder Frank (1998) and John Hobson (2004) have argued for the centrality of Asian economies, centuries before and underlying the rise of European economies.

In these views, human integration belongs to a deep dynamic in which shifting civilizational centers are but the front stage of history against a backdrop of much older and ongoing intercultural traffic. It does not matter all that much whether or not one would place these long-term processes under the umbrella of globalization, or at any rate that is a different kind of discussion (Nederveen Pieterse 2012b). What does matter is the general, underlying sense of history in relation to space. Thus for example, Robert Clark traces the "global imperative" back to pre-agricultural *Homo erectus*. In his view, "the essence of the human condition is a fundamental connectedness with parts of the universe across time and space" (1997: 2).

This kind of historical sensibility is profoundly different from the Eurocentric view that attributes human unification mainly to the journeys of modernity. If global integration is primarily a *modern* phenomenon, then it belongs to the historical chain of the European journeys of reconnaissance followed by expansion, imperialism, colonialism, and decolonization. Then the world was an archipelago of fragments that existed in bits and pieces until modernity and the moderns unified it. The Eurocentric view of history stands in contrast to the view that prevails among evolutionary historians, paleontologists, and anthropologists. The Eurocentric perspective prevails in many contemporary discussions, as with the sociologist Anthony Giddens for whom globalization is one of the "consequences of modernity" (1990) and all those who view modernity and its universalisms (which are rooted, in turn, in the classics) as the great unifying force in history. It follows that human integration stands or falls with the fate of modernity (read: the West) and all disruptive forces within and outside modernity detract from the great historical momentum of the moderns. Barbarians at the gate and within the citadel of civilization threaten human destiny. With this view comes a rhetoric of profound western chauvinism and, usually, pessimism concerning its course or destiny, which is reflected in somber perspectives on global cultural relations, the cultural contradictions of capitalism, and the fragmenting effects of ethnicity and religion toward a "Lebanonization" of global culture. The Eurocentric and "modernist" view of history appears superficial if only considered against the backdrop of the older universalisms rooted in religious worldviews; in fact, modern universalism replicates earlier religious universalism (Nederveen Pieterse 2010a: chapter 2). To contextualize modernities means to recover our collective history of forgotten migrations and lost routes of identity that wire the planet.

Taking a historical perspective on globalization, it makes sense to distinguish different stages of globalization—such as ancient, modern, and contemporary. Contemporary globalization, then, may be termed accelerated globalization. "Today's globalization process differs from that of earlier times in three ways: the volume of materials moved is larger; the speeds with which they are moved are faster; and the diversity of materials (matter, energy, information) moved is greater" (Clark 1997: 16).

While the attention is usually focused on cultural diffusion, we can also consider the human body as a site of global human integration. Large population movements and major turning points in cross-cultural contact have made for interethnic mingling and crisscrossing of gene pools and physiological features. They have also been marked by the spread of diseases. Asian-European contact overland was marked by the outbreak of the plague in medieval Europe (W. McNeill 1977).

European-American contact had a devastating impact on the Native Americans. Eventually also health care methods traveled widely. The spread of foodstuffs and eating habits has profoundly affected demographics and human densities. Forms of mobility (horse, saddle, bit, chariot, ship, compass, bicycle, automobile, airplane) have further affected human motion. Military technologies have shaped the logics and logistics of conquest (W. McNeill 1982). The diffusion of rhythms and music, movies, and advertising has influenced sensory experiences, aesthetics, forms of intimacy, and ways of experiencing the body. The same applies to clothing and fashions. The global spread of mass media and advertising dominated by western images has affected local beauty standards, fostering, for instance, practices of skin bleaching in various parts of the South. Conversely, Orientalism and other "nonwestern" influences have profoundly influenced western styles and sensibilities (Bruignac-La Hougue 1998, Nederveen Pieterse 1994). The human genome project shows the evolutionary intimacy of the human species. The Olympic Games and international beauty pageants are ceremonial arenas for nations to take their place among the "family of nations" (Malkki 1994). They do so by associating bodies and places. Women's bodies in particular are sites where borders are negotiated and renegotiated—witness the issues surrounding veiling, headscarves, and beauty pageants (Oza 2006). Thus in many ways, profound and superficial, human integration is being reflected and refracted in the changing experience of our bodies and those of others.

UTOPIAN VISIONS: HUMAN UNITY AS A THEME

> Are all nations communing? Is there going to be but one heart to the globe?
>
> —Walt Whitman

Prophecies and utopias across time and place have evoked human unity, from the Book of Daniel to Joachim de Fiore, whose "third age" predicted human integration, and from Akhenaton and Alexander to the Anabaptists.[1] Visions of common humanity have been evoked in the shift from tribal to universal religions. The shift from Judaism to Christianity, from the Old to the New Testament, opening the door of the gospel to the gentiles, is a case in point. In different ways, Taoism,

Buddhism, Hinduism, and Islam are universal in scope and appeal. In the Qur'an, cultural differences are presented as but a way for humanity to "know one another."

Under what circumstances do cultures flourish? In one view, cultural efflorescence requires or is more common in local, small-scale social units. Thus, according to the Indian philosopher and yogi Sri Aurobindo, "Collective life diffusing itself in too vast spaces seems to lose intensity and productiveness" (1999: 109). Nevertheless, Aurobindo believed in a general process of human unity (110). Advocates of localism oppose globalization or its current shape (Mander and Goldsmith 1996), or propose deglobalization (Bello 2001). A view that has become more common in recent times is that cultural efflorescence has usually been based on intercultural mingling. It has often arisen from the encounter of different cultures or human groups at the confluence of great rivers, along deltas, in major cities or centers where routes of travel and trade converged. It has often involved expansive or high-minded visions of human unity. Examples include Ashok, the Mongols and their ecumenical interests, and the Mughal Empire encompassing and being encompassed by multiple cultures as in the reign of Akbar.[2] In the Muslim world, the work of Rumi, Ibn Battuta, Ibn Khaldun, Ibn Rushd, and the efflorescence of al Andalus in Moorish times come to mind, and ramifying outward from its cultural radius, the troubadour culture of Provence. Other familiar episodes are the Italian Renaissance, the Enlightenment, and the romantics.

These episodes have in common that they were moments of intercultural synthesis uniting diverse elements in cultural achievement. The descendants often claimed them as expressions of regional genius (thus establishing their own virtue and claim to power) while their mixed history as an amalgam of diverse interregional currents and flows faded from memory, just as the flows themselves dried up or changed course over time. In this sense none of the achievements of the world's civilizational centers are local or regional: they are interregional achievements that are incomprehensible without their cross-cultural infrastructure. Human memory retains the façade but overlooks the back entrances, commemorates the peak but not the climb. Even so, with these episodes of intercultural efflorescence have come visions acknowledging or celebrating them—as with Erasmus, Goethe (and his *West-Östliche Divan*), Leibniz, Beethoven, Kant's cosmopolitanism, the Quakers. The Nahda in the Arab world, the Indian renaissance, Ethiopianism in Africa, and the Harlem renaissance have been great evocative moments, partly in protest against western colonialism.

Usually these universalisms have also been *centrisms*—one could write a history of the changing geographies and characters of civilizational centrisms over time. Unity has not generally been a level playing field. Often it involved a hierarchy organized in concentric circles around a core of accomplishment (such as attainment measured by purity of blood or faith), or along a ladder with the true believers or the accomplished on top, sliding down the rungs toward the outcasts at the bottom. Human unity and human hierarchy therefore have usually traveled together. China as the Middle Kingdom is an example. In Europe, the tripartite world of the Middle Ages (with the sons of Japheth, Sem, and Ham representing the three continents) comes to mind, the Adoration of the Magi (each representing a part of the world), the heavens and hells in Dante's *Divine Comedy* (as a concentric mapping of worlds spiritual and terrestrial), the Roman Catholic world image of the four rivers as represented in Bernini's fountains in Rome. These have been mandalas of unity and mandalas of power, of both inclusion and exclusion. They have inspired gestures of cross-cultural translation, hybridization, and unification as well as crusades, witch-hunts, genocides, holocausts—at times claiming the *same* paradigms, which turn out differently depending on whether one emphasizes the unity or the hierarchy. Unity has often been the inner meaning or intent and hierarchy the outward form or outcome. With the Enlightenment has come another series of Eurocentric views. Hierarchy has also been conceived in terms of political and military power (as in the balance of power and the hierarchy of superpowers, great powers, minor powers, and no power) and economic achievement. Thus the current hierarchy runs between advanced, developing, less, and least developed countries.

The Roman Catholic Church, the Renaissance humanists, the Jesuits, and the Freemasons all held transnational imaginaries. Political movements have taken up human integration translated into projects of political, cultural, and social internationalism. The Jacobins carried the republican ideals to England and Ireland, across the continent, and to the Americas, and the national movements took this momentum

further. Worker movements raised the banner of unity and struggle—
"workers of the world unite!" Women's movements merged with the
anti-slavery movements (Billington 1980). Nationalism implies internationalism. Thus Kemal Atatürk, while a fervent nationalist, also
proposed: "We should think of humanity as a body and of a nation as
one of its limbs. Pain in the fingertip affects the whole system" (quoted
in Keys 1982: 1). Cultural internationalism took off after 1914–1918
(Iriye 1997). Decolonization movements proclaimed the unity of all
the oppressed, "the wretched of the earth" (Fanon 1967). Indeed, to
a large extent the question of whether time has brought us closer to
human integration depends on how one interprets the history of conquest, slavery, and colonialism. I favor an interpretation that stresses
the dialectics of these episodes: empire and emancipation have been an
intricate historical interplay (chapter 4). Culture contact, in the end, is
a matter of collusion and not simply collision (Dathorne 1996).

The double character of unity and hierarchy, or hierarchical integration, also applies to the work of the Jesuit paleontologist Teilhard
de Chardin. His notion of growing planetary demographic density and
hence "complexification" and movement toward a noosphere points
toward the ultimate unification of humanity at point Omega. In the
process, critics argue, Teilhard underestimates global inequality and
stratification.[3] Taking a shortcut to human unity may have, so to speak,
a hierarchical effect. Hence taking human integration seriously means
taking inequality seriously.

UNEVEN GLOBALIZATION

An important account of contemporary globalization refers to the *exclusion* of the majority of humanity—the majority in large parts of Africa,
Asia, and Latin America who are excluded from life in the fast lane,
from the "interlinked economies" of the "Triad zone." But exclusion
may be too crude and blunt a term to describe the actual situation.

> The middle class in developing countries participates in the global
> circuits of advertising, brand name consumerism and high tech ser-
> vices, which, at another end of the circuitry, increasingly exclude the
> underclass in advanced economies. . . . The term exclusion ignores the
> many ways in which developing countries are *included* in global pro-

cesses: they are subject to global financial discipline (as in structural adjustment and interest payments, resulting in net capital outflows) and part of global markets (resource flows, distribution networks, diaspora and niche markets), global ecology, international politics, global communications, science and technology, international development cooperation, transnational civil society, international migration, travel, and crime networks. For instance, the public health sector in many African countries is increasingly being internationalised. Thus, it would be more accurate to speak of *asymmetrical inclusion* or hierarchical integration. (Nederveen Pieterse 1997: 80; cf. Krishna and Nederveen Pieterse 2008)

The import-export intensity of African economies, for example, is much higher than that of western countries. Thus, people in the South are within the reach of global mass communications and advertising, within the reach of the message but not necessarily the action. This is how an Albanian émigré describes the impact of Italian television on Albanians during the old days of seclusion:

> Step by step the entire advertising message is extracted from its (pragmatic) context. . . . The ultimate result is that ads are viewed as windows to an upper reality. This is the reality where people, and things, and behaviors, and actions are light, colorful, beautiful. People are almost always good looking, clean, and well dressed; they all smile and enjoy everything they do, and get extremely happy, even when confronted with a new toothbrush. . . . The repeated contact with mirages of a reality *beyond* the wall, not only created a diffuse desire, but also kept it alive for a sufficiently long time, so that desire could lose its initial property of being a[n] . . . impulse for action, and become a *state of mind*, similar to profuse, disinterested love. (Vebhiu 1999)

At another end of the television set, viewers experience "long distance suffering" and engage in schizophrenic behavior of limited or vague gestures of solidarity while finding shelter in the "chauvinism of prosperity" that is sustained by institutions and media. Electoral politics in the advanced countries tends to set up barriers to exclude terrorists and welfare recipients (Connolly 1991), which often extend to asylum seekers, refugees, and "illegal migrants."

North-South inequality runs deep *n'en déplaise* globalization and the "deterritorialization of poverty" (i.e., the rich in the South and the poor in the North). World images and perceptions of globalization are held also among the middle class in the South (Gopal 1998). Yet, the middle class and the poor majority in the South share national and regional destinies, suffer superpower geopolitics and geo-economics, western double standards, and domestic political incompetence. Do development policies stand a chance in relation to the vast global differentials of power, technology, and production? "Whither the North-South gap" is too large a question to take up here, but I should make at least these points. With global inequality comes the globalization of risk—political, security, economic, and ecological risk. Equally important, global inequality poses a profound moral challenge (Pogge 2002). Aurobindo, Habermas, the theologian Hans Küng (1997), and others have formulated planetary ethics. Confronting global inequality requires global reforms toward global equity and inclusion that can take many forms (Nederveen Pieterse 2000, Dallmayr 2001). I now turn to migration in relation to globalization and human integration.

WE ARE ALL MIGRANTS: MIGRATION AND HUMAN INTEGRATION

Taking a long view, globalization and migration are twin subjects. The earliest migrations on record (around the area of Harappa) go back two million years. In a historical sense we are all migrants because our ancestors have all traveled to the places where we have come from. States that impose border controls may go way back in time but their spread dates only from the nineteenth century and their covering the globe is more recent still (Torpey 2000). Few of our ancestors have lived under these dispensations. These are not merely academic considerations. In a profound way, our perspective on history shapes our perspective on migration. Presently the taken-for-granted way of looking at migration is from the point of view of the nation state. This implies a narrow take on migration, which in a growing body of literature is viewed in terms of political rights and constraints (citizenship, human rights), from a cultural point of view (identity, multiculturalism), or in a cost-benefit analysis from the point of view of the nation.

This reflection explores two considerations. The first is to bracket the conventional perspective on migration that takes the nation state as its point of departure, considering that the nation state is only a recent formation. A further consideration, mentioned above, is whether cultures flourish because of cultural mixing. This leads to familiar discussions of multiculturalism and associated moral, ideological, and cultural preferences and questions of citizenship; the point here is not to rehearse the pros and cons of multiculturalism, which is well-trodden ground, but to explore the socio-economics of migration. This is only a limited treatment of a large terrain, a contribution to the discussion.

Economic achievements are conventionally attributed to nations, reflecting nation state predilections in politics and social science since the nineteenth century. The contributions of foreigners, migrants, diasporas, and minorities have been generally ignored. They have been ignored in a fundamental sense because acknowledging them would go against the Zeitgeist, the nationalist ethos. If the period 1840 to 1960 has been the age of the nation, its peak time, it has been the age of oblivion of the migrant, the foreigner. In country after country, the dark side of nation building has been the marginalization, expulsion, expropriation, oppression of foreigners, as in politics of national cleansing. Turkey (Armenians and others), Germany (Jews), Uganda (Indians), Nigeria (Ghanaians), Bulgaria (ethnic Turks), India (Muslims) are familiar cases in point (Van Hear 1998), but they are only the tip of the iceberg.

During the past decades, nation-state pathos has been receding and in its stead have come globalization, regionalism, and an "age of ethnicity." Now that the nation state is no longer being taken for granted different sensibilities and problems emerge. New strands in economic analysis break with the conventions of nationalist historiography and credit the role of diasporas, minorities, and ethnic groups (Kotkin 1992). In this view many achievements routinely claimed by nations have to a significant extent been the work of travelers—traders, migrants, slaves, pilgrims, missionaries, itinerant craftsmen. Thus, the world of nations has all along been interspersed with the world of diasporas. Some have been recognized—such as the Jewish, Chinese, Irish, and Italian diasporas, also the African diaspora has been conspicuous, but many have been largely ignored except in local histories—such as the Greek, Armenian, Lebanese, Turkish, Egyptian, Yemeni, Indian, Malay, Mongol, Tibetan, Scottish diasporas, and so on. Some run so deep in time that the names used to identify them—derived from nation states or civilizational areas—are not adequate. Some terms used in conventional national historiography—such as Anglo-Saxon—obviously refer to earlier migrations. In effect, "national" identities are mélange identities, combinations of peoples that have been conventionally amalgamated under a political heading (such as Celts, Franks, and others in "France"). "African" and "Indian" migrations are obviously only approximations. "India," "Africa," and the "Middle East" did not exist until they were so named by Europeans. It has more often been regions (the Genoese), groups within regions (Ismailis from Gujarat, Parses from Mumbai), or ethnicities within nations (Fujianese from China) that have engaged in cross-cultural chain migration.

Leading perspectives on globalization and culture have been one-sided, polemical, and conservative in their implications (such as Huntington 1996). The World Commission on Culture and Development urges greater attention to cultural diversity and creativity (1996). A novel approach in economic research views intercultural contact as an engine of economic growth. According to the economist Keith Griffin (1996, 2000), the commingling of cultures has led to economic innovation and growth in the past and has the potential for doing so in the future. Intercultural contact in this view has accelerated the diffusion of technologies and knowledges and the development of new technologies and forms of social and economic cooperation. Trade routes that figure in historiography as nodes of economic activity (as in the work of Henri Pirenne and Fernand Braudel) also emerge as backbones of cultural transformation. In one of the many fascinating accounts of the Silk Roads, Sugiyama Jiro recounts: "In the third century B.C. King Asoka of Maurya sent groups of Buddhist missionaries to the West via the highway in western Asia completed by Alexander the Great" (1992: 55). This road leads via the Gandhara civilization to Mesopotamia and the Mediterranean. The account also tells of a Buddhist statue that is found among the remains of Viking ships in Scandinavia. This illustrates that, over time, roads of conquest turn into roads of commerce and roads of cultural exchange.

This approach means something radically different from considering migration as either an added value or cost to the nation. It goes beyond the preoccupation with ethnic economies, ethno-marketing, or intercultural management. Rather, we come to see nation states as a *grid* that has been temporarily superimposed upon a deeper and ongoing stratum of human migrations and diasporas. We could then ask the reverse question: how useful is the nation state structure (national economies, national sovereignty, border controls) to migration, considering that migration is a major site of cultural creativity and economic stimulus? Presently the nation-state grid as the central and preferred organizational form is gradually making way for a combination of different organizational structures and forms of governance—local, urban, regional, international, and supranational—such that institutional structures are increasingly becoming multiscalar. If we recognize the profound role of migration and intercultural contact in general and in economic history, what does this imply for current policies? Understanding multiculturalism as a vital economic force is not insignificant in an era dominated by market values. Thus, a key question is not merely whether immigration is culturally desirable, morally preferable, or politically feasible, but whether and how it contributes to economic development. It may not be really feasible to separate economic from other dimensions of migration, but since so many discussions follow different tracks this option is followed here.

According to the economist Thomas Sowell, migration and cultural diffusion are now separable: "The transportation of bodies and the dissemination of human capital have become increasingly separable operations, so that the historic role of immigration in advancing nations need not apply to its future role" (1996: 299). "In short, international migrations have tended to become a less and less effective way of transferring human capital, at least as compared to alternatives that have emerged or grown in importance" (Sowell 1996: 300). This is part of a wider argument against cultural relativism, affirmative action, and multiculturalism. Sowell concludes his study with an emphasis on the *creation of wealth* (and an implicit polemic with the emphasis on the distribution of wealth). There are several problems with this analysis. First, it overlooks the capacity of migrants to generate their own economic niches and resources. Second, in focusing on human capital it follows the liberal fallacy of viewing economics as an exchange among individuals, differentially endowed with skills and resources, and thus takes human capital as part of a liberal paradigm. In recent years this angle has been overtaken by the theme of social capital. Here the general perspective is that markets are socially embedded (à la Polanyi), economics is institutional, and what makes economies tick is not just individual skills and endowments (human capital) but social networks.

Empirical research shows that "embeddedness increases economic effectiveness along a number of dimensions that are crucial to competitiveness in a global economy—organizational learning, risk-sharing and speed-to-market" (Uzzi 1996: 694).

Much interest in social capital has concentrated on ethnic economies: trust within ethnic groups lowers transaction costs; within ethnic groups social capital densities are highest and payoffs greatest (Light and Karageorgis 1994). Social capital marshals economic resources: for example, the Vietnamese *hoa* releasing family labor and capital for small enterprises in the United States (Yoo 1998). While the ethnic economy argument demonstrates the role of social capital in wealth creation, it is confined to interactions *within* ethnic communities, which involves some limitations. One is the reification of ethnicity: the salience and boundaries of ethnicity should not be taken for granted; its actual boundaries and practices are fluid. The "ethnic economy" confirms ethnic boundaries, attributing greater solidity to them than may be justified, and involves an inward-looking take on ethnicity and social capital—while inward-looking ethnicity is but one modality of ethnicity and what matters is not merely in-group but also *intergroup* social capital. In-group social capital matches a conservative approach to social capital, as path dependence on the part of given social formations. It parallels a static take on multiculturalism as an archipelago of separate communities, a mosaic of fixed pieces, like a series of ghettos, or apartheid multiplied. Social capital in this sense would match a conservative approach, an economics of apartheid revisited. More fruitful is to view multiculturalism as intercultural interplay and mingling, a terrain of crisscrossing cultural flows, in the process generating new combinations and options; this applies in relation to political interests, lifestyle choices, and economic opportunities. Along these lines there are several ways further, such as considering "immigrant economies," transnational diaspora enterprise, and general perspectives on cultural difference and development.

Economic relations across cultural boundaries extend beyond employment and production, to trade and retail, credit and investment; and beyond immigrants, to natives or nationals, on the one hand, and overseas linkages, on the other. Since cultural differences often overlap with socioeconomic differences (as in the familiar race/class/gender patterns), in many contexts economic relations *across* culture/class differences may be as common as economic relations within culturally homogeneous settings. Thus, in Latin America this involves relations between urban *criollos*, Ladinos, and indigenes; in Africa, between urban entrepreneurs and rural workers or suppliers, often belonging to different ethnicities; in North America, between migrant labor and many types of employers. These relations are so numerous and diverse that they obviously involve many different types of relations across a wide continuum from exploitative to cooperative relations. The profound historical significance of such networks is well known, as shown in studies of Asian entrepreneurial minorities and their role in the making of the world economy (Dobbin 1996) and other diasporas (Kotkin 1992). Stereotypes of trading minorities (such as the Chinese in Southeast Asia, Indians in East Africa, Lebanese and Hausa in West Africa) exploiting local labor may conceal the actual diversity of cross-cultural social capital. We should not merely consider segmented societies but also their in-between spaces and adjacent border zones. We would need a typology of cross-cultural economic relations, and the finer the analytic maze the finer the yield.[4]

The transnational informal sector of small traders in foodstuffs, garments, and spare parts is part of huge transnational entrepreneurial networks that are invisible and unmonitored because they are informal. They typically operate in the economic and legal interstices of economic zones and connect migrant and home communities. They really bridge North-South development gaps. What would be the scope for policy interventions that can strengthen these entrepreneurial activities and deepen their contribution to bridging North-South worlds?

The glaring paradoxes of contemporary globalization include the free movement of capital, on the one hand, and the restricted movement of people and labor, on the other; on the one hand, restrictions on migration and, on the other, the wide North-South gap and growing labor demand in graying labor markets.[5] This in itself creates economic opportunity structures. Uneven development (such as differential wage rates, labor conditions, ecological standards, and brain drain from developing countries) serves as a major economic opportunity structure of different market niches. Migration involves boon and bane for sending and receiving regions. Diasporas and transnational communities utilize the differentials created by political boundaries in a host of ways, from grassroots transnational enterprises (Portes 1995) to criminal organizations (Williams and Vlassis 1997). To address the paradoxes of globalization would involve policy interventions from managing migration (Bhagwati 2003) to global social policy (Deacon et al. 1998).

In countries that have newly become immigration countries labor markets tend to be closed and institutional impediments stand in the way of integrating migrant labor. The Old World is becoming a New World for many but with old institutions. The dilemma is either to protect or to open the welfare state. A dilemma for migrants is to follow the official route and become deskilled and dependent in the process, or to become active in enterprise in the black economy and risk becoming illegal. The options for the Old World countries are either to lower or remove institutional impediments on labor markets and enterprise, or to accept hierarchical integration in the form of segmented labor markets to the disadvantage of migrants. The former may entail dismantling the welfare state to its residual form, as in the "New World" model of free enterprise, which entails ghettos and social gaps. This implies a scenario of "Californianization" while California is being "Brazilianized." Keynesianism is not likely to be revived on a national basis and EU-wide social settlements are slow in the making. Is the alternative to reduce institutional impediments and to go American? But part of the American way is individualism, ghettos, and crime.

Prophetic and utopian visions of human integration and unity have often been wide in spirit but not specific in the forms this might take. When they have been specific, they have often turned oppressive, as a critical literature testifies (Popper 1966, Dahrendorf 1967). Plato's Republic, Campanella's City of the Sun, Francis Bacon's New Atlantis, Fourier's phalanges, the utopian projects of Condorcet, Comte, Proudhon, and Saint-Simon, Lenin's democratic centralism—failed blueprints of social engineering litter the record of history. Speaking at a very general level, forms of human integration while enabling at some stage, turn disabling at a further juncture—the family, the clan, the village, tribe, empire, monarchy, nation state, republic, the concert of nations, the Pan movements, and so forth, have all led human integration up to a point and then become constraints and background music. The point is not to be anti-utopian but to be loosely utopian, not to give up on emancipatory human integration as a myth of Sisyphus, but to take the forms it takes sufficiently lightly. More precisely, both the intent and the forms need to be taken seriously but require combining different kinds of seriousness. Reforms require seriousness of detail and implementation but need to be taken lightly over time, as political circumstances change and can change with lightning speed.

Globalization, then, involves human integration, but this is a long-term, uneven, and paradoxical process. Intercultural relations have been crucial to "national accumulation" all along, though often their contribution has not been recognized. In the era of regionalization, crossborder intercultural relations build social and institutional tissue that is vital to present and future economic performance. Ethnic economies interweave regions spatially (as in the case of Chinese diasporas in the Pacific Basin) while interethnic economies weave links across segmented social formations. There are no easy shortcuts to the global equation. The nation state, the main form of human integration since the nineteenth century, is gradually making place for a wider variety of governance arrangements and different forms of integration including macro-regions and international and supranational forms of governance, which also open up democratic deficits. Migrations, diasporas and multiculturalism, decentralization and the emergence of nongovernmental organizations and social movements—local and transnational—are tugging away at this format, slowly prefiguring different kinds of political dispensation.

CHAPTER 3

GLOBALIZATION AND CULTURE: THREE PARADIGMS

Globalization or the trend of growing worldwide interconnectedness has been accompanied by several clashing notions of cultural difference. The awareness of the world "becoming smaller" and cultural difference receding coincides with a growing sensitivity to cultural difference. The increasing salience of cultural difference forms part of a general cultural turn, which involves a wider self-reflexivity of modernity. Modernization has been advancing like a steamroller, erasing cultural and biological diversity in its way, and now not only the gains (rationalization, standardization, control) but also the losses (alienation, disenchantment, displacement) are becoming apparent. Stamping out cultural diversity has been a form of disenchantment of the world.

Yet it is interesting to note how the notion of cultural difference itself has changed form. It used to take the form of *national* differences, as in prewar discussions of national character and identity. Now different forms of difference have come to the foreground, such as gender and identity politics, ethnic and religious movements, minority rights, and indigenous peoples. An argument prominent during the nineties was that we are experiencing a "clash of civilizations." In this view, cultural differences are regarded as immutable and generating rivalry and conflict. At the same time, there is a widespread understanding that growing global interconnectedness leads toward increasing cultural standardization and uniformization, as in the global sweep of consumerism. A shorthand version of this momentum is McDonaldization. A third position, altogether different from both these models of intercultural relations, is that what is taking place is a process of cultural mixing or hybridization across locations and identities.

This is a meta-theoretical reflection on cultural difference that argues that there are three, and only three, perspectives on cultural difference: cultural differentialism or lasting difference, cultural convergence or growing sameness, and cultural hybridization or ongoing mixing. Each of these positions involves particular theoretical precepts and as such they are paradigms. Each represents a particular *politics of difference*—as lasting and immutable, as erasable and being erased, and as mixing and in the process generating new translocal forms of difference. Each involves different subjectivities and larger perspectives. The first view, according to which cultural difference is immutable, may be the oldest perspective on cultural difference. The second, the thesis of cultural convergence, is as old as the earliest forms of universalism, as in the world religions. Both have been revived and renewed as varieties of modernism, respectively in its romantic and Enlightenment versions, while the third perspective, hybridization, refers to a postmodern sensibility of traveling culture. This chapter discusses the claims of these perspectives, their wider theoretical assumptions, and asks what kind of futures they evoke. Arguably there may be other takes on cultural difference, such as indifference, but none have the scope and depth of the three perspectives outlined here.

CLASH OF CIVILIZATIONS

In 1993 Samuel Huntington, as president of the Institute for Strategic Studies at Harvard University, published a controversial paper in which he argued that "a crucial, indeed a central, aspect of what global politics is likely to be in the coming years . . . will be the clash of civilizations. . . . With the end of the Cold War, international politics moves out of its Western phase, and its centerpiece becomes the interaction between the West and non-Western civilizations and among non-Western civilizations."

The imagery is that of civilizational spheres as tectonic plates at whose fault lines conflict, no longer subsumed under ideology, is increasingly likely. The argument centers on Islam: the "centuries-old military interaction between the West and Islam is unlikely to decline" (1993: 31–32), "Islam has bloody borders" (35). The fault lines include Islam's borders in Europe (as in former Yugoslavia), the Sudanic belt in Africa (animist or Christian cultures to the south and west), and Asia (India, China). Huntington warns against a "Confucian-Islamic military connection" that has come into being in the form of arms flows between East Asia and the Middle East. Thus "the paramount axis of world politics will be the relations between 'the West and the Rest'" and "a central focus of conflict for the immediate future will be between the West and several Islamic-Confucian states" (48). He therefore recommends greater cooperation and unity in the West, between Europe and North America; the inclusion of eastern Europe and Latin America in the West; cooperative relations with Russia and Japan; exploiting differences and conflicts among Confucian and Islamic states; and for the West to maintain its economic and military power to protect its interests.

The idea of dividing the world into civilizations has a long lineage. In Europe, it goes back to the medieval understanding of a tripartite world of descendants of the three sons of Noah (mentioned in chapter 2 above). Arnold Toynbee's world history divided the world into civilizational spheres. It informs the approach of the "Teen Murti" school of Contemporary Studies in Delhi (Sardar and Van Loon 1997: 78). Kavolis (1988) divides the world into seven incommensurable civilizational systems based on religion: Christian, Chinese (Confucian-Taoist-Buddhist), Islamic, Hindu, Japanese (Shinto-Buddhist-Confucian), Latin American syncretism, and non-Islamic African. Galtung (1981) argues that each civilization has different ways of knowing the world. Dividing the world into civilizations is a cliché that echoes in every encyclopedia of world history; but it is also old-fashioned and overtaken by new historiography and the emergence of global history (Mazlish and Buultjens 1993).

Huntington's position stands out for its blatant admixture of security interests and crude rendition of civilizational difference. In view of its demagogic character it obviously belongs to the genre of "new enemy" discourse. In fact, it merges two existing enemy discourses, the "fundamentalist threat" of Islam and the "yellow peril," and its novelty lies in combining them.

Huntington recycles the Cold War: "The fault lines between civilizations are replacing the political and ideological boundaries of the Cold War as the flash points for crisis and bloodshed" (29). "The Velvet Curtain of culture has replaced the Iron Curtain of ideology as the most significant dividing line in Europe" (31). Hence there will be no "peace dividend." The Cold War is over but war is everlasting. This has been referred to as a new politics of containment and a new round of hegemonic rivalry, which is translated from an ideological into a civilizational idiom. Huntington's thesis has given rise to extensive debate and his argument has been widely rejected (e.g., Rashid 1997, Camilleri and Muzaffar 1998) while acknowledging that its contribution has been to present culture as a significant variable in international relations. Huntington has developed his thesis in a book (1996) and followed up with a wider treatment of culture (Harrison and Huntington 2000). I will not reiterate the debate here but bring up key points that show Huntington's view as one of three paradigms of cultural difference.

Huntington constructs the West as a "universal civilization," "directly at odds with the particularism of most Asian societies and their emphasis on what distinguishes one people from another" (41). The charge against "the Rest" is that they attempt modernization without westernization. This may be the actual danger: the specter of *different modernities* and thus the breakdown of western civilizational hegemony. By now, multiple modernities are an accepted theme (see chapter 4 below).

The geopolitics is odd. Significant arms flows between the Middle East and East Asia do not involve Islamic countries but Israel and its arms sales to China, which have been of particular concern to the US because they re-export high-tech equipment of US origin. Another instance, which Huntington does cite, exchanges of military technology between Pakistan and China, also involves an American angle. Major concerns from an American security point of view, such as military relations between China and Iran (and more recently, arms exports from North Korea), are not mentioned.

What is overlooked in this geopolitical construction are the dialectics of the Cold War and the role the United States has been playing. It's not so much a matter of civilizational conflict as the unraveling of geopolitical security games, most of which have been initiated by the US in the first place (discussed in Johnson 2000), which the hegemon in its latter days can no longer control, so it calls on allied states to help channel them in a desirable direction. At the turn of the century, the British Empire in its latter days of waning economic and military power did the same, calling on the United States to "police" the Pacific, the Caribbean, and Latin America, on Japan to play a naval role in the China Sea and to contain the Russian empire, and seeking allies in the European concert of powers. Then as now, the waning hegemon calls on "civilizational" affinities: the White Man's Burden and his civilizing mission, and now "democracy," freedom, and the virtues of the free market.

The sociologist Malcolm Waters formulates a theory according to which "material exchanges localize, political exchanges internationalize and symbolic exchanges globalize" (1995: 156). This is difficult to maintain because it ignores how microeconomic dynamics at the level of firms propel the macroeconomic process of globalization; but interesting in this context is the view that the cultural, symbolic sphere is the first to globalize; a perspective diametrically opposed to Huntington's thesis. This shows the oddity of Huntington's view: it is a *political* perspective on culture coined in conventional national security language. Culture is politicized, wrapped in civilizational packages that just happen to coincide with geopolitical fault lines. Obviously, there is much slippage along the way and all along one wonders: what is national security doctrine doing in a world of globalization and in the sphere of cultural representations? While Huntington focuses on fault lines between civilizations, his pessimism is matched by gloomy views on growing ethnic conflict (as in Moynihan 1993, Kaplan 1996).

Indeed the most remarkable element of the thesis is its surface claim of a clash of *civilizations*. Why is *culture* being presented as the new fault line of conflict? Huntington's framework is a fine specimen of what he blames Asian societies for: "Their emphasis on what distinguishes one people from another." At a general level, this involves a very particular way of reading culture. Compare Immanuel Wallerstein on "culture as the ideological battleground of the modern world-system" (1991): note that culture and ideology are being merged in a single frame, and that culture is defined as "the set of characteristics which distinguish one group from another." Anthony King (1991: 13) uses a similar concept of culture as "collective articulations of human diversity."

If we would take this to its ultimate consequence then, for instance, bilingualism cannot be "cultural" because "it does not distinguish one group from another." Indeed any bicultural, intercultural, multicultural, or transcultural practices could not according to this definition be "cultural." Whichever mode of communication or intercourse different groups would develop to interact with one another would not be cultural for culture refers only to intergroup diversity. We have thus defined any form of intergroup or transnational culture out of existence for such per definition cannot exist. Intercultural diffusion through trade and migration, a lingua franca between cultures, returnees from abroad with bicultural experience, children of mixed parentage, travelers with multicultural experience, professionals interacting cross-culturally, the fields of cyberspace—all of these fall outside "culture."

Obviously, this notion of culture is one-sided to the point of absurdity. Diversity is one side of the picture but only one, and interaction, commonality, or the possibility of commonality is another. In anthropology this is cultural relativism and Ruth Benedict's view of cultures as single wholes—a Gestalt or configuration that can only be understood from within and in its own terms. It implies a kind of "billiard ball" model of cultures as separate, impenetrable units (similar to the way states have been represented in the realist view of international relations). Over time, this generated ethnomethodology, ethnosociology, and a trend toward the indigenization of knowledge. This is an anomalous definition of culture. More common a definition in anthropology is that culture refers to behavior and beliefs that are learned and shared: learned so it is not "instinctual" and shared so it is not individual. Sharing refers to social sharing but there is no limitation as to the boundaries of this sociality. No territorial or historical boundaries are implied as part of the definition. This understanding of culture is open-ended. Learning is always ongoing as a function of changing circumstances and therefore culture is always *open*. To sharing there are no fixed boundaries other than those of common social experience, therefore there are no territorial limitations to culture. Accordingly culture refers as much to commonality as to diversity. In the next chapter, I refer to these fundamentally different notions of culture as territorial culture and translocal culture.[1]

Cultural relativism represents an angle on culture that may be characterized as *culturalist differentialism* (Taguieff 1987, Al-Azmeh 1993). Its lineages are ancient. They are as old as the Greeks who deemed non-Greek speakers "barbarians." Next, this took the form of immutable cultural difference based on religion, separating the faithful from heathens, unbelievers, and heretics. The romantics such as Johann Gottfried Herder revived this view of strong cultural boundaries, now in the form of language as the key to nationhood. Both nationalism and race thinking bear the stamp of cultural differentialism, one emphasizing territory and language, and the other biology as destiny. Nation and race have long been twin and at times indistinguishable discourses. During the era of nationalism, all nations claimed cultural distinction for their own nation and inferiority for others, usually in racial terms. "Jewishness," "Germanness," "Japaneseness," "Englishness," "Turkishness," "Greekness," and so forth, all imply an inward-looking take on culture and identity. They are creation myths of modern times. They all share the problem of boundaries: who belongs, and since when?

Cultural differentialism can serve as a defense of cultural diversity. It may be evoked by local groups resisting the steamroller of assorted "developers," by ecological networks, anthropologists, and artists, as well as travel agencies and advertisers promoting local authenticity. Culture and development, a growing preoccupation in development thinking, may turn "culture" into an asset (Schech and Haggis 2000, Nederveen Pieterse 2010a). It calls to mind the idea of the "human mosaic." An upside of this perspective may be local empowerment; the downside may be a politics of nostalgia, a conservationist posture that ultimately leads to the promotion of open-air museums. Either way the fallacy is the reification of the local, sidelining the interplay between the local and the global. The image of the mosaic is biased, as the anthropologist Ulf Hannerz (1992) points out, because a mosaic consists of fixed, discrete pieces whereas human experience, claims and postures notwithstanding, is fluid and open-ended. Accordingly critical anthropology opts for deterritorialized notions of culture such as flows and "traveling culture."

Huntington's thesis is at odds with the common self-understandings of East and Southeast Asian societies, which run along the lines of East-West fusion, as in "western technology, Asian values." The Confucian ethic may carry overtones of East Asian chauvinism but also represents an East-West nexus of a kind because the neo-Confucianism it refers to owes its status to its reinterpretation as an "Asian Protestant ethic." While Confucianism used to be the reason why East Asian countries were stagnating, by the late twentieth century it has become the reason why the "Tigers" have been progressing. In the process, Confucianism has been recoded as a cross-cultural translation of the Weberian thesis of the Protestant ethic as the "spirit of modern capitalism." The Confucian ethic carries some weight in the "Sinic" circle of Singapore, Taiwan, China, and Korea; it carries less weight in Japan and no weight among the advocates of an "Asian way" such as Prime Minister Mahathir Mohamad of Malaysia and his "Look East" program (Mahathir and Ishihara 1995). Given the tensions between the ethnic Chinese and the "bumiputra" Malays in Malaysia, just as in Indonesia, here an Islamic-Confucian alliance is the least likely option.

While Huntington reproduces standard enemy images of "the Rest," he also rehearses a standard self-image of the West. "The West" is a notion conditioned by and emerging from two historical polarities: the North-South polarity of the colonizing and colonized world, and the East-West polarity of capitalism-communism and the Cold War. These were such overriding fields of tension that differences *within* the West/North, *among* imperialist countries and *within* capitalism faded into the background, subsiding in relation to the bigger issue, the seeming unity of imperialist or neocolonial countries and of the "free world" led by the US. In view of this expansionist history, we might as well turn the tables and say: the West has bloody borders. Thus, Huntington practices both Orientalism and Occidentalism. In reinvoking "the West," the differences between North America and Europe are papered over. In fact, historical revision may well show that there are much greater historical affinities, in particular similar feudal histories with their attendant consequences for the character of capitalisms, between Europe and Asia than between Europe and North America.[2]

In his usual capacity as a comparative political scientist, Huntington (1991) observes a worldwide "third wave" of democratization. Apparently, at this level of discourse civilizational differences *are* receding. In this domain, Huntington follows the familiar thesis of convergence, that is, the usual modernization paradigm of growing worldwide standardization around the model of the "most advanced country," and his position matches Fukuyama's argument of the universal triumph of the idea of liberal democracy.

MCDONALDIZATION

The McDonaldization thesis is a version of the recent idea of the worldwide homogenization of societies through the impact of multinational corporations. McDonaldization, according to the sociologist George Ritzer, is "the process whereby the principles of the fast-food restaurant are coming to dominate more and more sectors of American society as well as the rest of the world" (1993: 19). The expression "the rest of the world" bears contemplating. The process through which this takes place is rationalization in Weber's sense, that is, through formal rationality laid down in rules and regulations. McDonald's formula is successful because it is efficient (rapid service), calculable (fast and inexpensive), predictable (no surprises), and controls labor and customers.

McDonaldization is a variation on a theme: on the classical theme of universalism and its modern forms of modernization and the global spread of capitalist relations. Diffusionism, if cultural diffusion is taken as emanating from a single center (e.g., Egypt), has been a general form of this line of thinking. From the 1950s, this has been held to take the form of Americanization. Since the 1960s, multinational corporations have been viewed as harbingers of American modernization. In Latin America in the 1970s, this effect was known as Coca-colonization. These are variations on the theme of cultural imperialism, in the form of consumerist universalism or global media influence. This line of thinking has been prominent in media studies according to which the influence of American media makes for global cultural synchronization (e.g., Schiller 1989, Hamelink 1983; a critical view is Morley 1994).

Modernization and Americanization are the latest versions of westernization. If colonialism delivered Europeanization, neocolonialism under US hegemony delivers Americanization. Common to both is the modernization thesis, of which Marx and Weber have been the most influential proponents. Marx's thesis was the worldwide spread of capitalism. World-system theory is a current version of this perspective. With Weber, the emphasis is on rationalization, in the form of bureaucratization and other rational social technologies. Both perspectives fall within the general framework of evolutionism, a single-track universal process of evolution through which all societies, some faster than others, are progressing—a vision of universal progress such as befits an imperial world. A twentieth-century version of this line of thinking is Teilhard de Chardin's evolutionary convergence toward the noosphere.

Shannon Peters Talbott (1995) examines the McDonaldization thesis through an ethnography of McDonald's in Moscow and finds the argument inaccurate on every score. Instead of efficiency, queuing (up to several hours) and lingering are commonplace. Instead of being inexpensive, an average McDonald's meal costs more than a third of a Russian worker's average daily wage. Instead of predictability, difference and uniqueness attract Russian customers, while many standard menu items are not served in Moscow. Instead of uniform management control, McDonald's Moscow introduces variations in labor control ("extra fun motivations," fast service competitions, special hours for workers to bring their families to eat in the restaurant) and in customer control by allowing customers to linger, often for more than an hour on a cup of tea, to "soak up the atmosphere."

She concludes that McDonald's in Moscow does not represent cultural homogenization but should rather be understood along the lines of *global localization.* This matches the argument in business studies that corporations, also when they seek to represent "world products," only succeed if and to the extent that they adapt themselves to local cultures and markets. They should become insiders; this is the principle of "insiderization" for which the late Sony chairman Akio Morita coined the term *glocalization,* or "looking in both directions" (Ohmae 1992: 93). Firms may be multinational but "all business is local."

This can lead to counterintuitive consequences, as in the case of the international advertising firm McCann Erickson, whose Trinidad branch to justify a local presence promotes Trinidadian cultural specificity. "The irony is, of course, that . . . it is advertising including transnational agencies which have become the major investors in preserving and promoting images of local specificity, retaining if not creating the idea that Trinidad is different, and inculcating this belief within the population at large" (Miller 1995: 9). The profitability of the transnational firm hinges on the profitability of the branch office whose interest lies in persuading the firm that only local advertising sells.

So far, this only considers the angle of the corporation. The other side of global localization is the attitude of customers. The McDonald's Moscow experience compares with adaptations of American fast food principles elsewhere, for instance in East Asia (Watson 1997). Here fast food restaurants though outwardly the same as the American models serve quite different tastes and needs. They are not down-market junk food but cater to middle-class tastes. They are sought out for their "modern" aesthetics, are appreciated for food variation rather than uniformity, and generate "mixed" offspring, such as "Chinglish" or "Chamerican" restaurants in China. They offer a public space, a meeting place—in a sense culturally neutral because of its novelty—for new types of consumers, such as the consumer market of the young, of working women, and of middle-class families. They function in similar ways in southern Europe and the Middle East. In wintry Tokyo, upstairs in Wendy's young students spend hours doing their homework, smoking, and chatting with friends, because Japanese houses are small.

Thus, rather than cultural homogenization McDonald's and others in the family of western fast food restaurants (Burger King, KFC, Pizza Hut, Wendy's) usher in difference and variety, giving rise to and reflecting new, mixed social forms. Where they are imported, they serve different social, cultural, and economic functions than in their place of origin, and their formula is accordingly adapted to local conditions. In western metropoles, we now see oriental fast food restaurants and chains along with Latino, Middle Eastern, Turkish, and French eateries. Fast food may well have originated outside the West, in the street-side food stalls of the Middle East, Asia, and Africa. American fast-food restaurants serve German food (hamburgers, frankfurters) with French (fries, dressing) and Italian elements (pizza) in American management style. American contributions besides ketchup are assembly-line standardization, in American Taylorist and managerial traditions, and marketing. Thus, it would make more sense to consider McDonaldization as a form of intercultural hybridization, partly in its origins and certainly in its present globally localizing variety of forms.

McDonaldization has sparked growing resistance and wide debate (Alfino et al. 1998, Smart 1999). In its home country, McDonald's is past its peak, its shares declining and franchises closing. Obesity as a national disease and changing diets, saturation of the fast food market, resistance, and litigation contribute to the decline. Beyond "rationalization" this takes us to the shifting shapes of contemporary capitalism. Is contemporary capitalism a homogenizing force? A stream of studies examines the cultures of late capitalism, a problematic often structured by world system thinking (Wallerstein 1991) or at least vocabulary (King 1991). The commodification of labor, services, and information takes myriad forms, under headings each of which are another lament: McJobs, McInformation, McCitizens, McUniversity, McTourism, McCulture, McPrisons, McCourts, McMafia (Gottdiener 2000, Ritzer 2002, Stojkovic et al. 1999, Glenny 2009). One study seeks "to intervene in discourses on transnational capitalism whose tendency is to totalize the world system" (Lowe and Lloyd 1997: 15), but in the process finds that "capitalism has proceeded not through global homogenization but through differentiation of labor markets, material resources, consumer markets, and production operations" (13). The economist Michael Storper finds a combined effect of homogenization and diversification across the world:

> The loss of "authentic" local culture in these places [smaller U.S. cities] is a constant lament. But on the other hand, for the residents of such places—or of Paris, Columbus, or Belo Horizonte, for that matter—there has been an undeniable increase in the variety of material, service, and cultural outputs. In short, the perceived loss of diversity would appear to be attributable to a certain rescaling of territories: from a world of more internally homogeneous localities, where diversity was found by traveling between places with significantly different material cultures to a world where one travels between more similar places but finds increasing variety within them. (Storper 2001: 114–15)

Most studies of capitalism and culture find diverse and hybrid outcomes.[3] This suggests that capitalism itself hosts more diversity than is usually assumed—so the appropriate analytic would rather be capitalisms; and its cultural intersections are more diverse than is generally assumed. The rhizome of capitalism twins then with the rhizome of culture, which brings us to the theme of hybridization.

HYBRIDIZATION: RHIZOMES OF CULTURE

Mixing has been perennial as a process but new as an imaginary. As a perspective, it differs fundamentally from the previous two paradigms. It does not build on an older theorem but opens new windows. It is fundamentally excluded from the other two paradigms. It springs from the taboo zone of race thinking because it refers to that which the doctrines of racial purity and cultural integrism could not bear to acknowledge the existence of: the half-caste, mixed-breed, métis. If it was acknowledged at all, it was cast in diabolical terms. Nineteenth-century race thinking abhorred mixing because, according to Comte de Gobineau and many others, in any mixture the "lower" element would predominate. The idea of mixing goes against all the doctrines of *purity* as strength and sanctity, ancient and classical, of which "race science" and racism have been modern, biologized versions.

Hybridization is an antidote to the cultural differentialism of racial and nationalist doctrines because it takes as its point of departure precisely those experiences that have been banished, marginalized, tabooed in cultural differentialism. It subverts nationalism because it privileges border crossing. It subverts identity politics such as ethnic or other claims to purity and authenticity because it starts out from the fuzziness of boundaries. If modernity stands for an ethos of order and neat separation by tight boundaries, hybridization reflects a postmodern sensibility of cut 'n' mix, transgression, subversion. It represents, in Foucault's terms, a "resurrection of subjugated knowledges" because it foregrounds those effects and experiences which modern cosmologies, whether rationalist or romantic, would not tolerate.

Hybridization goes under various aliases such as syncretism, creolization, métissage, mestizaje, crossover. Related notions are global ecumene, global localization, and local globalization. The next two chapters develop this perspective and discuss several objections to the hybridity thesis. Hybridization may conceal the asymmetry and unevenness in the process and the elements of mixing. Distinctions need to be made between different times, patterns, types, and styles of mixing; besides, mixing carries different meanings in different cultural settings.

Hybridization occurs of course also among cultural elements and spheres *within* societies. In Japan, "Grandmothers in kimonos bow in gratitude to their automated banking machines. Young couples bring hand-held computer games along for romantic evenings out" (Green-feld 1994: 230). Is the hybridization of cultural styles then typically an urban phenomenon, a consequence of urbanization and industrialization? If we look into the countryside virtually anywhere in the world, we find traces of cultural mixing: the crops planted, planting methods and agricultural techniques, implements and inputs used (seeds, fertilizer, irrigation methods, credit) are usually of translocal origin. Farmers and peasants throughout the world are wired, directly or indirectly, to the fluctuations of global commodity prices that affect their economies and decision making. The ecologies of agriculture may be local, but the cultural resources are translocal. Agriculture is a prime site of globalization (Richards 1996, Goodman and Watts 1997).

An interesting objection to the hybridization argument is that what are actually being mixed are cultural *languages* rather than *grammars*. The distinction runs between surface and deep-seated elements of culture. It is, then, the folkloric, superficial elements of culture—foods, costumes, fashions, consumption habits, arts and crafts, entertainments, healing methods—that travel, while deeper attitudes and values, the way elements hang together, the structural ensemble of culture, remain contextually bound. There are several implications to this argument. It would imply that contemporary "planetarization" is a surface phenomenon only because "deep down" humanity remains divided in historically formed cultural clusters. Does this also imply that the new social technologies of telecommunication—from jet aircraft to electronic media—are surface phenomena only that don't affect deep-seated attitudes? If so, the implications would be profoundly conservative. A midway position is that the new technologies are profound in themselves while each historically framed culture develops its own takes on the new spaces of commonality.

Another issue is immigrant and settler societies where intermingling over time represents a historical momentum profound enough to engage cultural grammar and not just language. A prime example is North America. Probably part of the profound and peculiar appeal of American popular culture is precisely its mixed and "traveling" character, its "footloose" lightness, unhinged from the feudal past. In this culture, the grammars of multiple cultures mingle, and this intercultural density may be part of the subliminal attraction of American popular media, music, film, television: the encounter, and often enough the clash, but an intimate clash, of ethnicities, cultures, histories. The intermingling of cultural grammars then makes up the deeply human appeal of American narratives and its worldly character, repackaging elements that came from other shores, in a "Mississippi Masala."

Intercultural mingling itself is a deeply creative process not only in the present phase of accelerated globalization but stretching far back in time. Cees Hamelink notes: "The richest cultural traditions emerged at the actual meeting point of markedly different cultures, such as Sudan, Athens, the Indus Valley, and Mexico" (1983: 4). This sheds a different light on the language/grammar argument: presumably, some grammars have been mingling all along. Thus, a mixture of cultural grammars is part of the intrinsic meaning of the world religions (as against tribal, national religions). More fundamentally, the question is whether the distinction between cultural language and cultural grammar can be maintained at all, as a distinction between surface and depth. Certainly we know that in some spheres nothing has greater depth than the surface. This is the lesson taught by art and aesthetics. Superficial mingling then may have deep overtones. Even so we have been so trained and indoctrinated to think of culture in territorial packages of assorted "imagined communities" that to seriously address the windows opened and questions raised by hybridization in effect requires a decolonization of imagination.

A schematic précis of the three paradigms of cultural difference is in table 3.1.

FUTURES

The futures evoked by these three paradigms are dramatically different. McDonaldization evokes both a triumphalist Americanism and a gloomy picture of a global "iron cage" and global cultural disenchantment. The clash of civilizations likewise offers a horizon of a world of iron, a deeply pessimistic politics of cultural division as a curse that dooms humanity to lasting conflict and rivalry; the world as an archipelago of incommunicable differences, the human dialogue as a dialogue of war, and the global ecumene as an everlasting battlefield. The political scientist Benjamin Barber in *Jihad vs. McWorld* (1995) presents the clash between these two perspectives without giving a sense of the

Table 3.1. Three Ways of Seeing Cultural Difference

Dimensions	Differentialism	Convergence	Mixing
Cosmologies	Purity	Emanation	Synthesis
Analytics	Territorial culture	Cultural centers and diffusion	Translocal culture
Lineages	Differences in language, religion, region. Caste.	Imperial and religious universalisms. Ancient "centrisms"	Mixing technologies, languages, institutions, religions, cuisine, fashion
Modern times	Romantic differentialism. Race thinking, chauvinism. Cultural relativism.	Rationalist universalism. Evolutionism. Modernization. Coca-colonization.	Métissage, syncretism, creolization, hybridization
Present	Clash of civilizations. Ethnic cleansing. Ethnodevelopment, ethnonationalism	McDonaldization, Disneyfication, Barbiefication. Homogenization.	Postmodern views of culture, cultural flows, crossover, cut 'n' mix
Futures	A mosaic of immutably different cultures, civilizations	Global cultural standardization	Open-ended ongoing mixing, new combinations

third option, mixing. Mixing or hybridization is open-ended in terms of experience as well as in a theoretical sense. Its newness means that its ramifications over time are not predictable because it doesn't fit an existing matrix or established paradigm but itself signifies a paradigm shift.

Each paradigm represents a different politics of *multiculturalism*. Cultural differentialism translates into a policy of closure and apartheid. If outsiders are let in at all, they are preferably kept at arm's length in ghettos, reservations, or concentration zones. Cultural communities are best kept separate, as in colonial "plural society" in which communities are not supposed to mix except in the marketplace, or as in gated communities that keep themselves apart. Cultural convergence translates into a politics of assimilation with the dominant group as the cultural center of gravity. Cultural mixing refers to a politics of integration without the need to give up cultural identity while cohabitation is expected to yield new cross-cultural patterns of difference. This is a future of ongoing mixing, ever-generating new commonalities and new differences.

At a deeper level, each paradigm resonates with particular sensibilities and cosmologies. The paradigm of differentialism follows the principle of *purity*, as in ritual purity in the caste system, the *limpieza de sangre* in Spain after the Reconquest, and the preoccupation with purity of blood and lineage among aristocracies, a concern that was subsequently translated into thinking about "race" and class (Nederveen Pieterse 1989: chapter 11). The paradigm of convergence follows the theory of *emanation*, according to which phenomena are the outward expressions of an ultimate numinous realm of being. In its sacred version, this reflects a theology and cosmogony of emanation outward from a spiritual center of power (as in Gnosticism). What follows upon the cycle of emanation, dissemination, and divergence is a cycle of "in-gathering," or a process of convergence. A temporal reflection of this cosmology is the ancient imperial system in which the empire is the circumference of the world and the emperor its center (as in the case of the Pharaoh, the emperor of China as the "middle of the middle kingdom," and imperial Rome) and divine kingship, in which the king embodies the land and the people. Western imperialism and its *mission civilisatrice* or White Man's Burden was a variation on this perspective. Since decolonization, the principle of radiation outward from an imperial center has retained its structure but changed its meaning, from positive to negative, as in dependency theory and the critique of cultural imperialism and Eurocentrism.

The third view is the synthesis that acts as the solvent between these polar perspectives. As such, it owes its existence to the previous two principles and is meaningful only in relation to them. It resolves the tension between purity and emanation, between the local and the global, in a dialectic according to which the local is in the global and the global is in the local. An example in which we see this synthetic motion in operation is Christmas: "The ability of this festival to become potentially the very epitome of globalization derives from the very same quality of easy syncretism which makes Christmas in each and every place the triumph of localism, the protector and legitimation for specific regional and particular customs and traditions" (Miller 1993: 25).[4]

Each paradigm involves a different take on *globalization*. According to cultural differentialism, globalization is a surface phenomenon only: the real dynamic is regionalization, or the formation of regional blocs, which tend to correspond with civilizational clusters. Therefore, the future of globalization is interregional rivalry. According to the convergence principle, contemporary globalization is westernization or Americanization writ large, a fulfillment in installments of the classical imperial and the modernization theses. According to the mixing approach, the outcome of globalization processes is open-ended and current globalization is as much a process of easternization as of westernization, as well as of many interstitial influences.

In the end it turns out that the two clashing trends noted at the beginning, growing awareness of cultural difference and globalization, are not simply contradictory but interdependent. Growing awareness of cultural difference is a function of globalization. Increasing cross-cultural communication, mobility, migration, trade, investment, tourism, all generate awareness of cultural difference. The other side of the politics of difference is that the very striving for recognition implies a claim to equality, equal rights, same treatment: in other words, *a common universe of difference.* Accordingly, the clash between cultural diversity and globalization may well be considered a creative clash.

These views find adherents in each setting and their dispute echoes in every arena. Arguably, cultural self-understandings and empirical evidence confirm the third perspective more than the others do. Through most of Asia, ideas of East-West fusion are a dominant motif. In Africa, recombinations of local and foreign practices are a common notion. Latin America and the Caribbean are steeped in syncretism and creolization. But the imprint of other paradigms runs deep, disputes over identity and meaning are ubiquitous, and besides there is disagreement over the meaning and dynamics of hybridity.

Since 2002 the growth of the Golden Arches has begun to sag in the United States and beyond because of growing criticism of its menus, competition from other fast food chains, and market saturation. Meanwhile other chains such as Starbucks have been expanding. While McDonaldization as a paradigm has been widely criticized, McDonaldization as a theme continues to proliferate—as in the McDonaldization of information, cyberspace, news, churches, labor, and higher education. Parallel notions such as the Disneyfication, Barbiefication, and CNN-ization of society have been sprawling.[5]

The literature on fast food has grown steadily and in different directions from the original McDonaldization thesis. That fast food chains pursue not just strategies of global expansion but different *regional* strategies is now taken as a given. Rather than producing global standardization, they pursue regional strategies or strive toward localization—in menus, advertising, design, and look. McDonald's in Greece sells a Greek salad and in Italy McDonald's offers quality coffee. A report informs, "A new 'food studio' will open in Hong Kong in May, where chefs will devise meals aimed at specific local markets in the region. The studio is similar to the one already open in Paris, which is doing the same for European palates" (Grant 2006). Localization is in line with the business model of the franchise system in which local owners carry risk.

In a further installment of the "glocalization of cuisine," American chains set up restaurants abroad that offer not just American food but domestic food with an American twist—such as Taco Bell serving tacos in Mexico and East Dawning selling Chinese food in China. Both are part of Yum Brands of Louisville, Kentucky, the owner of KFC, Pizza Hut, and other fast food restaurants (Cullen 2008). In this trend American chains primarily sell a management formula, with a service style, an aesthetic and, last, if it applies, brand recognition and a product. At any rate, a common variable is the spread of processed foods and fast food, which follows urbanization and media and marketing culture, and brings in its trail diabetes, obesity, and other ailments of life in the fast lane (Schlosser 2002).

Attention now goes also to foreign restaurants and fast food in the United States and Europe. As Jennifer Lee notes, there are about forty thousand Chinese restaurants in the United States, more than the number of McDonald's, Burger Kings, and KFCs combined. Traveling the world to trace the origins of fortune cookies and General Tso and chop suey recipes, she finds them in the United States (Lee 2008).

This trend includes McDonaldization in reverse. A case in point is the "globalization of sushi" (Bestor 2000, Issenberg 2007). Yoshinoya, which started in Tokyo's fish market district in 1899, is now a global corporation with 92 franchise stores in California. Jollibee, a McDonald's imitator that pushed McDonald's into second place in the Philippines, now also runs 11 branches in California. In Japan 7-Eleven is now Japanese owned, and the new owner has started to open convenience store branches in California (Stein 2007). In other words, the business and management model exported by the United States can be followed by others and brought back to the United States.

To the familiar rivalry between film industries—Hollywood, Bollywood, Nollywood (Nigerian film), European, Latin American, Chinese and Middle Eastern film and television (Tyrrell 2008, Cowen 2002)—there are new turns. The interspersion of Hong Kong movies in the Hollywood movie industry was long established, as in movies starring Bruce Lee and Jackie Chan. Immigrant experiences and sensibilities have been a rising theme in literature and movies. Films such as *Mississippi Masala* (1991), *The Namesake* (2006), and *The Reluctant Fundamentalist* (2013) by the Indian-born movie director Mira Nair typically deal with Indian and Pakistani immigrants in the United States, just as works written by Hanif Kureishi, such as the film *My Beautiful Laundrette* (1985) and *The Buddha of Suburbia* novel (1990) and BBC television series (1993), deal with Pakistani and South Asian experiences in the UK.

A recent twist is the cooperation between Hollywood and Bollywood, as seen in the agreement between DreamWorks and India's Reliance Big Entertainment, owned by Anil Ambani. Ambani will provide financing in the amount of $500 million to the Hollywood production company owned by Steven Spielberg and David Geffen in an attempt to enter the American movie market with joint productions (Garrahan and Leahy 2008). In time this will lead to new combinations and interspersions. This crossover also seeks to appeal to NRI (non-resident Indian) audiences. Another twist in 2008 was Abu Dhabi Media's investing $1 billion in Warner Brothers to make movies and video games.

Cross flow in crafts, music and art, Internet and computers, and video games has been far more pervasive than in movies. John Rockwell notes that "the music business is more flexible than the movie business" mostly because of "the relatively small cost of recording and pressing a CD as opposed to making a film." Thus the music of Youssou N'Dour is "both borderless and indigenous" and "challenges the fear of globalization" (Rockwell 2003). Salif Keita likewise combines similar multiple resonances: African, griot, and French. In fact, much contemporary African music has been recorded in Paris (Orlean 2002).

Indian singers and musicians in the Caribbean combine calypso and creole with Indian instruments and themes in chutney while Afro-West Indians combine calypso and American R&B in soca. In Britain, "Asian Kool, a mix of bhangra, rap, reggae, and hip-hop music, could be the next big thing," as shown by the popularity of fusion artists such as Style Bhai, Apache Indian, Fun-da-Mental, and DJ Ritu (Raghavan 1994). This is the London of the "desi beats," Brick Lane, 2nd Generation Magazine, "Little Bombay" in Southall, the monthly club night at the Bombay Bronx club, and Gautam Malkani's evocative novel *Londonstani*.

Scrambling traditions is a musical style in hip-hop and rap, DJing and dubbing, and graffiti. Hip-hop and rap have become transnational repertoires ("hip-hop has been the CNN of the street"), as in Moroccan rap, Berber rap, Turks rapping in Berlin, Africans rapping in Paris, and rap in Malawi. They serve as musical meeting places—intercultural up to a point—and as ways of marking turf and ethnic and masculinist identity. The thesis of "Americanization" is, as usual, exaggerated. "Take a taxi in any foreign city and listen to the driver's radio. Chances are it will be playing the local pop music, and chances are that music will be both familiar and, refreshingly, unfamiliar. I've had this experience in Mexico, in India, in Thailand, in Romania, in China, in Russia. Despite the dominance of American marketing and the genuine popularity of some American artists, the local traditions have enough vitality to make use of the internationalized technology, not to be submerged by it" (Rockwell 2003).

The vivid paintings of the Kinshasa artist Chéri Samba flaunt contradictions and inconsistencies. And a historian comments, "He is hybrid because that's the way his world is" (Jewsiewicki 1995: 18). Imagination is borderless. The next chapters develop the theme of hybridity as a major departure in understanding cultural difference.

CHAPTER 4

GLOBALIZATION AS HYBRIDIZATION

The most common interpretations of globalization are the idea that the world is becoming more uniform and standardized, through a technological, commercial, and cultural synchronization emanating from the West, and that globalization is tied up with modernity. These perspectives are interrelated, if only in that they are both variations on an underlying theme of globalization as westernization. The former is critical in intent while the latter is ambiguous. My argument takes issue with both these interpretations as narrow assessments of globalization and instead argues for viewing globalization as a process of hybridization that gives rise to a global mélange.

GLOBALIZATIONS PLURAL

Globalization, according to Albrow, "refers to all those processes by which the peoples of the world are incorporated into a single world society, global society" (1990: 9). Since these processes are plural, we may as well conceive of globalizations in the plural. Thus, in social science there are as many conceptualizations of globalization as there are disciplines. In economics, globalization refers to economic internationalization and the spread of capitalist market relations. "The global economy is the system generated by globalising production and global finance" (Cox 1992: 30). In international relations, the focus is on the increasing density of interstate relations and the development of global politics. In sociology, the concern is with increasing world-wide social densities and the emergence of "world society." In cultural studies, the focus is on global communications and worldwide cultural standardization, as in Cocacolonization and McDonaldization, and on postcolonial culture. In history, the concern is with conceptualizing "global history" (Mazlish and Buultjens 1993). *All* these approaches and themes are relevant if we view globalization as a multidimensional process, which, like all significant social processes, unfolds in multiple realms of existence simultaneously. Accordingly, globalization may be understood in terms of an open-ended synthesis of several disciplinary approaches. This extends beyond social science—for instance, to ecological concerns, technology, and agricultural techniques. Another way to conceive of globalizations plural is that there are as many modes of globalization as there are globalizing agents and dynamics or impulses. Historically these range from long-distance cross-cultural trade, religious organizations, and knowledge networks to contemporary multinational corporations, banks, international institutions, technological exchange, and transnational social movements networks. We can further differentiate between globalization as policy and project, as in the case of Amnesty International, which is concerned with internationalizing human rights standards; or as unintended consequence, as in the case of the "globalizing panic" of AIDS. *Globalism* is the policy of furthering or managing (a particular mode of) globalization. In political economy, it refers to policies furthering economic internationalization or to the corporate globalism of transnational enterprises; and in foreign affairs, to the global stance in US foreign policy, both in its initial postwar posture (Ambrose 1971) and its post–Cold War stance. These varied dimensions all point to the inherent fluidity, indeterminacy, and open-endedness of globalizations. If this is the point of departure it becomes less obvious to think of globalizations in terms of standardization and less likely that globalizations can be one-directional processes, either structurally or culturally.

GLOBALIZATION AND MODERNITY

Modernity is a keynote in reflections on globalization in sociology. In several prominent conceptualizations, globalization is the corollary of modernity (e.g., Giddens 1990).[1] It's not difficult to understand this trend. In conjunction with globalization, modernity provides a structure and periodization. In addition, this move reflects the general thematization of modernity in social science from Jürgen Habermas to Marshall Berman. Together globalization and modernity make up a ready-made package. Ready-made because it closely resembles the earlier, well-established conceptualization of globalization: the Marxist theme of the spread of the world market. The timing and pace are the same in both interpretations: the process starts in the 1500s and experiences its high tide from the late nineteenth century. The structures are the same: the nation state and individualization—vehicles of modernity or, in the Marxist paradigm, corollaries of the spread of the world market. In one view, universalism refers to the logic of the market and the law of value, and in the other, to modern values of achievement. World-system theory is the most well known conceptualization of globalization in the Marxist lineage; its achievement has been to make "society" as the unit of analysis appear a narrow focus, while on the other hand it faithfully replicates the familiar constraints of Marxist determinism (Nederveen Pieterse 1989).

There are several problems associated with the modernity/globalization approach. In either conceptualization, whether centered on capitalism or modernity, globalization begins in and emanates from Europe and the West. In effect, it is a theory of westernization by another name, which replicates all the problems associated with Eurocentrism: a narrow window on the world, historically and culturally. With this agenda, it should be called westernization and not globalization. Another problem is that globalization theory turns into or becomes an annex of modernization theory. While modernization theory is a passed station in sociology and development theory it is making a comeback under the name of globalization—the 1950s and 1960s revisited under a wide global umbrella. Roland Robertson takes issue with the prioritization of modernity in Giddens' work (1990: 138–45). Robertson's approach to globalization is multidimensional with an emphasis on sociocultural processes. Yet his preoccupation with themes such as "global order" is, according to Arnason, "indicative of a Parsonian approach, transferred from an artificially isolated and unified society to the global condition" (1990: 222). The re-thematization of modernity (Tiryakian 1991) indicates the continuing interest in modernization thinking, but the problems remain. The tendency to focus on social structure produces an account from which the dark side of modernity is omitted. What of modernity in the light of Bauman's *Modernity and the Holocaust*? While the Marxist perspective involves a critical agenda, the thematization of modernity, whether or not it serves as a stand-in for capitalism, does not: "The ambiguities involved in this discourse are such that it is possible, within it, to lose any sense of cultural domination: to speak of modernity can be to speak of cultural change as 'cultural fate' in the strong sense of historical . . . inevitability. This would be to abandon any project of rational cultural critique" (Tomlinson 1991: 141).

Generally, questions of power are marginalized in both the capitalism and modernity perspectives. Another dimension that is conspicuously absent from modernity accounts is imperialism. Modernity accounts tend to be societally inward looking, in a rarefied sociological narrative, as if modernity precedes and conditions globalization, and not the other way round: globalization constituting one of the conditions for modernity. The implication of the modernity/globalization view is that the history of globalization begins with the history of the West. But is it not precisely the point of globalizations as a perspective that globalizations begin with world history? The modernity/globalization view is not only geographically narrow (westernization) but also historically shallow (1500 plus). The time frame of some of the relevant perspectives is as follows (table 4.1).

Apparently the broad heading of globalization accommodates some very different views. The basic understanding is usually a neutral formulation, such as "Globalization can thus be defined as the intensification of worldwide social relations which link distant localities in such a way that local happenings are shaped by events occurring many miles away and vice versa" (Giddens 1990: 64). The "intensification of worldwide social relations" can be thought of as a long-term

Table 4.1. Timing of Globalization

Author	Start	Theme
Manning	1000 BCE	Commercial revolution
Hobson	500	Oriental globalization
Marx	1500s	Modern capitalism
Wallerstein	1500s	Modern world-system
Robertson	1500s, 1870–1920s	Multidimensional
Habermas, Giddens	1800	Modernity
Tomlinson	1960s	Cultural planetarization

process that finds its beginnings in the first migrations of peoples and long-distance trade connections, and subsequently accelerates under particular conditions (the spread of technologies, religions, literacy, empires, capitalism). Or, it can be thought of as consisting only of the later stages of this process, from the time of the accelerating formation of global social relations, and as a specifically global momentum associated with particular conditions (the development of a world market, western imperialism, modernity). It can be narrowed down further by regarding globalization as a particular epoch and formation—as in Tomlinson's view of globalization as the successor to imperialism (rather than imperialism being a mode of globalization), Jameson's view of the new cultural space created by late capitalism, and David Harvey's argument that associates globalization with the postmodern condition of time-space compression and flexible accumulation. But, whichever the emphasis, globalization as the "intensification of worldwide social relations" presumes the prior existence of "worldwide social relations," so that globalization is the conceptualization of a *phase* following an existing condition of *globality* and part of an ongoing process of the formation of worldwide social relations. This recognition of historical depth brings globalizations back to world history and beyond the radius of modernity/westernization.

One way around the problem of modernization/westernization is the idea of multiple *paths* of modernization, which avoids the onus of Eurocentrism and provides an angle for reproblematizing western development. Benjamin Nelson advances this as part of his concern with "intercivilizational encounters" (1981). The idea that "all societies create their own modernity," or at any rate of alternative modernities, is now a salient theme (Gaonkar 2001, Eisenstadt 2002).

The modernizations plural approach matches the notion of the *historicity* of modernization, which is common in South and East Asia (Singh 1989). That Japanese modernization has followed a different path from that of the West is a cliché in Japanese sociology (Tominaga 1990) and well established in Taiwan and China (Li 1989, Sonoda 1990). It results in an outlook that resembles the argument of poly-centrism and multiple paths of development (Amin 1990). But this remains a static and one-dimensional representation: the multiplication of centers still hinges on centrism. It's not much use to make up for Eurocentrism and occidental narcissism by opting for other centrisms such as Sinocentrism, Indocentrism, Afrocentrism, or polycentrism. In effect, this echoes the turn of the century Pan-movements: Pan-Slavism, Pan-Islamism, Pan-Arabism, Pan-Turkism, Pan-Europeanism, Pan-Africanism, and so forth, in which the logic of nineteenth-century racial classifications is carried further under the heading of civiliza-tional provinces turned into political projects. This may substitute one centrism and parochialism for another and miss the fundamental point of the "globalization of diversity," of the mélange effect pervading ev-erywhere, from the heartlands to the extremities and vice versa.

STRUCTURAL HYBRIDIZATION

With respect to cultural forms, hybridization is defined as "the ways in which forms become separated from existing practices and recombine with new forms in new practices" (Rowe and Schelling 1991: 231). This principle also applies to structural forms of social organization.

It is by now a familiar argument that nation state formation is an expression and function of globalization and not a process contrary to it (Greenfield 1992). At the same time it is apparent that the pres-ent phase of globalization involves the relative weakening of nation states—as in the weakening of the "national economy" in the context of economic globalism and, culturally, the decline of patriotism. But this too is not simply a one-directional process. Thus, the migration move-ments that make up demographic globalization can engender absentee patriotism and long-distance nationalism, as in the political affinities of Irish, Jewish, and Palestinian diasporas and émigré or exiled Sikhs in Toronto, Tamils in London, Kurds in Germany, and Tibetans in India (B. Anderson 1992).

Globalization can mean the reinforcement of or go together with localism, as in "Think globally, act locally." This kind of tandem operation of local/global dynamics, or glocalization, is at work in the case of minorities who appeal to transnational human rights standards beyond state authorities, or indigenous peoples who find support for local demands from transnational networks. The upsurge of ethnic identity politics and religious revival movements can also be viewed in the light of globalization. "Identity patterns are becoming more complex, as people assert local loyalties but want to share in global values and lifestyles" (Ken Booth quoted in Lipschutz 1992: 396). *Particularity*, notes Robertson, is a *global* value and what is taking place is a "universalization of particularism" or "the global valorization of particular identities" (1992: 130).

Global dynamics such as the fluctuations of commodity prices on the world market can result in the reconstruction of ethnic identities, as occurred in Africa in the 1980s (T. Shaw 1986). State development policies can engender a backlash of ethnic movements (Kothari 1988). Thus "globalisation can engender an awareness of political difference as much as an awareness of common identity; enhanced international communications can highlight conflicts of interest and ideology, and not merely remove obstacles to mutual understanding" (Held 1992: 32).

Globalization can mean the reinforcement of both supranational and subnational regionalism. The European Union is a case in point. Formed in response to economic challenges from Japan and the United States, it represents more than the internal market and is becoming an administrative, legal, political, and cultural formation, involving multiple Europes: a Europe of the nations, the regions, "European civilization," Christianities, and so on. The dialectics of unification mean, for instance, that constituencies in Northern Ireland can appeal to the European Court of Human Rights in Strasbourg on decisions of the British courts, or that Catalonia can outflank Madrid and Brittany outmaneuver Paris by appealing to Brussels or by establishing links with other regions (e.g., between Catalonia and the Ruhr area). Again, there is an ongoing flow or cascade of globalization–regionalism–subregionalism. Or, "Globalization encourages macro-regionalism, which, in turn, encourages micro-regionalism" (Cox 1992: 34).

Micro-regionalism in poor areas will be a means not only of affirming cultural identities but of claiming pay-offs at the macro-regional level for maintaining political stability and economic good behaviour. The issues of redistribution are thereby raised from the sovereign state level to the macro-regional level, while the manner in which redistributed wealth is used becomes decentralised to the micro-regional level. (Cox 1992: 35)

What globalization means in structural terms, then, is the *increase in the available modes of organization:* transnational, international, macro-regional, national, microregional, municipal, local. This ladder of administrative levels is being crisscrossed by *functional networks* of corporations, international organizations, nongovernmental organizations, as well as professionals and computer users. This approximates Rosenau's "postinternational politics," made up of two interactive worlds with overlapping memberships: a state-centric world, in which the primary actors are national, and a multicentric world of diverse actors such as corporations, international organizations, ethnic groups, churches (1990). These multicentric functional networks in turn are nested within broader sprawling "scapes," such as finanscapes and ethnoscapes (Appadurai 1990). Furthermore, not only these modes of organization are important but also the informal spaces that are created in between, the interstices. Inhabited by diasporas, migrants, exiles, refugees, nomads, these are sites of what the sociologist Michael Mann (1986) calls "interstitial emergence" and identifies as important sources of social renewal.

Also in political economy, we can identify a wide range of hybrid formations. The articulation of modes of production follows a principle of hybridization. The dual economy argument saw neatly divided economic sectors while the articulation argument sees interactive sectors giving rise to mélange effects, such as "semi-proletarians" who have one foot in the agrarian subsistence sector. Counterpoised to the idea of the dual economy split in traditional/modern and feudal/capitalist sectors, the articulation argument holds that what has been taking place is an interpenetration of modes of production. Uneven articulation in turn gives rise to asymmetric integration (Terhal 1987). Dependency theory may be read as a theory of structural hybridization in which dependent capitalism is a mélange category in which the logics of capitalism and imperialism have merged. Recognition of this hybrid condition is what distinguishes neo-Marxism from classical Marxism (in which capital was regarded as a "permanently revolutionizing force"): that is, regular capitalism makes for development but dependent capitalism makes for the "development of underdevelopment." The contested notion of semiperiphery may also be viewed as a hybrid formation.[2] In a wider context, the mixed economy, the informal sector, and the "third sector" of the "social economy," comprising cooperative and nonprofit organizations, may be viewed as hybrid economic formations. Social capital, civic entrepreneurship, and corporate citizenship—all themes of our times—are thoroughly hybrid in character.

Hybrid formations constituted by the interpenetration of diverse logics manifest themselves in *hybrid sites* and spaces. Thus, urbanization amid the fusion of precapitalist and capitalist modes of production, as in parts of Latin America, may give rise to "cities of peasants" (Roberts 1978). Border zones are the meeting places of different organizational modes—such as free enterprise zones and offshore banking facilities (hybrid meeting places of state sovereignty and transnational enterprise), overseas military facilities, and surveillance stations (Enloe 1989). Borderlands generally are a significant topos (Anzaldúa 1987). The blurring and reworking of public and private spaces is a familiar theme (Helly and Reverby 1992). Global cities and ethnic mélange neighborhoods within them (such as Jackson Heights in Queens, New York) are other hybrid spaces in the global landscape. The use of information technology in supranational financial transactions (Wachtel 1990) gives rise to a hyperspace of capital.

Another dimension of hybridity concerns the experience of time, as in the notion of *mixed times* (tiempos mixtos) common in Latin America, where it refers to the coexistence and interspersion of premodernity, modernity, and postmodernity (Calderón 1988, Vargas 1992). A similar point is that "intrinsic asynchrony" is a "general characteristic of Third World cultures" (Hösle 1992: 237).

Globalization, then, increases the range of organizational options, all of which are in operation simultaneously. Each or a combination of these may be relevant in specific social, institutional, legal, political, economic, or cultural spheres. What matters is that no single mode has a necessary overall priority or monopoly. This is one of the salient differences between the present phase of globalization and the preceding era from the 1840s to the 1960s, the great age of nationalism when by and large the nation state was the single dominant organizational option. While the spread of the nation state has been an expression of globalization, the dynamic has not stopped there.

The overall tendency toward increasing global density and interdependence, or globalization, translates, then, into the pluralization of organizational forms. Structural hybridization and the mélange of diverse modes of organization give rise to a pluralization of forms of cooperation and competition as well as to novel mixed forms of cooperation. This is the structural corollary to flexible specialization and just-in-time capitalism and, on the other hand, to cultural hybridization and multiple identities. Multiple identities and the decentering of the social subject are grounded in the ability of individuals to avail themselves of several organizational options at the same time. Thus globalization is the framework for the diversification and amplification of "sources of the self."

A different concern is the scope and depth of the historical field. The westernization/modernity views on globalization only permit a global momentum with a short memory. Globalization taken widely, however, refers to the formation of a worldwide historical field and involves the development of global memory, arising from shared global experiences. Such shared global experiences range from intercivilizational encounters such as long-distance trade and migration to slavery, conquest, war, imperialism, colonialism. It has been argued that the latter would be irrelevant to global culture:

> Unlike national cultures, a global culture is essentially memoryless. When the "nation" can be constructed so as to draw upon and revive latent popular experiences and needs, a "global culture" answers to no living needs, no identity-in-the-making. . . . There are no "world memories" that can be used to *unite* humanity; the most global experiences to date—colonialism and the World Wars—can only serve to remind us of our historic cleavages. (A. Smith 1990: 180)

If, however, conflict, conquest, and oppression would *only* divide people, then nations themselves would merely be artifacts of division for they too were mostly born out of conflict (e.g., Hechter 1975). Likewise, on the larger canvas, it would be shallow and erroneous to argue that the experiences of conflict merely divide humanity: they also unite humankind, even if in painful ways and producing an ambivalent kind of unity (Abdel-Malek 1981, Nederveen Pieterse 1989). Unity emerging out of antagonism and conflict is the ABC of dialectics. It is a recurrent theme in postcolonial literature, for example, *The Intimate Enemy* (Nandy 1983). The intimacy constituted by repression and resistance is not an uncommon notion either, as hinted in the title of the Israeli author Uri Avneri's book about Palestinians, *My Friend the Enemy* (1986). A conflictual unity bonded by common political and cultural experiences, including the experience of domination, has been part of the makeup of hybrid postcolonial cultures. Thus, the former British Empire remains in many ways a unitary space featuring a common language, common elements in legal and political systems, infrastructure, traffic rules, an imperial architecture that is in many ways the same in India as in South Africa, along with the legacy of the Commonwealth (King 1990).

Robertson makes reference to the deep history of globality, particularly in relation to the spread of world religions, but reserves the notion of globalization for later periods, starting in the 1500s, considering that what changes over time is "the scope and depth of consciousness of the world as a single place." In his view, "contemporary globalization" also refers to "cultural and subjective matters" and involves *awareness* of the global human condition, a global consciousness that carries reflexive connotations (1992: 183). No doubt this reflexivity is significant, also because it signals the potential capability to act upon the global human condition. On the other hand, there is no good reason why such reflexivity should halt at the gates of the West and not also arise from and be cognizant of the deep history of intercivilizational connections including the influence of the world religions.

GLOBAL MÉLANGE

How do we come to terms with phenomena such as Thai boxing by Moroccan girls in Amsterdam, Asian rap in London, Irish bagels, Chinese tacos, and Mardi Gras Indians in the United States, or "Mexican schoolgirls dressed in Greek togas dancing in the style of Isadora Duncan" (Rowe and Schelling 1991: 161)? How do we interpret Peter Brook directing the Mahabharata, or Ariane Mnouchkine staging a Shakespeare play in Japanese Kabuki style for a Paris audience in the Théâtre Soleil? Cultural experiences, past or present, have not been simply moving in the direction of cultural uniformity and standardization. This is not to say that the notion of global cultural synchronization (Schiller 1989) is irrelevant, on the contrary, but it is fundamentally incomplete. It overlooks the countercurrents—the impact nonwestern cultures have been making on the West. It downplays the ambivalence of the global- izing momentum and ignores the role of local reception of western culture—for example, the indigenization of western elements. It fails to see the influence nonwestern cultures have been exercising on one another. It has no room for crossover culture, as in the development of "third cultures" such as world music. It overrates the homogeneity of western culture and overlooks the fact that many of the standards exported by the West and its cultural industries themselves turn out to be of culturally mixed character if we examine their cultural lineages. Centuries of South-North cultural osmosis have resulted in interconti- nental crossover culture. European and western culture are *part* of this global mélange. This is an obvious case if we reckon that Europe until the fourteenth century was invariably the recipient of cultural influ- ences from the "Orient."[3] The hegemony of the West dates only from very recent time, from 1800 and, arguably, from industrialization.

One of the terms offered to describe this interplay is the *creolization* of global culture (Hannerz 1987). This approach is derived from Creole languages and linguistics. Creolization is itself an odd, hybrid term. In the Caribbean and North America it stands for the mixture of African and European (the Creole cuisine of New Orleans, etc.), while in Latin America *criollo* originally denoted those of European descent born on the continent.[4] "Creolization" means a Caribbean window on the world. Part of its appeal is that it goes against the grain of nineteenth- century racism and the accompanying abhorrence of métissage as miscegenation, as in the view that race mixture leads to decadence and decay for in every mixture the lower element is bound to predominate. The doctrine of racial purity involves the fear of and *dédain* for the half- caste. By stressing and foregrounding the *mestizo* factor, the mixed and in-between, creolization highlights what has been hidden and valorizes boundary crossing. It also implies an argument with westernization: the West itself may be viewed as a mixture and western culture as a Creole culture.

The Latin American term *mestizaje* also refers to boundary-crossing mixture. Since the early 1900s, however, this has served as a hegemonic elite ideology, which refers to "whitening" or Europeanization as the overall project for Latin American countries: the European element is supposed to maintain the upper hand and through the gradual "whitening" of the population and culture, Latin America is supposed to achieve modernity (Graham 1990, Whitten and Torres 1992). A limitation of both creolization and mestizaje is that they are confined to the experience of the post-sixteenth-century Americas.

Another terminology is the "orientalization of the world," which is referred to as "a distinct global process" (Featherstone 1990). In Duke Ellington's words, "We are all becoming a little Oriental" (quoted in Fischer 1992: 32). It is reminiscent of the theme of "East wind prevails over West wind" that runs through Sultan Galiev, Mao, and Abdel-Malek. In the setting of the rise of China and the Asian newly industrialized countries, it evokes the twenty-first century as an "Asian century" and the Asian Renaissance (Park 1985, Ibrahim 1996).

Each of these terms—creolization, mestizaje, orientalization—opens a different window on the global mélange. In the United States, *crossover* culture denotes the adoption of black cultural characteristics by European Americans and of white elements by African Americans. As a general notion, crossover culture may aptly describe long-term global intercultural osmosis and global mélange. Still what are not clarified are the *terms* under which cultural interplay and crossover take place. In terms such as global mélange, what is missing is acknowledgment of the actual unevenness, asymmetry, and inequality in global relations.

THEORIZING HYBRIDITY

Given the backdrop of nineteenth-century discourse, it's no wonder that those arguments that acknowledge hybridity often do so on a note of regret and loss—loss of purity, wholeness, authenticity. Thus according to the sociologist Hisham Sharabi, neopatriarchal society in the contemporary Arab world is "a new, hybrid sort of society/culture," "neither modern nor traditional" (1988: 4). The "neopatriarchal petty bourgeoisie" is likewise characterized as a "hybrid class" (1988: 6). This argument is based on an analysis of "the political and economic conditions of distorted, dependent capitalism" in the Arab world (1988:

5), in other words, it is derived from the framework of dependency theory.

In arguments such as these hybridity functions as a negative trope, in line with the nineteenth-century paradigm according to which hybridity, mixture, mutation are negative developments that detract from prelapsarian purity—in society and culture as in biology. Since the development of Mendelian genetics in the 1870s and subsequently in early-twentieth-century biology, however, a revaluation has taken place according to which crossbreeding and polygenic inheritance have come to be positively valued as enrichments of gene pools. Gradually this has been seeping through in wider circles; the work of the anthropologist Gregory Bateson (1972), as one of the few to connect the natural sciences and the social sciences, has been influential in this regard.

In poststructuralist and postmodern analysis, hybridity and syncretism have become key words. Thus, hybridity is the antidote to essentialist notions of identity and ethnicity (Lowe 1991). Cultural syncretism refers to the methodology of montage and collage, to "cross-cultural plots of music, clothing, behaviour, advertising, theatre, body language, or . . . visual communication, spreading multi-ethnic and multi-centric patterns" (Canevacci 1993: 3; 1992). Interculturalism, rather than multiculturalism, is a keynote of this kind of perspective. But it also raises different problems. What is the political portée of the celebration of hybridity? Is it merely another sign of perplexity turned into virtue by those grouped on the consumer end of social change? According to Ella Shohat, "A celebration of syncretism and hybridity per se, if not articulated in conjunction with questions of hegemony and neo-colonial power relations, runs the risk of appearing to sanctify the *fait accompli* of colonial violence" (1992: 109). Hence, a further step is not merely to celebrate but to theorize hybridity.

A theory of hybridity would be attractive. We are so used to theories that are concerned with establishing boundaries and demarcations among phenomena—units or processes that are as neatly as possible set apart from other units or processes—that a theory that instead would focus on fuzziness and mélange, cut 'n' mix, crisscross and crossover, might well be a relief in itself. Yet, ironically, of course, it would have to prove itself by giving as neat as possible a version of messiness, or an unhybrid categorization of hybridities.

By what yardstick would we differentiate hybridities? One consideration is in what context hybridity functions. At a general level, hybridity concerns the mixture of phenomena that are held to be different, separate; hybridization then refers to a *cross-category* process. Thus with the linguist Bakhtin (1968) hybridization refers to sites, such as fairs, that bring together the exotic and the familiar, villagers and townspeople, performers and observers. The categories can also be cultures, nations, ethnicities, status groups, classes, and genres, and hybridity by its very existence blurs the distinctions among them. Hybridity functions, next, as part of a power relationship between center and margin, hegemony and minority, and indicates a blurring, destabilization, or subversion of that hierarchical relationship.

One of the original notions of hybridity is *syncretism,* the fusion of religious forms. Here we can distinguish syncretism as *mimicry*—as in Santeria, Candomble, Vodûn, in which Catholic saints serve as masks behind which non-Christian forms of worship are practiced (R. F. Thompson 1984). The Virgin of Guadalupe as a mask and disguise for Pacha Mama is another example. On the other hand, we find syncretism as a mélange not only of forms but also of beliefs, a merger in which both religions, Christian and native, have changed and a "third religion" has developed (as in Kimbangism in the Congo).

Another phenomenon is hybridity as migration mélange. A common observation is that second-generation immigrants, in the West and elsewhere, display mixed cultural traits—a separation between and, next, a mix of a home culture and language (matching the culture of origin) and an outdoor culture (matching the culture of residence), as in the combination "Muslim in the daytime, disco in the evening" (Feddema 1992).

In postcolonial literature, hybridity is a familiar and ambivalent trope. Homi Bhabha (1990) refers to hybrids as intercultural brokers in the interstices between nation and empire, producing counternarratives from the nation's margins to the "totalizing boundaries" of the nation. At the same time, refusing nostalgic models of precolonial purity, hybrids, by way of mimicry, may conform to the "hegemonized rewriting of the Eurocentre." Hybridity, in this perspective, can be a condition tantamount to alienation, a state of homelessness. Smadar Lavie comments: "This is a response-oriented model of hybridity. It lacks agency, by not empowering the hybrid. The result is a fragmented Otherness in the hybrid" (1992: 92). In the work of Gloria Anzaldúa and others, she recognizes, on the other hand, a community-oriented mode of hybridity, and notes that "reworking the past exposes its hybridity, and to recognize and acknowledge this hybrid past in terms of the present empowers the community and gives it agency" (Lavie 1992).

An ironical case of hybridity as intercultural crossover is mentioned by Michael Bérubé, interviewing the African American literary critic Houston Baker Jr.: "That reminds me of your article in *Technoculture,* where you write that when a bunch of Columbia-graduate white boys known as Third Bass attack Hammer for not being black enough or strong enough . . . *that's* the moment of hybridity" (1992: 551).

Taking in these lines of thought, we can construct a *continuum of hybridities:* on one end, an assimilationist hybridity that leans over toward the center, adopts the canon, and mimics hegemony and, at the other end, a destabilizing hybridity that blurs the canon, reverses the current, subverts the center. Hybridities, then, may be differentiated according to the components in the mélange: an assimilationist hybridity in which the center predominates—as in V. S. Naipaul, known for his trenchant observations such as there's no decent cup of coffee to be had in Trinidad; a posture that has given rise to the term Naipaulitis—and on the other hand, a hybridity that blurs (passive) or destabilizes (active) the canon and its categories. Perhaps this spectrum of hybridities can be summed up as ranging from Naipaul to Salman Rushdie (cf. Brennan 1989), Edward Said, and Subaltern Studies. Still, what does it mean to destabilize the canon? It is worth reflecting on the politics of hybridity.

POLITICS OF HYBRIDITY

Relations of power and hegemony are inscribed and reproduced *within* hybridity for wherever we look closely enough we find the traces of asymmetry in culture, place, descent. Hence, hybridity raises the question of the *terms* of mixture, the conditions of mixing. At the same time it's important to note the ways in which hegemony is not merely reproduced but *refigured* in the process of hybridization. Generally, what is the bearing of hybridity in relation to political engagement?

At times, the anti-essentialist emphasis on hybrid identities comes dangerously close to dismissing all searches for communitarian origins as an archaeological excavation of an idealized, irretrievable past. Yet, on another level, while avoiding any nostalgia for a prelapsarian community, or for any unitary and transparent identity predating the "fall," we must also ask whether it is possible to forge a collective resistance without inscribing a communal past. (Shohat 1992: 109)

Isn't there a close relationship between political mobilization and collective memory? Isn't the remembrance of deeds past, the commemoration of collective itineraries, victories and defeats—such as the Matanza for the FMLN in El Salvador, Katipunan for the NPA in the Philippines, Heroes Day for the ANC—fundamental to the symbolism of resistance and the moral economy of mobilization? Still, this line of argument involves several problems. While there may be a link, there is no necessary symmetry between communal past and collective resistance. What is the basis of bonding in collective action—past or future, memory or project? While communal symbolism may be important, collective symbolism and discourse merging a heterogeneous collectivity in a common project may be more important. Thus while Heroes Day is significant to the ANC (December 16 is the founding day of Umkhonto we Sizwe), the Freedom Charter and, specifically, the project of nonracial democracy (non-sexism has been added later) has been of much greater importance. These projects are not of a communal nature: their strength is precisely that they transcend communal boundaries. Generally, emancipations may be thought of in the plural, as an ensemble of projects that in itself is diverse, heterogeneous, multivocal.[5] The argument linking communal past/collective resistance imposes a unity and transparency which in effect reduces the space for critical engagement, for plurality *within* the movement, diversity within the process of emancipation. It privileges a communal view of collective action, a primordial view of identity, and ignores or downplays the importance of *intra*-group differences and conflicts over group representation, demands, and tactics, including reconstructions of the past. It argues as if the questions of whether demands should be for autonomy or inclusion, whether the group should be inward or outward looking, have already been settled, while in reality these are political dilemmas. The nexus between communal past/collective engagement is one strand in political mobilization, but so are the hybrid past/plural projects, and in everyday politics the point is how to negotiate these strands in roundtable politics. This involves going beyond a past to a future orientation—for what is the point of collective action without a future? The lure of community, powerful and prevalent in left as well as right politics, has been questioned often enough. In contrast, hybridity when thought through as a politics may be subversive of essentialism and homogeneity, disruptive of static spatial and political categories of center and periphery, high and low, class and ethnos, and in recognizing multiple identities, widen the space for critical engagement. Thus, the nostalgia paradigm of community politics has been contrasted to the landscape of the city, along with a reading of "politics as relations among strangers" (Young 1990).

What is the significance of this outlook in the context of global inequities and politics? Political theory on a global scale is relatively undeveloped. Traditionally political theory is concerned with the relations between sovereign and people, state and society. It's of little help to turn to the "great political theorists" from Locke to Mill for they are all essentially concerned with the state-society framework. International relations theory extrapolates from this core preoccupation with concepts such as national interest and balance of power. Strictly speaking, international relations theory, at any rate neorealist theory, precludes global political theory. In the absence of a "world society," how can there be a worldwide social contract or global democracy? This frontier has opened up through ideas such as global civil society and the transnational networks of nongovernmental organizations: "The growth of global civil society represents an ongoing project of civil society to reconstruct, re-imagine, or re-map world politics" (Lipschutz 1992: 391). While global society and postinternational politics are relevant, a limitation to these reconceptualizations remains the absence of legal provisions that are globally binding rather than merely in interstate relations. Hence new initiatives such as the International Criminal Court and the Kyoto Protocol are particularly significant.

The question remains what kind of conceptual tools we can develop to address questions such as the double standards prevailing in global politics: perennial issues such as western countries practicing democracy at home and imperialism abroad; the edifying use of terms such as self-determination and sovereignty while the United States invades

Panama, Grenada, or Iraq. The term *imperialism* may no longer be adequate to address the present situation. It may be adequate in relation to US actions in Panama or Grenada, but less so to describe the Gulf War. Empire is the control exercised by a state over the domestic and foreign policy of another political society (Doyle 1986: 45), which is not an adequate terminology to characterize the Gulf War episode. If we consider that major actors in today's global circumstance are the IMF, World Bank, and World Trade Organization, transnational corporations, and regional investment banks, it is easy to acknowledge their influence on the domestic policies of countries from Brazil to the Philippines; but the situation differs from imperialism in two ways: the actors are not states and the foreign policy of the countries involved is not necessarily affected. The casual use of terms such as recolonization or neocolonialism to describe the impact of IMF conditionalities on African countries remains just that, casual. The situation has changed also since the emergence of regional blocs which can potentially exercise joint foreign policy (e.g., the European Union) or which within themselves contain two or more "worlds" (e.g., NAFTA, APEC). Both these situations differ from imperialism in the old sense. Literature in international political economy shows a shift from "imperialism" to "globalization." According to Tomlinson,

> the distribution of global power that we know as "imperialism" . . . characterised the modern period up to, say, the 1960s. What replaces "imperialism" is "globalisation." Globalisation may be distinguished from imperialism in that it is a far less coherent or culturally directed process. . . . The idea of "globalisation" suggests interconnection and interdependency of all global areas which happens in a less purposeful way. (1991: 175)

This is a particularly narrow interpretation in which globalization matches the epoch of late capitalism; still what is interesting is the observation that the present phase of globalization is less coherent and less purposeful than imperialism. Domination may be more dispersed, less orchestrated, more heterogeneous. To address global inequalities and develop global political theory a different kind of conceptualization is needed. We are not without points of reference but we lack a theory of global political action. The sociologist Alberto Melucci has discussed the "planetarization" of collective action (1989). Some of the implications of globalization for democracy have been examined by Held (1992). As regards the basics of a global political consensus, the UN Declaration of Human Rights, and its amendments by the Movement of Nonaligned Countries, may be a point of reference (Parekh 1992).[6]

POST-HYBRIDITY?

Cultural hybridization refers to the mixing of Asian, African, American, European cultures: hybridization is the making of global culture as a global mélange. As a category, hybridity serves a purpose based on the assumption of *difference* between the categories, forms, beliefs that go into the mixture. Yet the very process of hybridization shows the difference to be relative and, with a slight shift of perspective, the relationship can also be described in terms of an affirmation of *similarity*. Thus, the Catholic saints can be taken as icons of Christianity but can also be viewed as holdovers of pre-Christian paganism inscribed in the Christian canon. In that light, their use as masks for non-Christian gods is less quaint and rather intimates transcultural pagan affinities.

Ariane Mnouchkine's use of Kabuki style to stage a Shakespeare play leads to the question, which Shakespeare play? The play is *Henry IV,* which is set in a context of European high feudalism. In that light, the use of Japanese feudal Samurai style to portray European feudalism (Kreidt 1987: 255) makes a point about transcultural historical affinities. "Mexican schoolgirls dressed in Greek togas dancing in the style of Isadora Duncan," mentioned before, reflects transnational bourgeois class affinities, mirroring themselves in classical European culture. Chinese tacos and Irish bagels reflect ethnic crossover in employment patterns in the American fast food sector. Asian rap refers to cross-cultural stylistic convergence in popular youth culture.

An episode that can serve to probe this more deeply is the influence of Japanese art on European painting. The impact of *Japonisme* is well known: it inspired impressionism, which in turn set the stage for modernism. The color woodcuts that made such a profound impression on Seurat, Manet, Van Gogh, Toulouse-Lautrec, Whistler belonged to the Ukiyo school, a genre sponsored by the merchant class, that flourished in Japan between the seventeenth and nineteenth centuries. Ukiyo-e typically depicted urban scenes of ephemeral character, such as entertainments, theater, or prostitution, and landscapes. It was a popular art form that, unlike the high art of the aristocracy, was readily available at reasonable prices in bookstores (rather than cloistered in courts or monasteries) and therefore also accessible to Europeans (Budde 1993). This episode, then, is not so much an exotic irruption in European culture, but rather reflects the fact that bourgeois sensibilities had found iconographic expression in Japan earlier than in Europe. In other words, Japanese popular art was modern before European art was. Thus, what from one angle appears as hybridity to the point of exoticism, from another angle, again, reflects transcultural class affinities in sensibilities vis-à-vis urban life and nature. In other words, the other side of cultural hybridity is transcultural compatibility.

What makes it difficult to discuss these issues is that two quite distinct concepts of *culture* are generally being used indiscriminately. The first concept of culture (culture 1) views culture as essentially territorial; it assumes that culture stems from a learning process that is, in the main, localized. This is culture in the sense of *a culture,* that is, the culture of a society or social group: a notion that goes back to nineteenth-century romanticism and that has been elaborated in twentieth-century anthropology, in particular cultural relativism—with the notion of cultures as a whole, a Gestalt, configuration. A related idea is the organic or "tree" model of culture.

A wider understanding of culture (culture 2) views culture as a general human "software" (Banuri 1990: 77), as in nature/culture arguments. This notion has been implicit in theories of evolution and diffusion, in which culture is viewed as, in the main, a *translocal* learning process. These understandings are not incompatible: culture 2 finds expression in culture 1; cultures are the vehicles of culture. But they do reflect different emphases in relation to historical processes of culture formation and hence generate markedly different assessments of cultural relations. Divergent meta-assumptions about culture underlie the varied vocabularies in which cultural relations are discussed (table 4.2).

Culture 2 or translocal culture is not without place (there is no culture without place), but it involves an *outward looking* sense of place, whereas culture 1 is based on an *inward looking* sense of place. Culture 2 involves what the geographer Doreen Massey calls "a global sense of place": "the specificity of place which derives from the fact that each

Table 4.2. Assumptions about Culture

Territorial Culture	Translocal Culture
Endogenous	Exogenous
Orthogenetic	Heterogenetic
Societies, nations, empires	Diasporas, migrations
Locales, regions	Crossroads, borders, interstices
Community-based	Networks, brokers, strangers
Organic, unitary	Diffusion, heterogeneity
Authenticity	Translation
Inward looking	Outward looking
Community linguistics	Contact linguistics
Race	Half caste, half-breed, métis
Ethnicity	Ethnicities, new ethnicity
Identity	Identification, agency

place is the focus of a distinct *mixture* of wider and more local social relations" (1993: 240).

The general terminology of cultural pluralism, multicultural society, intercultural relations, and so on, does not clarify whether it refers to culture 1 or culture 2. Thus, relations among cultures can be viewed in a static fashion (in which cultures retain their separateness in interaction) or a fluid fashion (in which cultures interpenetrate) (table 4.3).

Hybridization as a perspective belongs to the fluid end of relations between cultures: the mixing of cultures and not their separateness is emphasized. At the same time, the underlying assumption about culture is that of culture/place. Cultural forms are called hybrid/syncretic/mixed/creolized because the elements in the mix derive from different cultural contexts. Thus, Hannerz defines Creole cultures as follows: "Creole cultures like creole languages are those which draw in some way on two or more historical sources, often originally widely different. They have had some time to develop and integrate, and to become

Table 4.3. Cultural Relations

Static	Fluid
Plural society (Furnivall)	Pluralism, melting pot
Multiculturalism (static)	Multiculturalism (fluid), interculturalism
Global mosaic	Cultural flows in space (Hannerz)
Clash of civilizations	Third cultures

elaborate and pervasive" (1987: 552). But in this sense would not every culture be a Creole culture? Can we identify any culture that is *not* Creole in the sense of drawing on one or more different historical sources?[7] A scholar of music makes a similar point about world music: "All music is essentially world music" (Bor 1994: 2).

A further question is: Are cultural elements different merely because they originate from different cultures? More often, what may be at issue, as argued above, is the *similarity* of cultural elements when viewed from the point of class, status group, lifestyle, or function. Hence, at some stage, toward the end of the story, the notion of cultural hybridity itself unravels or, at least, needs reworking. To explore what this means in the context of globalization, we can contrast the vocabularies and connotations of globalization-as-homogenization and globalization-as-hybridization (table 4.4).

What is common to some perspectives on both sides of the globalization/ homogenization/ heterogenization axis is a territorial view of culture. The territoriality of culture, however, itself is not constant over time. For some time we have entered a period of accelerated globalization and cultural mixing. This also involves an overall tendency toward the deterritorialization of culture, or an overall shift in orientation from culture 1 to culture 2. Introverted cultures, which have been prominent over a long stretch of history and overshadowed translocal culture, are gradually receding into the background, while translocal culture made up of diverse elements is coming to the foreground. This transition and the hybridization processes themselves unleash intense and dramatic nostalgia politics, of which ethnic upsurges, ethnicization of nations, and religious revivalism form part.

Table 4.4.   Globalization as Homogenization or as Diversification

Homogenization	*Diversification*
Cultural imperialism	Cultural planetarization
Cultural dependence	Cultural interdependence
Cultural hegemony	Cultural interpenetration
Autonomy	Syncretism, synthesis, hybridity
Modernity	Modernities
Westernization	Multipolarity, global mélange
Cultural convergence	New combinations, crossover
Global culture, world civilization	Global ecumene

Hybridization refers not only to the crisscrossing of cultures (culture 1) but also and by the same token to a transition from the provenance of culture 1 to culture 2. Another aspect of this transition is that due to advancing information technology and biotechnology different *modes* of hybridity emerge on the horizon: in the light of hybrid forms such as cyborgs, virtual reality, and electronic simulation, intercultural differences may begin to pale to relative insignificance—although of great local intensity. Biotechnology opens up the perspective of "merged evolution," in the sense of the merger of the evolutionary streams of genetics, cultural evolution, and information technology, and the near prospect of humans intervening in genetic evolution, through the matrix of cultural evolution and information technologies (Goonatilake 1991).

FORWARD MOVES

Globalization/hybridization makes, first, an empirical case: that processes of globalization, past and present, can be adequately described as processes of hybridization. Second, it is a critical argument: against viewing globalization in terms of homogenization, or of modernization/westernization, as empirically narrow and historically flat.

The career of sociology has been coterminous with the career of nation state formation and nationalism, and from this followed the constitution of the object of sociology as society and the equation of society with the nation. Culminating in structural functionalism and modernization theory, this career in the context of globalization is in for retooling. A global sociology is taking shape around notions such as social networks (rather than "societies"), border zones, boundary crossing, diaspora, and global society. In other words, a sociology conceived within the framework of nations/societies is making place for a post-inter/national sociology of hybrid formations, times, and spaces.

Institutional and structural hybridization, or the increase in the range of organizational options, and cultural hybridization, or the doors of erstwhile imagined communities opening up, are signs of an age of boundary crossing, but not, surely, of the erasure of boundaries. Thus, state power remains strategic, but it is no longer the only game in town. The tide of globalization reduces the room of maneuver of states while international institutions, transnational transactions, regional cooperation, subnational dynamics, and nongovernmental organizations expand in impact and scope (Cooperrider and Dutton 1999).

In historical terms, writing diaspora histories of global culture may deepen this perspective. Due to nationalism as a dominant paradigm since the nineteenth century, cultural achievements have been routinely claimed for nations and culture has been "nationalized," territorialized. A different historical record can be constructed based on the contributions to culture formation and diffusion by diasporas, migrations, strangers, and brokers, as in chapter 2 above. A related project would be histories of the hybridization of metropolitan cultures, that is, a counterhistory to the narrative of imperial history. Such historical inquiries may show that hybridization has been taking place all along but has been concealed by religious, national, imperial, and civilizational chauvinisms. Moreover, they may deepen our understanding of the temporalities of hybridization: how certain junctures witness downturns or upswings of hybridization, slowdowns or speedups. At the same time it follows that, if we accept that cultures have been hybrid *all along,* hybridization is in effect a tautology: contemporary accelerated globalization means the hybridization of hybrid cultures.

As such, the hybridization perspective remains meaningful only as a critique of essentialism. Essentialism will remain strategic as a mobilizational device as long as the units of nation, state, region, civilization, ethnicity remain strategic: and for just as long hybridization remains a relevant approach. Hybridity unsettles the introverted concept of culture that underlies romantic nationalism, racism, ethnicism, religious revivalism, civilizational chauvinism, and cultural essentialism. Hybridization, then, is a perspective that is meaningful as a counterweight to introverted notions of culture; at the same time, the very process of hybridization unsettles the introverted gaze, and accordingly, hybridization eventually ushers in post-hybridity, or transcultural cut-and-paste.

Hybridization is a factor in the reorganization of social spaces. Structural hybridization, or the emergence of new practices of social cooperation and competition, and cultural hybridization, or new translocal cultural expressions, are interdependent: new forms of cooperation require and evoke new cultural imaginaries. Hybridization is a contribution to a sociology of the in-between, a sociology from the interstices. This involves merging endogenous/exogenous understandings of culture. Significant perspectives include Hannerz's work on mapping micro-macro linkages (1989) and work in geography and cultural studies (e.g., Bird et al. 1993).

In relation to the global human condition of inequality, the hybridization perspective releases reflection and engagement from the bounds of nation, community, ethnicity, or class. Fixities have become fragments as the kaleidoscope of collective experience is in motion. It has been in motion all along, and the fixities of nation, community, ethnicity, and class have been grids superimposed upon experiences more complex and subtle than reflexivity and organization could accommodate.

One of the problems in discussing boundaries, ethnicity, hybridity, and so forth is that history plays tricks. First, historical situations are layered and complex, and judgments concern representations of situations rather than situations. The representations are themselves interpretations and responses to other judgments, so our views are a matter of judgments upon judgments, and so forth, with *couleur locale* and thick description diminishing at every turn. Second, boundaries and boundary pathos are temporal and temporary; even minor shifts in place or time can make a considerable difference. Third, the exercise of judgment upon judgment may become a polemical play in its own right, with increasingly predictable outcomes (and politically correct judgments) and shrinking bearing on actual situations. To do justice to actual processes usually takes far more historical fine print. These provisos also apply to the treatments in this book; I am aware of the shortcuts because in other work I have dealt with many of these issues with much greater historical and graphic detail and nuance (e.g., Nederveen Pieterse 1989, 1992).

For a century the British in India had been mingling and intermarrying with Indians, and in several domains British-Indian culture unfolded as a mestizo culture. That began to change in the course of the nineteenth century due to a new sense of superiority on the part of English reformers, of which Macaulay is a well-known representative. Doctrines of racial difference imported from Europe also made their mark. But the major turning point was the Indian Mutiny of 1857. Then a pathos of difference and distinction set in, combined with fierce and brutal boundary policing. At that time views such as these became common: "Lord made the Whites, Lord made the Blacks but the Devil made the half-castes" and signs said, "No entrance for dogs and half-castes." This pathos of cultural tension carried, of course, its own undoing, and segregation and violence hastened the demise of the British raj in India.

Not so long ago immigrants to the United States such as Hispanics found themselves "racialized" once they were in America, coded in racial categories foreign to them. A white Brazilian based in Washington explains, "'In this country if you are not quite white, then you are black.' But in Brazil, 'If you are not quite black, then you are white'" (Fears 2003). Most Latinos mark the census box "some other race" and write in identities such as Mayan, Tejano, and mestizo, or indicate that they belong to two or more races. Yet in recent years, in the United States and generally, there have been marked changes in discourses of "race." According to conservative commentator George Will, race is "now an anachronism" (2003). Cupid is becoming color-blind (Kristof 2002a). A new "Mongrel America" is taking shape. "Generation E.A.: Ethnically Ambiguous" is a new theme. "Ambiguity is chic." In DJ language, "We are the remix." "To marketers, the multiracial face of youth is the new American beauty. It doesn't hurt in getting a date either" (La Ferla 2003). Barack Obama arrived at his current outlook via feelings of alienation and "racial confusion," even in Hawaii where "hapa" (or half, for combinations of white, Hawaiian or Asian, or other biracial mixtures) is ordinary (Obama 1995). "Mixing is the new norm" (Zachary 2000: ix). This means the census categories (which assume that ethnic identities are like fixed and separate pieces of mosaic) are gradually losing meaning and the rationale for affirmative action is weakening too. "Mixed" in this setting is not mixed up as in cultural confusion, but mixed as in bridging worlds. These trends parallel the "after race" discourses by Paul Gilroy, Kwame Appiah, and others.

Hybridity as a perspective and sensibility is often associated with high modern or postmodern times, with postcolonial conditions, postcolonial studies, multicultural salad bowls, and tutti-frutti cocktails. Surely the hybridity conversations owe much to contemporary accelerated globalization and to crossborder media, marketing, and consumption scapes, as the sign language of a world that leaves behind, or seems to leave behind, the national, ethnic, and at least some of the religious boundaries of the past. Yet this common sense is also shallow. It tacitly assumes that mixing is something that has occurred only recently, courtesy of "globalization." In doing so it takes for granted the preexisting grid lines of difference. This implies fundamental misrepresentations. Realities are far more complicated and nuanced. In general, each time period, each epoch has its own boundaries *and* fluidity. Second, mingling and mixing are of all times, regardless of boundaries. Third, each period has its own pathos of difference—in which some differences count and others rank as insignificant.

There was separation, of course, in ancient and past times—such as the Greek "barbarians," Homer's and Herodotus' tales of monstrous beings at the boundaries of the known world; the Chinese "foreign devils"; the Crusades; the Inquisition; the religious wars of sixteenth- and seventeenth-century Europe, and so forth. Yet even the Middle Ages, which rank as a compartmentalized world, show much more mobility and wide-ranging interaction than is generally thought (Hoerder 2002). Much of the practice and pathos of separation—in relation to which we mark contemporary hybridity—comes with the moderns of the seventeenth to nineteenth centuries. The moderns adopted biological classifications, thought of in terms of race and race science, developed civilizational arrogance ("mission civilisatrice") in relation to "the rest," and drew lines of separation between races, ethnicities, nations, and cultures in relation to which our contemporary hybridity is a transcendence and relief.

This implies that many of the polemics that criticize hybridity for being a recent, faddish trend, a postcolonial or postmodern affectation (e.g., Cashmore 2003, Nanda 2001; see chapter 5 below) bark up the wrong tree. It implies that the genealogies of hybridity matter, for they destabilize the foundations of Eurocentrism, chauvinism, and cultural narcissism. One of the markers of early and ongoing intermingling is of course language. About half the words in the English language are borrowed from other cultures. "Cushy" has nothing to do with cushions but comes from *khush*, Hindi for "pleasant," and so forth (Hitchings 2008).

Hybridity, of course, involves a wide register of meanings. Often hybridity simply means in-between. Thus a discussion of "the hybrid regimes of Central America" asks, "What are the prospects for democracy in Central America? Will the region's policies regress to frank authoritarian rule, consolidate their democratic gains, or remain stuck in some middle 'hybrid' terrain?" (Karl 1995: 72).

Usually the term hybrid is reserved for *combinations of diverse elements*—as in the hybrid car. Microsoft's "Live Mesh," which combines

Internet and desktop software, is described as a "hybrid computing platform" (R. Waters 2008). Indeed, the point of "hybridity" is often the merger of contrasting or opposite components. Describing the international order in the 1990s as a "hybrid uni-multipolar system" (in which the United States has limited veto power), Samuel Huntington uses hybridity in this sense, as a fusion of the contrasting frameworks of unipolarity and multipolarity (1999). In this case the contrast stems from the definitions. Generally the implication of the term hybridity is that the elements are held to be contrasting or opposed—that is, from a certain viewpoint. This is the recurring refrain in hybridity, cultural and otherwise. Hybridity implies boundaries; without boundaries, no hybridity. Yet, of course, boundaries are contextual and changing. Besides, while the components are dissimilar, they are apparently similar enough to allow their combination. According to Marwan Kraidy, "The notion of hybridity invokes the fusion of two (or more) components into a third term irreducible to the sum of its parts. By unhinging the identities of its ingredients without congealing into a stable third term, hybridity enters a vicious circle where its condition of existence is at the same time its kiss of death" (2005: 66). This is perfectly true but a tad melodramatic. Indeed, once hybridity becomes the "new norm," the components lose dissimilarity through their merger in the new compound. Newcomers or a new generation may no longer be aware that it is a hybrid, or if it is, that it matters. Thus much of our contemporary concern with hybridity is essentially a response to and negotiation of nineteenth-century assumptions, categories, and sensibilities that are out of sync with twentieth-century trends. By the same token, much of our hybridity talk is "so twentieth century" and is likely to lose much of its distinctiveness or salience in the course of the twenty-first century for by then other boundaries and differences will emerge. Thus, unity-separation-hybridity (by way of shorthand; there are many other sequences and relations) are simply part of a historical process, and what matters, rather than either celebrating or bemoaning hybridity, or bemoaning its passing, is understanding the process and the *longue durée*.

Some combinations are unremarkable, such as French-German articulations along the Rhine like the Alsace cuisine of choucroute or sauerkraut, for the elements are not dissimilar enough. Hybridity doesn't apply to French-Italian combinations in southern France, also taking into account that some parts such as Nice used to be part of Italy (and was called Nizza). Take, however, Chinese-Italian, which is not a mere combination but a hybrid, for the elements are unlike and too geographically and culturally distant to easily interrelate. Yet this too depends on the context. Italian-Chinese connections include Marco Polo and the Jesuit scholar Matteo Ricci, who after years in China was able to view western culture in Chinese terms and translated Confucian classics into Latin. Besides, if our setting would be Tientsin (Tianjin), Chinese-Italian combinations would not be unusual, for a concession in this autonomous municipality was granted to Italy (1901–1947). Besides this, can we envision a time when, for instance, Chinese-Italian would no longer be a hybrid?

Cultural hybridity is a common trope, but less often discussed is institutional hybridity—for instance, public-private partnerships, participatory budgeting in local government, and interactive decision making. Still less discussed are hybrids of human agency and material formations, such as Donna Haraway's cyborgs (cybernetic organisms) and Paul Virilio's point that the US military's combining of human and technological components, such as satellite vision, extends human perception. Actor-network theory takes a further step and argues for material agency.[8] Functional foods that combine nutrition and medicinal functions are a rising trend.

One of the criticisms of "hybridity theory" is that it exaggerates cultural flux and assumes cultural or linguistic freedom, but this bears little relation to actual hybridity. Usually necessity is the mother of hybridity. As James Clifford notes, hybridity is often simply a matter of necessity and, quite unlike what critics allege, is rather "a pragmatic response, making the best of given (often bad) situations. The cultural inventiveness at stake is a matter of specific juxtapositions, selections, and overlays offered and imposed in limited historical conjunctures." He concludes, "If there is utopia here, it is utopia in a minor key, or . . . a utopic/dystopic tension" (1998: 366).

Western hospitals and clinics in sub-Saharan Africa increasingly cooperate with traditional healers, if only because there are not enough modern amenities to go around. Barefoot doctors in China and elsewhere have done the same. In South Africa, cooperation with sangomas, or traditional healers, has long been institutionalized, a cooperation that is not without frictions, such as different standards of hygiene and different diagnostics. Laotian Hmong immigrants in the United States develop a syncretism of folk beliefs and western biomedical practices, simply making the best out of the situation they find themselves in (Hickman 2007). The pharmaceutical industry cooperates with indigenous peoples in order to extract and design new herbal remedies from the rain forest.

Diversity and hybridity enter in management and business studies as variables in the knowledge economy, creative economy, and cultural economy. This goes far beyond the marketing and the world product ad campaigns of Coca-Cola and Benetton; it concerns conception, design, engineering, and every aspect from research and development to production to marketing. Richard Florida celebrates diversity as a feature of creative dynamic cities. Diversity and hybridity enter into accounts of the global economy as a cosmopolitan sphere and a condition of "globality" in which firms must organize into project teams that scout for talent and combine diverse skills from across the world, from engineering to regulatory regimes and law to local cultural savvy, in order to compete.[9]

Chapter 5

Hybridity, So What?
The Anti-hybridity
Backlash and the
Riddles of Recognition

Opening up to politics of difference is one of the changes of recent times. As the goalposts shift to difference and recognition, new problems arise. As identity politics come to the fore, does interest politics fade into the background? What is the relationship between identity and class, between recognition and social justice? What about recognition of the steepest difference of all, the world's development gap? This inquiry focuses on the question of when we recognize "others," according to which boundaries do we identify "others"? When we recognize difference, what about "difference within"? What about those who straddle or are in-between categories and combine identities? To what extent is recognition a function of the available categories of knowledge and cognitive frames in which self and others are identifiable and recognizable? Can it be that recognition is an exercise in reproduction, recycling the categories in which existing social relations have been coded while stretching their meaning? Recognition, then, stretches or revalues social boundaries but does not transgress them. To what extent is politics of recognition a politics of musical chairs—as one more identity is acknowledged, another is left behind? As the spotlight turns to one identity, does another fade into the shadow? Does politics of recognition chase a social horizon that ever recedes as one comes closer? To what extent is progress (such a difficult word) measured not simply in attainment (because any attainment is partial and entails a price) but in process and motion? And then what would such an acknowledgment of process entail?

"Recognition" refers to the willingness to socially or publicly validate or affirm differences as they are perceived, but what about differences that are not being perceived? Recognition and difference are a function of the existing identities and boundaries that are available on the social and cultural maps. Recognition is part of a process of struggle over cognition. Hybridity is a journey into the riddles of recognition. Take any exercise in social mapping and it is the hybrids that are missing. Take most models and arrangements of multiculturalism and it is hybrids that are not counted, not accommodated. So what? This chapter addresses this question. The 2000 Census in the United States is the first to permit multiple identifications: for the first time one can identify as Caucasian, African American, Hispanic, for example, and as all of those. This public recognition of multiple identity has been controversial particularly for minorities whose entitlements depend on recognition of their numbers.

The first section of this treatment discusses the varieties of hybridity and the widening range of phenomena to which the term now applies. According to anti-hybridity arguments hybridity is inauthentic and "multiculturalism lite." Examining the current anti-hybridity backlash provides an opportunity to deepen and fine-tune our perspective on hybridity. Part of what is missing in these arguments is historical depth; the third section deals with the *longue durée* and proposes multiple historical layers of hybridity. The fourth section concerns the politics of boundaries, for in the end the real problem is not hybridity, which is common throughout history, but boundaries and the social proclivity to boundary fetishism. Hybridity is unremarkable and noteworthy only from the point of view of boundaries that have been essentialized. What hybridity means varies not only over time but also in different cultures, and this informs different patterns of hybridity. Then we come back to the original question: So what? The importance of hybridity is that it problematizes boundaries.

VARIETIES OF HYBRIDITY

Fairly recent on the horizon, after Latino rock, is Mandarin pop, a Cantonese and Pacific American combination of styles. One of its original inspirations is Hong Kong crooners doing Mandarin cover versions of Japanese popular ballads. The Japanese ballads were already a mixture of Japanese and American styles that featured for instance saxophone backgrounds. Mandarin pop (or Mandopop) is part of the soundscape of the Pacific Chinese diaspora. Its audience ranges from youngsters in China, Hong Kong, and Taiwan to prosperous second-generation Chinese immigrants in the United States (Tam 2000).

Many have these kinds of cultural phenomena in mind when they think of hybridity. We could call it the world music model of hybridity. Its general features are that it concerns cultural expressions that are new and recent, recombine existing combinations, and involve a limited range in expression and a distinctive audience, usually urban and newly prosperous. And while they are significant because they reflect and cater to a new class or stratum, their meaning is clearly restricted.

New hybrid forms are significant indicators of profound changes that are taking place as a consequence of mobility, migration, and multiculturalism. However, hybridity thinking also concerns existing or, so to speak, old hybridity, and thus involves different ways of looking at historical and existing cultural and institutional arrangements. This is a more radical and penetrating angle that suggests not only that things are no longer the way they used to be but were never really the way they used to be, or used to be viewed.

For some time hybridity has been a prominent theme in cultural studies.[1] It follows older themes of syncretism in anthropology and creolization in linguistics. In cultural studies hybridity denotes a wide register of multiple identity, crossover, cut 'n' mix, experiences, and styles, matching a world of growing migration and diaspora lives, intensive intercultural communication, everyday multiculturalism, and erosion of boundaries. In optimistic takes on hybridity, "hybrids were conceived as lubricants in the clashes of culture; they were the negotiators

like the cover of Sen

who would secure a future free of xenophobia" (Papastergiadis 1997: 261). This angle that is both instrumental and celebratory may overlook that hybridity is also significant in its own right, as the experience of hybrids. An Afro-German writes:

> I always liked being a "mulatto," even in the terrible times of National Socialism. I have been able to manage the black and white in me very well. I remember when a colleague once asked me during the terrible 1940s whether I was very unhappy having to live as mulatto. I said, "No, you know, what I have experienced in my life because of my ethnic origin, you will never in your entire life experience." (Quoted in Beck 2000: 125)

Hybridity thinking has been criticized for being a "dependent" thinking that makes sense only on the assumption of purity (Young 1995). In addition, of late there has been a polemical backlash against hybridity thinking. Hybridity, it is argued, is inauthentic, without roots, for the elite only, does not reflect social realities on the ground. It is multiculturalism lite, highlights superficial confetti culture and glosses over deep cleavages that exist on the ground. The downside of this anti-hybridity backlash is that it recycles the nineteenth-century parochialism of an ethnically and culturally compartmentalized world, whose present revival and rearticulation is baffling. In my understanding, hybridity is deeply rooted in history and quite ordinary. Indeed, what is problematic is not hybridity but the fetishism of boundaries that has marked so much of history. That history should not be seen this way and hybridity is somehow viewed as extraordinary or unusual is baffling. Besides, as noted in the introduction, I'm hybrid myself. Engaging the anti-hybridity backlash offers an opportunity to enter more deeply into the hybridity perspective, and polemics offers a certain kind of clarity.

The first point to consider is the varieties of hybridity, as phenomena and as perspective (a schema is in table 5.1).

Hybridization as a process is as old as history but the pace of mixing accelerates and its scope widens in the wake of major structural changes, such as new technologies that enable new phases of intercultural contact. Contemporary accelerated globalization is such a new phase. A major terrain of newly emerging mixtures is the new middle

Table 5.1. Varieties of Hybridity

New hybridity:	Old hybridity:
Recent combinations of cultural and institutional forms. Dynamics: migration, trade, ICT, multiculturalism, globalization. Analytics: new modernities. Examples: Punjabi pop, Mandopop, Islamic fashion shows.	Existing cultural and institutional forms are translocal and crosscultural combinations already. Dynamics: crosscultural trade, conquest and contact. Analytics: history as collage. Examples: too many.
Objective: as observed by outsiders.	Subjective: as experience and self-awareness.
As process: hybridization.	As discourse and perspective: hybridity consciousness.
As outcome: hybrid phenomena.	

classes and their cultural and social practices arising in the context of migration and diaspora and the new modernities of the "emerging markets." For almost two decades, the growth rates of the Asian Tiger economies and other emerging markets have been twice as high as western countries. This entails vast applications of new technologies and the emergence of new social mores and consumption patterns. They are typically fusion cultures that combine new technologies and existing social practices and cultural values. Nilufer Göle discusses changes in Islam in Turkey in terms of "hybridization between Islamists and modernity" (2000: 112).

> As can be observed in the Turkish context, not only are Islamists using the latest model of Macintosh computers, writing best-selling books, becoming part of the political and cultural elite, winning elections, and establishing private universities, but they are also carving out new public spaces, affirming new public visibilities, and inventing new Muslim lifestyles and subjectivities. . . . An Islamic service sector offers luxury hotels that advertise facilities for an Islamic way of vacationing; they feature separate beaches and nonalcoholic beverages. Islamic dress and fashion shows, Islamic civil society associations, Islamic pious foundations, associations of Islamic entrepreneurs, and Islamic women's platforms all attest to a vibrant and rigorous social presence. (Göle 2000: 94)

If practices of mixing are as old as the hills, the thematization of mixing as a discourse and perspective is fairly new. In one sense, it dates from the 1980s. In a wider sense, it concerns the general theme of bricolage and improvisation. Its lineages include psychoanalysis and bringing together widely diverse phenomena—such as dreams, jokes, Freudian slips, and symbols—under new headings relevant to psychological diagnosis.[2] Psychoanalysis synthesized sensibilities ranging from Nietzsche to nineteenth-century novels and art. Dada made mixing objects and perspectives its hallmark and inspired the collage. Marcel Duchamp hybridized art itself. Surrealism moved further along these lines and so did conceptual and installation art

The domains in which hybridity plays a part have been proliferating over time:

- The term hybridity originates in pastoralism, agriculture, and horticulture.[3] Hybridization refers to developing new combinations by crossbreeding one plant or tree with another.
- A further application is genetics. When belief in "race" played a dominant part, miscegenation and "race mixture" were prominent notions.
- Previously hybridity referred to combinations of different animals, such as the griffin, or animals and humans, such as the centaur and satyr; now it also refers to cyborgs (cybernetic organisms), combinations of humans or animals and technology (pets carrying chips for identification, biogenetic engineering).
- Hybridity first entered social science via anthropology of religion and the theme of syncretism. Roger Bastide defined syncretism as "uniting pieces of the mythical history of two different traditions in one that continued to be ordered by a single system" (1970: 101).
- Creole languages and creolization in linguistics was the next field to engage social science interest. Bakhtin's work on polyphony develops a related strand. In time, creolization became a wider metaphor (e.g., Richards 1996).
- Presently the main thrust of hybridity thinking concerns cultural hybridity, including art (e.g., P. Harvey 1996).
- Other strands concern structural and institutional hybridization, including governance (Ruijter 1996; see also chapter 4 above).
- Organizational hybridity (Oliver and Montgomery 2000) and diverse cultural influences in management techniques are common themes (e.g., Beale 1999).

- Interdisciplinarity in science has given rise to "new hybrids" such as ecological economics (D. McNeill 1999: 322).
- "Menus have increasingly become monuments to cultural hybridity" (Warde 2000: 303).
- Most common of all is everyday hybridity in identities, consumer behavior, lifestyle, and so forth.

International relations, education, the hybrid car (combining petrol and electricity), and so forth: nowadays there is no end to the travel and spread of hybridity. The current polemic on hybridity, however, only considers cultural hybridity, which captures but a small slice of the domains indicated above. The world music model of hybridity is narrower still and only concerns recent cultural blends. Besides shortchanging the varieties of hybridity, other fundamental considerations are oddly missing in the current anti-hybridity arguments. One concerns the historical depth of hybridity viewed in the *longue durée*. The second is the circumstance that boundaries and borders can be matters of life or death and the failure to acknowledge hybridity is a political point whose ramifications can be measured in lives.

In the end, the anti-hybridity backlash is a minor debate. The issue is not whether to be for or against hybridity; the debate concerns another question: Hybridity, so what? What is the significance of hybridity? To take this further means to unpack hybridity in its varieties and to distinguish patterns of hybridity. Meanwhile the other side of this question is: Boundaries, so what?

THE ANTI-HYBRIDITY BACKLASH

Criticisms of particular versions of hybridity arguments and quirks in hybridity thinking are familiar. The most conspicuous shortcoming is that hybridity skips over questions of power and inequality: "Hybridity is not parity."[4] Some arguments make no distinction between different levels: "The triumph of the hybrid is in fact a triumph of neo-liberal multiculturalism, a part of the triumph of global capitalism" (Araeen 2000: 15). These wholesale repudiations of hybridity thinking belong in a different category: this is the anti-hybridity backlash, which this argument takes on. In the discussion below, most arguments against hybridity thinking have been taken from the anthropologist Jonathan

Table 5.2.   Arguments For and Against Hybridity

Contra Hybridity	Pro Hybridity
Hybridity is meaningful only as a critique of essentialism.	There is plenty of essentialism around.
Were colonial times really so essentialist?	Enough for hybrids to be despised
Hybridity is a dependent notion.	So are boundaries
Asserting that all cultures and languages are mixed is trivial.	Claims of purity have long been dominant
Hybridity matters to the extent that it is a self-identification.	Hybrid self-identification is hindered by classification codes and boundaries
Hybridity talk is a function of the decline of western hegemony.	It also destabilizes other hegemonies
Hybridity talk is carried by a new cultural class of cosmopolitans.	Would this qualify an old cultural class of boundary police?
"The lumpenproletariat real border-crossers live in constant fear of the border."	Crossborder knowledge is survival knowledge.
"Hybridity is not parity"	Boundaries don't usually help either.

Friedman (1997, 1999) as representative of a wider view.[5] A précis of anti-hybridity arguments and rejoinders is in table 5.2.

"Hybridity Is Meaningful
Only as a Critique of Essentialism"

There is plenty of essentialism to go around. Boundary fetishism has long been and in many circles continues to be the norm. After the nation, one of the latest forms of boundary fetishism is "ethnicity." Another reification is the "local." Friedman cites the statement above (Nederveen Pieterse 1995: 63) and then concludes that "hybridization is a political and normative discourse" (1999: 242). Indeed, but so of course is essentialism and boundary fetishism. "In a world of multiplying diasporas, one of the things that is not happening is that boundaries are disappearing" (241). That, however, is much too sweeping a statement to be meaningful. On the whole, crossboundary and crossborder activities have been on the increase, as a wide body of work in international relations and international political economy testifies, where the erosion of boundaries is one of the most common accounts of contemporary times and globalization.

WERE COLONIAL TIMES REALLY SO ESSENTIALIST?

This is a question raised by Young (1995). Here we can distinguish multiple levels: actual social relations, in which there was plenty border crossing, and discourse, which is differentiated in turn between mainstream and marginal discourses. Discourse and representation were also complex and multilayered, witness for instance the mélange of motifs in Orientalism (e.g., Mackenzie 1995, Clarke 1997). While history then is a history of ambivalence, attraction and repulsion, double takes, and zigzag moves, nevertheless the nineteenth- and early-twentieth-century colonial world was steeped in a Eurocentric pathos of difference, *dédain*, distinction.[6] All the numerous countermoves in the interstices of history do not annul the *overall* pathos of the White Man's Burden and *mission civilisatrice* nor its consequences.

> But the imperial frontiers are not only geographical frontiers, where the "civilized" and the "barbarians" confront and contact one another; they are also frontiers of status and ethnicity which run through imperialized societies, as in the form of the colonial "colour bar." Here colonizers and colonized are segregated and meet, here slave masters and slaves face one another and here, where imperial posturing is at its most pompous and hatred is most intense, the imperial house of cards folds and paradox takes over. For this frontier is also the locus of a *genetic dialectic*, a dialectic which in the midst of the most strenuous contradictions gives rise to that strangest of cultural and genetic syntheses—the *mulatto, mestizo*, half-caste. The mestizo is the personification of the dialectics of empire and emancipation. No wonder that in the age of empire the mestizo was dreaded as a monster, an infertile hybrid, an impossibility: subversive of the foundations of empire and race. The mestizo is the living testimony of an attraction that is being repressed on both sides of the frontier. The mestizo is proof that East and West *did* meet and that there is humanity on either side. (Nederveen Pieterse 1989: 360–61)

HYBRIDITY IS A DEPENDENT NOTION

"In the struggle against the racism of purity, hybridity invokes the dependent, not converse, notion of the mongrel. Instead of combating essentialism, it merely hybridizes it" (Friedman 1999: 236). The mongrel, half-caste, mixed race, métis, mestizo was a taboo figure in the colonial world. When so much pathos was invested in boundaries, boundary crossing involved dangerous liaisons. In an era of thinking in biological terms boundaries were biologized ("race") and by extension so was boundary crossing. Status, class, race, nation were all thought of as *biological* entities in the lineage from Comte de Boullainvilliers and Gobineau to Houston Stewart Chamberlain and Hitler (cf. Nederveen Pieterse 1989: chapter 11).

By the turn of the century, genetics underwent a paradigm shift from a dominant view that gene mixing was weakening and debilitating (decadence) to the view in Mendelian genetics that gene mixing is invigorating and that combining diverse strains creates *hybrid vigor*. This principle still guides plant-breeding companies now. Social and cultural hybridity thinking takes this further and revalorizes the half-castes. The gradual emergence of hybrid awareness (in nineteenth-century novels, psychoanalysis, modernism, bricolage) and its articulation in the late twentieth century can be sociologically situated in the rapid succession of waning aristocracy (as represented in the theme of *décadence*), bourgeois hegemony, and its supersession and reworking from the second half of the twentieth century.

Hybridity as a point of view is meaningless *without* the prior assumption of difference, purity, fixed boundaries. Meaningless not in the sense that it would be inaccurate or untrue as a description, but that without an existing regard for boundaries it would not be a point worth making. Without reference to a prior pathos of purity and boundaries, of hierarchy and gradient of difference, the point of hybridity would be moot.

ASSERTING THAT ALL CULTURES AND LANGUAGES ARE MIXED IS TRIVIAL (FRIEDMAN 1999: 249)

Trivial? After for time immemorial the dominant idea has been that of pure origins, pure lineages, as in perspectives on language, religion, nation, race, culture, status, class, gender? The hieratic view was preoccupied with divine or sacred origins. The patriarchal view posited strong gender boundaries. The aristocratic view cultivated blue blood. The philological view saw language as the repository of the genius of peoples, as with Herder and the subsequent "Aryan" thesis. The racial view involved a hierarchy of races. The Westphalian system locked sovereignty within territorial borders. Next came the nation and chauvinism. All these views share a preoccupation with pure origins, strong boundaries, firm borders. The contemporary acknowledgment of mixture in origins and lineages indicates a sea change in subjectivities and consciousness that correlates, of course, with sea changes in social structures and practices. It indicates a different ethos that in time will translate into different institutions. To regard this as trivial is to profoundly misread history.

HYBRIDITY MATTERS TO THE EXTENT THAT IT IS SELF-IDENTIFICATION

"Hybridity only exists as a social phenomenon when it is identified as such by those involved in social interaction. This implies that where people do not so identify, the fact of cultural mixture is without social significance. . . . Hybridity is in the eyes of the beholder, or more precisely in the practice of the beholder" (Friedman 1999: 249, 251).

Hybrid self-identification *is* in fact common: obvious instances are second-generation immigrants and indeed hyphenated identities. Tiger Woods, the champion golfer, describes himself as "Cablinasian": "a blend of Caucasian, black, Indian and Asian" (Fletcher 1997). Donald Yee, who is part black, part Asian, and part Native American, can sympathize. "When Mr. Yee fills out racial questionnaires, he frequently checks 'multiracial.' If that is not an option, he goes with either black or Asian. 'Nothing bothers me,' he said. 'It is just that it doesn't capture all of me'" (Fletcher 1997).

Creolization in the Caribbean, mestizaje in Latin America, and fusion in Asia are common self-definitions. In some countries, national identity is overtly hybrid. Zanzibar is a classic instance (Gurnah 1997). Mexico and Brazil identify themselves as hybrid cultures. Nepal is a mélange of Tibetan, Chinese, and Indian culture of the Gangetic plains (Bista 1994), and the same applies to Bhutan. Singapore's identity is often referred to as Anglo-Chinese (Wee 1997).

Even so, the view that in relation to hybridity only self-identification matters presents several problems. (1) The obvious problem is how to monitor hybrid self-identification since most systems of classification and instruments of measurement do not permit multiple or in-between identification. In the United States, "Until 1967 states were constitutionally permitted to ban mixed-race marriages. More than half the states had anti-miscegenation statutes in 1945; 19 still had them in 1966" (Fletcher 1997). The US census is a case in point. The 2000 census is the first that, after much resistance and amid ample controversy, permits multiple self-identification, that is, white as well as African American, Latino, and so forth. (2) What about the in-betweens? The point of hybridity thinking is that the in-betweens have been numerous all along and because of structural changes have been growing in number. (3) Only the eye of the beholder counts? Going native as epistemological principle? Because most people in the Middle Ages thought the earth was flat, it *was* flat? Because between 1840 and 1950 many people were racist, there were races? Or, there were as long as most people thought so? Jews were bad when most Germans under National Socialism thought so? *Vox populi, vox dei*—since when? This is unacceptable in principle and untenable in practice.

Hybridity Talk Is a Function of the Decline of Western Hegemony

This is true in that the world of Eurocentric colonialism, imperialism, and racism is past. It is only partially true because hybridity talk can refer just as much to the passing of other centrisms and hegemonies, such as China the middle kingdom, Japan and the myth of the pure Japanese race (Yoshino 1995), Brahmins in India, Sinhala Buddhists in Sri Lanka and their claim to "Aryan" origins, Israel the Jewish state, Kemalist Turkism centered on Anatolia, Greekness among the Greeks. For all hegemonies, the claim to purity has served as part of a claim to power. This applies to all status boundaries, not just those of nation, ethnicity, or race. The Church clamped down on heresies; the aristocracy and then the bourgeoisie despised mésalliance. Status requires boundaries and with boundaries comes boundary policing.

Hybridity Talk Is by a New Cultural Class of Cosmopolitans Who Seek Hegemony

Hybridity represents "a new 'elite' gaze," "a new cosmopolitan elite" (Friedman 1999: 236; cf. Ahmad 1992, Dirlik 1992). Here innuendo comes in. *Ad hominem* reasoning, casting aspersion on the motives of the advocates of an idea, rather than debating the idea, is not the most elevated mode of debate. Then, should we discuss the motives of those who talk homogeneity? Of those who talk of boundaries allegedly on behalf of the working class and "redneck" virtues? Of those who create a false opposition between working class locals and cosmopolitan airheads? According to Friedman, "Cosmopolitans are a product of modernity, individuals whose shared experience is based on a certain loss of rootedness. . . . Cosmopolitans identify with the urban, with the 'modern.' . . . They are the sworn enemies of national and ethnic identities" (1999: 237).

Aversion to cosmopolitanism and the decadence of city life was part of Hitler's outlook and the Nazi ideology of blood and soil. With it came the Nazi idealization of the German peasant and, on the other hand, anti-Semitism. According to a German source in 1935, "Dangers threaten the nation when it migrates to the cities. It withers away in a few generations, because it lacks the vital connection with the earth. The German must be rooted in the soil, if he wants to remain alive" (quoted in Linke 1999: 199).

It is odd to find this combination of elements restated. For one thing, it is an ideological and not an analytical discourse. Brief rejoinders are as follows: (1) The specific discourse of cosmopolitanism does not really belong in this context; there is no necessary relationship. But if it is brought in, one would rather say that humanity is a cosmopolitan species. Adaptability to a variety of ecological settings is inherent in the species. (2) Also if this view is not accepted, cosmopolitanism still predates modernity and goes back to the inter-civilizational travel of itinerant craftsmen, traders, and pilgrims. (3) The stereotype that is implicitly invoked here echoes another stereotype, that of Ahasverus, the wandering Jew. (4) Why or by which yardstick would or should "rootedness" be the norm? Have nomadism and itinerancy not also a long record? (5) Why should affinity with the urban (if it would apply at all) necessarily involve animosity to national and ethnic identities? The romantics thought otherwise. Cities have been central to national as well as regional identities. (6) According to Friedman, "Modernist identity as an ideal type is anti-ethnic, anti-cultural and anti-religious" (1999: 237). "Anti-cultural" in this context simply does not make sense. Apparently this take on modernism excludes Herder and the romantics and assumes a single, ideal-type modernity.

"WHILE INTELLECTUALS MAY CELEBRATE BORDER-CROSSING, THE LUMPENPROLETARIAT REAL BORDER-CROSSERS LIVE IN CONSTANT FEAR OF THE BORDER" (FRIEDMAN 1999: 254)

Experiences with borders and boundaries are too complex and diverse to be captured under simple headings. Even where boundaries are strong and fences high, knowing what is on either side is survival knowledge. This is part of the political economy of mobility. Geographical mobility is an alternative key to social mobility. In negotiating borders, hybrid bicultural knowledge and cultural shape-shifting acquire survival value. "Passing" in different milieus is a survival technique. This applies to the large and growing transborder informal sector in which migrant grassroots entrepreneurs turn borders to their advantage.

Friedman sees it otherwise. "But for whom, one might ask, is such cultural transmigration a reality? In the works of the post-colonial border-crossers, it is always the poet, the artist, the intellectual, who sustains the displacement and objectifies it in the printed word. But who reads the poetry, and what are the other kinds of identification occurring in the lower reaches of social reality?" (1997: 97). (Elsewhere: "This author, just as all hybrid ideologues, takes refuge in literature" [1999: 247].) This is deeply at odds with common experience. Thus, research in English and German major cities finds that it is precisely lower class youngsters, second-generation immigrants who develop new, mixed lifestyles (Räthzel 1999: 213).[7] Also, Friedman recognizes this among Turks in Berlin but then neutralizes this finding by arguing that "the internal dynamics of identification and world-definition aim at coherence" (1999: 248). Why not? Hybridity is an argument against homogeneity, not against coherence. The point is precisely that homogeneity is not a requirement for coherence. When Friedman does acknowledge hybridity, he shifts the goalposts. "Now this combination of cultural elements might be called hybridization, but it would tell us nothing about the processes involved" (1999: 248). The processes involved indeed may vary widely. And probably there is something like a stereotyping of hybridity—of world music stamp.

Friedman's argument against hybridity is inconsistent, contradictory, and at times far-fetched, so it's not worth pursuing far. Friedman argues that all cultures are hybrid but that boundaries are not disappearing: these two statements alone are difficult to rhyme. He argues that hybridity talk is trivial unless it is self-identification, but if hybridity is part of self-identification it is overruled by coherence, and we should examine the processes involved. However, if all cultures are hybrid all along, then the problem is not hybridity but boundaries: how is it that boundaries are historically and socially so significant? How come that while boundaries continuously change shape in the currents and tides of history, boundary fetishism remains, even among social scientists? If hybridity is real but boundaries are prominent, how *can* hybridity be a self-identification: in a world of boundaries, what room and legitimacy is there for boundary-crossing identities, politically, culturally?

How to situate the anti-hybridity argument? At one level it is another installment of the critique of "postmodernism," which in these times recurs with different emphases every ten years or so. In the present wave a polemical emphasis is "Marxism versus cultural studies," which is obviously a broad stroke target. At another level, the argument reflects unease with multiculturalism. When these two lines coincide, we get the novel combination of redneck Marxism. In this view, multiculturalism is a fad that detracts from, well, class struggle.[8] A positive reading is that this refocuses the attention on political economy, class, social justice, and hard politics, which is surely a point worth making in relation to Tinkerbell postmodernism. At the same time this is an exercise in symbolic politics unfolding on a narrow canvas, for it mainly concerns positioning within academia. Would this explain why so much is missing from the debate? Among the fundamental considerations that are missing in the anti-hybridity backlash is the historical depth of hybridity viewed in the *longue durée*. More important still is the circumstance that boundaries and borders can be issues of life and death; and the failure to recognize and acknowledge hybridity then is a political point that may be measured in lives.

HYBRIDITY AND THE *LONGUE DURÉE*

Hybridization is common in nature. Carrying pollen between flowers, bees and other insects contribute to the variety of flora. While cross-pollination is inherent in nature, hybridity is common in human history as well. Thousands of years of dividing and policing of space, territorial and symbolic, stand between us and our mixed evolutionary and long-term history, or, more precisely, are interspersed with it. Thanks to boundaries, civilizations have flourished and suffocated. Boundaries have come and gone. Been erected, fought over, and then walked over.

Many contemporary debates take as their point of departure recent history rather than the *longue durée*. According to Friedman, "The current stage is one in which culture has begun to overflow its boundaries and mingle with other cultures, producing numerous new breeds or hybrids" (1999: 237). A historically more plausible view is that cultures have been overflowing boundaries all along and that boundaries have been provisional and ever contentious superimpositions upon substrata of mingling and traffic. Not recent times are the yardstick (or, they would be only from a superficial point of view) but evolutionary times. A distinctive feature of contemporary times is that they are times of *accelerated mixing*. Thus, not mixing is new but the scope and speed of mixing.

Population movements, cross-cultural trade, intercultural contact, and intermarriage have been common throughout history. Occasionally there have been forced population transfers, diaspora, or exile. Sometimes this involved so to speak population grafting; in Babylon, Alexander compelled 7,000 of his soldiers to marry 7,000 Persian women. At times large public works involved the relocation of thousands of craftsmen.

We can think of hybridity as *layered* in history, including precolonial, colonial, and postcolonial layers, each with distinct sets of hybridity, as a function of the boundaries that were prominent and accordingly a different pathos of difference. (For colonizing countries, these are precolonial, imperial, and postimperial periods. A précis is in table 5.3.)

Table 5.3. Historical Layers of Hybridity

Colonies	Colonizing countries	Boundaries
	Prehistory	Ecology, geography, plus cultural
	Precolonial	difference (language, religion)
Colonial, dependent	Imperial, metropolitan	"Victorian" hierarchies (modes of production, race)
Postcolonial	Postimperial	Development hierarchies (GNP and other indices)

But we should add prehistory as an earlier phase of mixing. The evolutionary backdrop of our common origins in Africa confirms that humanity is a hybrid species.[9] The species' subsequent "clustering" in different regions of the world has not precluded large-scale contact and population movements across and between the continents (Gamble 1993). This mixed heritage is confirmed by the "cultures" identified by archaeologists which in Paleolithic and Neolithic times sprawl widely and do not coincide with the boundaries of much later times. The diffusion of technologies—of pastoralism, agriculture, horse riding, the stirrup, chariot, saddle, bow and arrow, bronze and iron, and so forth—rapidly and over vast distances, is a further indication of long-distance communication early on (W. McNeill 1982). Half the world's population speaks languages that derive from a single common root—an Indo-European root (Mallory 1991). A further indicator is the spread of the world religions. The spread of diseases is another marker of episodes of intercultural contact (W. McNeill 1977). Besides technologies, language, and religions, the travel of symbols is another indicator of cross-cultural communication, examined in art history (a fine source is Wittkower 1989). Anthropologists have studied the travel of customs and foodstuffs. In other words, our foundations are profoundly, structurally, inherently mixed, and it could not be otherwise. Mixing is intrinsic to the evolution of the species. History is a collage (see table 5.3).

Superimposed upon the deep strata of mixing in evolutionary time are historical episodes of long-distance cross-cultural trade, conquest, and empire, and specific episodes such as trans-Atlantic slavery and the triangular trade. Within and across these levels we can distinguish further types of hybridity. Taking a political economy approach, we can identify the following general types of historical hybridity:

- *Hybridity across modes of production.* This gives rise to mixed social formations. It entails combinations between hunting/gathering and cultivation or pastoralism, agriculture and industry, craft and industry, within and across social formations. Semifeudalism, feudal capitalism are other instances. As the debate on the articulation of modes of production shows (Foster-Carter 1978) modes of production did not simply succeed one another but coexisted.

- *Hybridity before and after industrialization.* The agricultural revolution was the first major break in history and industrialization was the second, and this introduced a global development gap. It refers to 1800 as a marker indicating the first use of fossil fuels (steam engine).
- *Hybrid modes of regulation.* The social market, Fordism, market socialism, and the Third Way are examples of mixed forms of regulation.[10]

Besides hybrid nations, there are *hybrid regions* that straddle geographic and cultural areas such as the Sudanic belt in Africa. Southeast Asia combines Indo-Chinese and Malay features. The Malay world, Indo-China, Central and South Asia, Middle Eastern, North African, and Balkan societies are ancient mélange cultures. As Willis points out, there are "societies with creoles and creole societies" (2001b: 175). *Hybrid societies* include all contact cultures, on the crossroads of trade and traffic, or straddling civilizational zones. The island cultures of the Caribbean and the Pacific and Indian oceans are contact cultures that have developed creole languages. Central and Latin American countries from Mexico to Brazil define themselves as mestizo. *Hybrid cities* are typically located at civilizational crossroads, ports, major arteries of trade, or involve significant immigrant populations. Istanbul, Venice, and Toledo are classic examples and so are Baghdad and Cairo, Lahore and Delhi, Calcutta and Bombay, Hong Kong and Singapore, Marseille and Mombasa, New Orleans and San Francisco.[11]

Among hybrid societies, we can distinguish those whose conventional self-definition is hybrid, such as Mexico and Zanzibar, and those whose conventional self-understanding is monocultural and where plural, multicultural identity is a recent transition. Portugal and Spain are mixed cultures but owe their national identity to the Reconquista. Greece has been part of the Byzantine and Ottoman empires and while this shapes its folk culture, its national identity turns its back to the East. In England, English and British identities represent monocultural ("little England") and plural identities. This ignores that English identities are a multiethnic mix all along including Celts, Angles, Saxons, Danes, Romans, and Normans (MacDougall 1982). All nations share this kind of plural heritage. As the saying goes, it took two hundred years to create Frenchmen. National identity has been a specific historical project, which is now being redefined again.

Also in nations where hybridity doesn't form part of national identity, it looms in the background. A caption in a museum in Norway notes that a particular type of jewelry is found "from Dublin to the Volga." Regional and folklore museums usually reveal the transborder cultural continuities that national museums militantly ignore; they relate to deeper cultural strata and a different historical awareness.

Next are *hybrid communities* within societies, such as the Khacharas in Nepal (offspring of a Nepali father and Tibetan mother), the Burghers in Sri Lanka, the Coloreds in Cape Town (Februari 1981), and countless others throughout the world. For instance, in Japan, "With the growth and expansion of transnational Pacific Rim entrepôt, Pacific Creole communities appeared and flourished: Kobe Creoles, San Francisco Creoles, Yokohama Creoles, and others" (Willis 2001b: 175). A recent site of hybridization is international education (Willis coins the term "eduscapes"). With growing transnationalism come generations of "third culture kids."

Against the backdrop of deep time, the current hybridity discussion seems superficial, for it is entirely dominated by the episodes of colonialism and nationalism of the last two hundred or so years. What is striking is the spell these episodes cast and the preoccupation with boundaries this involves (cf. Nederveen Pieterse 2002).

BOUNDARY FETISHISM AND LIFE AND DEATH

In the United States, demographers speak of a silent explosion in the number of mixed-race people. Between 1960 and 1990, the number of interracial married couples went from 150,000 to more than 1.1 million, and the number of interracial children leaps accordingly. "Since 1970, the number of mixed-race children in the United States has quadrupled. And there are six times as many intermarriages today as there were in 1960" (Etzioni 1997). No wonder that a commentator observes, "Look at Tiger Woods and see the face of America's future. . . . It was Tiger Woods's *face* that provided the real benchmark—showing how far Americans have come on an unstoppable national journey: the journey from the time-honored myth of racial clarity to the all-mixed up reality of multiracialism" (Overholser 2000).

In addition to the choice of sixteen racial categories that the Census Bureau used to offer Americans, Etzioni and others proposed a new "multiracial" category. This idea has been infuriating to some African American leaders who regard it as undermining black solidarity. "African-American leaders also object to a multiracial category because race data are used to enforce civil rights legislation in employment, voting rights, housing and mortgage lending, health care services and educational opportunities" (Etzioni 1997). The proponents argue that this category—and a "category of 'multiethnic' origin, which most Americans might wish to check"—would help soften the racial and ethnic divisions that now run through American society. This is only an example of the clash between the politics of recognition based on the allocation of collective rights and the idea of fluid group boundaries.

Most of the world population now lives on less than $2 a day while a few hundred billionaires own as much as half the world's population. Technical explanations for the world's development gaps are plenty but insufficient. A superficial impression is that there is a lack of circulation or flow. Overall, human capabilities are evenly spread and capacitation or empowerment is possible, so presumably what stand in the way are boundaries, barriers, or borders of various kinds. Ecology and geography map bioregions and climate zones. Boundaries are a central theme in social science. Economics measures boundaries such as GNP and income; microeconomics examines investment and location strategies; political science studies systems of organization and representation within given boundaries; sociology examines how boundaries such as nation, class, caste, and region inform social practices (Moore and Buchanan 2003). But invariably it is through cultural codes that boundaries are experienced, lived, upheld.

We could follow this with a history of boundaries—boundaries of clan, tribe, language, region, culture, civilization, empire, religion, state, nation, race, ethnicity, and a history of *centrisms*, that is, hegemonic positions of power and points of view from which social landscapes have been viewed, mapped, and defined. At no time have these boundaries precluded crossborder contact, though attempts have been made to control them. We could then follow with a history of boundary and border crossing, smuggling, piracy, cross-cultural traffic, migration, travel, diaspora, pilgrimage, trade: the hybridity angle on history unsettles the boundaries as well as the codes that sustain them.

According to Zbigniew Brzezinski, in the twentieth century 167,000,000 to 175,000,000 lives have been deliberately extinguished through politically motivated carnage (quoted in Hirsch 1995: xii). If we consider this death toll, a major and perhaps a greater part of ethnonationalist and ethnic killing involves internecine strife, that is, political factions eliminating competitors within their own camp. The targets include crossover factions who threaten to blur the lines of conflict, rivals for leadership, forces that defy the political and military hegemony of the leading faction, and all those who would wage peace rather than war. Episodes of "ethnic cleansing," genocide, communal violence, and civil war involve the militant suppression of the in-between, the elimination of hybridity. This refers to political as well as cultural in-betweens.

In Bosnia, about a third of the population was hybrid—intermarried or of mixed parentage—but none of the wartime counts of Bosnian Muslims, Bosnian Croats, or Bosnian Serbs acknowledged this. "No provisions are made for the more than 26 percent of the population that is intermarried, for the substantial numbers of urban dwellers who refused to describe themselves as either Serbs, Muslims, or Croats in the last census; or for the Serbs and Croats who support and have fought for the Bosnian government against their ethnic fellow nations that are trying to destroy Bosnia. All of that has been buried under the assumption that the *only* civic links that remain in Bosnia are those of the ethnic community" (Denitch 1994: 7; Nederveen Pieterse 1998b).

The opportunistic and political character of the markers of "ethnicity" has also been apparent in Bosnia: "Each side will alternately emphasize their common roots when it indeed suits its purposes. Before the war, for example, when the Serbs still hoped to keep Bosnia in Yugoslavia, the media frequently highlighted similarities with the Muslims, while Croats often stressed that Bosnia had been part of historical Croatia and that most Bosnian Muslims were originally of Croatian descent" (Bell-Fialkoff 1993: 121). In Vojvodina, the region of former Yugoslavia where cultural mixing, measured by rate of intermarriage, was highest, conflict was absent (Botev 1994). In the region where intermarriage was lowest, at 0.2 percent in Kosovo, conflict was sparked off.

DIFFERENT CULTURAL TAKES ON HYBRIDITY

Hybridity involves different meanings not only across time but also across cultural contexts. In "high" and classical cultural settings, the gatekeepers of "standards" easily repudiate hybridity as infringement of the canon (without awareness or acknowledgment of the mixed character of the canon itself). In popular culture, mixing of elements and styles may pass unnoticed, be taken for granted, or welcomed (Frow 1992). Creativity and innovation often turn on unlikely combinations, so in art and sciences hybridity is common and at times more readily acknowledged than in other domains.

Hybridity carries different meanings in different cultures, among different circles within cultures and at different periods. Radhakrishnan (1996) distinguishes between metropolitan and peripheral hybridity; but the meaning of hybridity is not the same in all metropolises or peripheries. The meaning of hybridity differs according to the way it has come about. In the United States, where race is such an overriding preoccupation, hybridity talk centers on race (Chideya 1999). However "mixed race" carries meaning only where "race" counts. It has no meaning in places that do not share a history of racial division and where, for instance, religious or ideological boundaries count. Hybridity is entirely contextual, relational. What is strikingly hybrid in one setting may not even be noticeable in another. The significance of hybridity extends only so far as the reach of the boundaries that it transgresses. If hybridity subverts a provincialism, outside the province it has no meaning.

In Asia, on the whole it carries a different ring than in Latin America. In Asia, the general feeling has been upbeat, as in East-West fusion culture. Hybridity tends to be experienced as chosen, willed, though there are plenty of sites of conflict. In Latin America, the feeling has long been one of fracture, fragmentation, *tiempos mixtos*. Hybridity used to be experienced as a fateful condition that is inflicted rather than willed. An example is the Mexican "Malinche complex" discussed by Octavio Paz (1967). This goes back to the duality at the foundation of the Latin American experience: the experience of conquest and the divide between *criollos* and *indigenes*, which led to Latin American societies being characterized as "dual societies" (a diagnosis that ignores other identities such as descendants of African slaves, Asian immigrants, and again the in-betweens, the Ladinos). In recent Latin American accounts the notion of hybridity as an affliction has turned into a growing recognition of popular creativity (Canclini 1995, 2000; Ortiz 2000). "Latinity" as bricolage is now a common perception.

An equivalent of Malinche in Japan is Okichi: "The story of Okichi, the mistress to the first US envoy to Japan, is seen as a tragic metaphor for purity sullied and the demise of the nation (read male nation)" (Willis 2001a: 32). Here trauma has made place for explorations of Japanese-American or "JAmerican" culture (Willis 2001a: 32). In everyday talk in Asia, one often hears of the negative consequences of rapid modernization, for instance, in Indonesia: "Just how successful has the government been at developing the spiritual and cultural sectors in order to counter the negative impacts of rapid modernization?" (*Jakarta Post*, 9 March 1995). Modernization has never been universally embraced and there has been a wide spectrum of interests and positions, which, however, have typically been *interpreted* through the lens of modernity, with modernity as a yardstick, from "traditionalists" to "modernizers," anti- or pro-modernization, and conservative or defensive modernization.

In sub-Saharan Africa, key themes in relation to modernity have been traditional social institutions and values—as in négritude, African socialism, and ujama. Slavery, the gun-slave cycle, and European colonialism have sidetracked the development of African societies; here colonialism has been fresher and more destructive than anywhere else and decolonization has been the most recent. Revisionist history inspires Afrocentric readings of Egyptian civilization, and indigenization informs language politics and Afrocentric ethnosociology. At the same time, "reworking modernity" is a prominent strand in African societies (Pred and Watts 1992, Appiah 1992).

It would not be difficult to make a general case for modernization and development in the global South as processes of hybridization. In anthropology, this terminology is widely used.[12] The anthropologist Bayart (1992) refers to social and political "hybridation" to characterize African modernities. Hybridity is common terminology in Latin America and terms such as fusion are common in Asia. Neotraditionalism is common and another example is neopatriarchy in the Arab world (Sharabi 1988). Everywhere a language of combinations, articulations, and improvisations describes the various changes in the wake of anti-colonialism, decolonization, and development.

In the West, hybridity thinking is à la mode but borders persist—witness issues of migration, racism and illegal aliens, the class divisions of ghettos, and the vagaries of international development discourse. Still it makes a huge difference whether the argument is that there is too much multiculturalism or not enough, and this remains unclear in the anti-hybridity argument.

PATTERNS OF HYBRIDITY

In cultural, literary, and postcolonial studies, hybridity, syncretism, creolization, métissage have become common tropes. Usually the reference is to cultural rather than institutional or structural hybridity. Hybridity is fast becoming a routine, almost trite point of reference in reflections on global culture that speak of the "mongrel world" and the "hybridity factor" (Zachary 2000, Iyer 2000). Yet, as hybridity becomes a ubiquitous attribute or quality, by the same token it becomes increasingly meaningless, a universal soup: if everything is hybrid what does hybridity mean? Hence the next question to come up is what kind of hybridity? Radhakrishnan (1996) distinguishes between metropolitan (ludic) and postcolonial (critical) hybridity, Werbner (1997) between organic and intentional hybridity, Bhavnani (1999) between situational and organic hybridity. Patterns of hybridity in relation to modes of production and regulation are explored above. A standard criticism of hybridity is that it sidesteps power differences: "Hybridity is not parity."[13] According to Raewyn Connell, "The idea of 'hybridization,' so popular in the discourse of globalization, is deeply misleading. All these lines of difference involve power, or struggles for power, and construct continuing privilege" (2013: 69). This assumes that it is either/or: either we talk hybridity or we talk power; but, of course, it is and/and: we can talk hybridity *and* power.

So the critical variable is power. Thus in assessing varieties of multiculturalism, pertinent criteria are power and equality, or degrees of symmetry and the extent to which culture is centered on a standard or canon. *Mestizaje* in Latin America has a cultural center of gravity; it is an ideology of whitening, Europeanization, parallel to modernization. Creolization in the Caribbean is more fluid, though it remains centered

Table 5.4. Patterns of Hybridity

Axes	Implications
Asymmetric/symmetric	The relative power and status of elements in the mixture. E.g., colonial society and American hegemony are asymmetric. It is difficult to give an example of the perfectly symmetric extreme of the continuum.
With or without center	Hybridities with or without a center are polarities of a continuum. Again it is difficult to think of an example of completely free-floating mixture, for even at a carnival the components are charged with different values, polarities.

on "browning" and the color hierarchy of "shadism." "If you're black, stay back. If you're brown, stick aroun'. If you're white, you're alright" (D. P. Thompson 1999). A précis of patterns of hybridity is in table 5.4.

SO WHAT?

It is not obvious why the term "hybridity" has stuck as the general heading for these phenomena. As a word it came of age in the nineteenth century (Young 1995: 6). In French *bricolage* has long been a common term. Mixing, blending, melding, and merging are other terms and nuances with longer lineages than the quasi-scientific term hybridity. Mixing plays a part in agriculture (mixing crops), cooking (ingredients), weaving (tissues, motifs), healing (herbs, methods), art (genres, materials), fashion (styles), and so forth. Amalgamation and fusion of different substances are fundamental processes in alchemy, producing transubstantiation or decay. This returns in chemistry, metallurgy (alloys), and the pharmaceutical industry. Osmosis plays a part in cell biology and chemistry. Why of all terms hybridity has stuck is probably because of the preoccupation with biological and "racial" differences and the intellectual imprint of genetics, which are essentially eighteenth- and nineteenth-century problematics.[14]

Now let's come back to the original question: Hybridity, so what? In the previous chapter I ask: "How do we come to terms with phenomena such as Thai boxing by Moroccan girls in Amsterdam, Asian rap in London, Irish bagels, Chinese tacos?" Friedman cites this and asks: "What is it that we must come to terms with here?" (1999: 236) What we must come to terms with is the circumstance that nowadays we are *all* "Moroccan girls doing Thai boxing in Amsterdam," that is, we are all mixing cultural elements and traces *across* places and identities.[15] This is not simply an issue of classification or fancy cosmopolitan experience; rather the point is that this has become an *ordinary* experience. A Greek restaurant called Ipanema serving Italian food in Brighton: such crossovers are now common in all spheres of life.

This is only the tip of the iceberg. Boundaries themselves are tricky. Thus, the *meanings* of boundaries are by no means constant. For instance, the anthropologist Fiona Wilson (2000) discusses the radically changing meanings of the categories of Indian and Mestizo over time and by class in Andean Peru. More revealing still is that boundaries themselves are often bricolage improvisations. Thus, the claims of racial, ethnic, and religious "fundamentalisms" are often cobbled together from diverse and hybrid sources. For instance, Stephen Howe (1998) shows how Afrocentrism derives several of its claims and methods from European sources. All this does not mean that boundaries fade or vanish; they never will because boundaries are a function of power and social life. It does not mean that the emotions associated with boundaries wane, nor do their consequences, such as racist murder. Then, does this mean that "hybridity," as so many argue, is merely a plaything of bourgeois or bohemian elites? Rather the point is that the flux of our times is such that across classes the contingency of boundaries is now a more common experience than ever before.

Hybridity is a terminology and sensibility of our time in that boundary and border crossing mark our times. Thus with regard to national borders these are times of postnationalism. Sovereignty changes meaning, and is now increasingly being pooled in regional and international arrangements and covenants; neomedievalism is one of the accounts for current political conditions (Kobrin 1998). Class and gender boundaries are less strict than before. Aesthetic boundaries are increasingly permeable with high and low cultures mingling. In the sciences, disciplinary boundaries are increasingly old-fashioned. And so on.

As a perspective, hybridity entails three different sets of claims: empirical (hybridization happens), theoretical (acknowledging hybridity as an analytical tool), and normative (a critique of boundaries and valorization of mixtures, in certain contexts and particular relations of power). Hybridity is to culture what deconstruction is to discourse: transcending binary categories. Another account of hybridity is "in-betweenness." Recognizing the *in-between* and the *interstices* means going beyond dualism, binary thinking, Aristotelian logic. Methodologically this is the hallmark of poststructuralism and deconstruction; it represents an epistemological shift outside the box of Cartesian epistemology. Postmodernism has been a general heading for this change in outlook. In its affirmative sense it involves a profound moment of collective reflexivity that includes the awareness that boundaries are historical and social constructions and cognitive barriers whose validity depends on epistemic orders, which are ultimately of an arbitrary or at least contingent nature. This awareness in itself is not new; what is new is its expansion among broader strata of the population and its widening scope in relation to phenomena. Thomas Kuhn's paradigm shifts in science, the emergence of "new science" beyond Newtonian science, Foucault on epistemic orders, Derrida on deconstruction, Deleuze and Guattari on deterritorialization, feminist boundary crossings, Lyotard on the space in between language games, Bhabha on "third space"—these are all different moments and ways of stepping out of the Cartesian box of knowledge and order.

This overall movement has so many ramifications that its significance is difficult to map—as if any mapping exercise in the process validates maps while the point is to recognize the limited and contingent status of any kind of map. One account is that the space across and between boundaries is a liminal space and current changes involve liminality of a kind becoming a collective awareness.[16] This awareness may be described as a kind of Trickster knowledge, in which the Trickster is the joker in the pack, the jester, the fool, the shape-shifter who does not take seriously what all society around regards as sacred rules. Along the Mexican-US border, people smugglers are nicknamed "coyotes." Among Native Americans, Coyote is a Trickster, Wily Coyote, like Anansi the spider in West Africa and Brer Rabbit in rural America. In this sense hybridity consciousness represents a return of the Trickster, now at a collective scale.

This does not mean that boundary crossing is a free-for-all. There is free cheese only in the mousetrap. As some boundaries wane, others remain or come in. Thus, as national borders and governmental authority erode, ethnic or religious boundaries, or boundaries of consumption patterns and brand names emerge in their place. NGOs carve out new spaces of power. Or, as some boundaries fade, people's differential capacities for border crossing and mobility come to the foreground. In virtual space, cognitive boundaries and cyberwars emerge. Another complex issue is the relationship between cultural diversity and bio-diversity. Acknowledging the contingency of boundaries and the significance and limitations of hybridity as a theme and approach means engaging hybridity politics. This is where critical hybridity comes in, which involves a new awareness of and new take on dynamics of group formation and social inequality. This critical awareness is furthered by acknowledging rather than by suppressing hybridity.

Chapter 6

Globalization Is Braided: East-West Osmosis

True, neither East nor West is what it used to be.

—K. G. Subramanyan

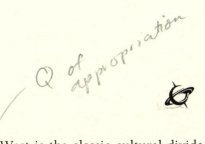

East-West is the classic cultural divide that gave rise to Orientalism. Showing crossover and hybridization between East and West means pulling the carpet from under one of the major cultural fissures in world history. Doing so, of course, is by no means new. Orientalism itself is profoundly ambivalent, oscillating between attraction and repulsion, part fascination and part disdain (Baudet 1965).

Borrowing and cross fertilization between East and West is as old as the hills. Much is now on record and is no longer or less controversial, particularly since revisionist historical studies of recent decades. European Ethiopianism, Egyptomania, Chinoiserie, Turquerie, Indophilia, and so forth have been extensively documented (e.g., Nederveen Pieterse 1994). Nevertheless, while some crossovers are familiar, others are not, and the overall picture remains West-centric. This chapter first sketches a genealogy of East-West divides and then turns to the braiding and intertwining of East-West influences, with a section devoted to the Islamic world.

East-West mixing is a meaningful theme for several reasons. The first, of course, is overcoming Eurocentrism and instead developing a polycentric perspective on global history. Perspectives on history, modernity, and globalization are still steeped in Eurocentric assumptions, for instance, world-system theory and its preoccupation with the "long sixteenth century" and Anthony Giddens' shallow view that globalization is "a consequence of western modernity." In fact, what is at stake is not just decolonizing world history but making visible *how* the world's peoples have become more interconnected over time. This matters also because it sheds light on contemporary trends. Thus, if the rise of Asia is not merely a rise but a comeback, it places ongoing economic, cultural, and political trends in a deeper perspective. Third, it is a matter of deepening our understanding of globalization, viewed not just from a western viewpoint but from global viewpoints. It is probably a good idea that globalization thinking should be global. Fourth, uncovering the many layers of East-West relations and looking beyond present times contributes to a sophisticated, more refined take on hybridity. Like much else, hybridity thinking suffers from presentism; considering hybridity in the *longue durée* deepens our insight.

Global history is in vogue, but Eurocentric habits die hard. Thus in a recent work the Cambridge historian Christopher Bayly, although an adherent of global history, offers a periodization of globalization that is thoroughly conventional and Eurocentric. According to Bayly (2004), the main phases of globalization are *archaic globalization* in the sixteenth century; *early modern globalization* during the seventeenth and eighteenth centuries (with the emergence of a European-Atlantic economy and 1760–1830 as the "first global imperialism"); and *modern globalization* from the nineteenth century onward. This periodization recycles all the hallmarks of a Eurocentric view: the late start privileges Europe, featuring Europe as the central stage and the lead actor. The timeline matches the categories of Europeanist history (in which early modern and modern history are mainstays of the curriculum) and echoes the Eurocentric preoccupation with the post-1500 period, the "long sixteenth century." This narrative marginalizes or conceals from view the role of the East, for all other contributions become a mere prelude or sideshow to western globalization (a critical discussion is Nederveen Pieterse 2005). "Modern" is, as usual, used as a Eurocentric category.

A revisionist literature follows global history, critiques Eurocentrism, and presents an "Orient first" thesis, according to which *oriental globalization* precedes occidental or West-centric globalization (Hobson 2004, Nederveen Pieterse 2006). In this general framework, "early globalization," which is also termed "primary globalization," begins much earlier than in Eurocentric accounts. Different time frames and accents include the Bronze Age from 3000 BCE (Goody 2010) and 500–1000 CE (Hobson) or 1250 (Abu-Lughod 1989), centered in the Middle East. The next phase of early globalization is centered in China and South Asia from circa 1100 (Hobson) or 1400 (Frank 1998, Pomeranz 2000) and Southeast Asia (Reid 1993, Gunn 2003). Table 6.1 sums up this literature and offers an account of the phases of globalization that differs fundamentally from the conventional Eurocentric view, in

Table 6.1. Phases of Globalization

Phases	Start time	Central nodes	Dynamics
Bronze Age	3000 BCE	Eurasia	Migrations, trade, conquest
Oriental globalization 1	500 CE	Middle East	World economy
Oriental globalization 2	1100	East and South Asia	Productivity, technology, trade
Early modern	1500	Multipolar and Europe	Triangular trade, Americas
Modern	1800	Euro-Atlantic economy	Colonialism, colonial division of labor, new imperialism
Postwar accelerated globalization	1950	US, Europe, Japan	Multinational corporations, Cold War, new international division of labor
Neoliberal globalization	1980	United States	Washington consensus, IMF, World Bank, WTO
Twenty-first-century globalization	2000	Emerging economies	Multipolarity

Table 6.2.   Twentieth- and Twenty-first-Century Globalization

Phases	Central nodes	Dynamics
1950	US, Europe, Japan	Multinational corporations, Cold War
1970	Rise of new industrializing economies	New international division of labor (basic industries relocate to low wage zones)
1980	US, East Asia, US-Asia codependence	Neoliberal globalization, flexible accumulation; offshoring, outsourcing; combined role of Wall Street, Treasury, IMF, World Bank, WTO
2000	BRICS (Brazil, Russia, India, China, South Africa)	New industrialization, rising trade and demand for commodities, energy; new South-South combinations

shorthand. Table 6.2 (discussed below) views twentieth- and twenty-first-century globalization in a finer grain.

The thesis of oriental globalization corrects the conventional paradigm of occidental globalization, which is an important contribution. Even so, more important than establishing a merry-go-round of leading centers and hegemonies is growing insight in the interconnected and parallel histories of East, West, North, and South (as in Lieberman 1999). A more radical view holds that the developments in Asia may be viewed not just as early globalization but also as an "early modernity" (e.g., Subrahmanyam 1997, 1998), but it leads too far to take up this case here. The point of tracing East-West hybridities is to uncover these interrelations. Part of this involves taking a step back and holding the categories themselves to the light.

EAST-WEST

East-West is a special way of dividing up the world. As a trope it goes back to the divide between the Greeks and Persians, dramatized in the Trojan War. The classical education of European elites and their immersion in the Greek and Latin legacies bequeathed a sense of cultural boundaries. Some of the pathos of difference of the ancients passed on to the moderns. The influence the East-West divide exercised as part of the European and later American classical legacy concealed the long-term osmosis of East and West and of the East and the Hellenic world.

From the outset, of course, it was an artificial and polemical division, a cultural posture, and not a description of actual relations. The divide played a much larger role in rhetoric and representation than in reality. Population movements and the travel of Stone Age tools and bronze and iron technologies go back to evolutionary time (W. McNeill 1982, Goody 2010), so East and West, of course, were woven of the same cloth long before they were, allegedly, divided. We can view evolutionary time as the prehistory of globalization: prehistory because relations across space were sparse and irregular (and unrecorded), and globalization because they laid the infrastructure for later traffic.[1] The ecological adaptability of the species enables its global spread. Large-scale population movements during the prehistory of globalization established the infrastructure; during early phases of globalization the density and volume of traffic increased and a world economy took shape.

Ancient Egypt traded with Mohenjo-Daro and Harappa; Rome traded wine with Cochin in India. The interconnections were increasingly substantial. That Chinese silk played an important part in the foreign trade of the Roman Empire (W. Cohen 2000: 11) is possible only if the supplies were substantial, regular, and direct. The ancient civilization centers of the great rivers, the Nile, the Euphrates and Tigris, the Indus river valley, and the Yangtze and Yellow River, became interconnected over time, sharing technologies, knowledge, and the rites of mystery schools. Plato learned in academies in Egypt and Egypt traded and shared knowledge with Asia. As Martin Bernal argues in *Black Athena*, ancient Greece was shaped by influences from Egypt, Mesopotamia, Phoenicia, and Persia, which in turn were influenced by Asian civilizations.

A saying in Rome was *ex Oriente lux*. From the outposts of empire, legionnaires brought eastern cults to Rome: the Mithras cult from Persia, Isis worship from Egypt, Mesopotamian cults such as Baal worship, and the chthonic cults of Pan, Dionysus, and Bes (Tiryakian 1996). One of the eastern cults, Christianity, became the religion of the empire and a world religion. Relations ran in multiple directions, as suggested in Karl Jaspers' axial age from 800 to 200 BCE when Zoroastrianism, Buddhism, Confucianism, and early Greek philosophy took shape. This long period of civilizational osmosis is part of the foundations of early globalization and saw early intimations of global consciousness.

Early East-West braiding includes the travel of fundamental technologies such as literacy and numeracy. Until the sixteenth century the arrows of influence mostly pointed from East to West, but at times West-East influences played a part. Alexander's conquests as far as the Punjab and the Indus and Ganges rivers are an early instance (327 BCE) and left in what is now the Afghan border and northwest Pakistan, near Peshawar and Taxila, the legacy of the *Gandhara civilization*, a style of Buddhist art with Hellenic traits and a mixture of Greek, Roman, Iranian, and Central Asian cultures. Hellenic and Roman influences are other instances of influence from West to East. Of course, establishing flows and directions of influence implies accepting the East-West divide in the first place, which is tenuous (if it mattered at all, it did in limited spheres) and anachronistic (at the time when it mattered it carried quite different meanings than have been attributed to it subsequently).

The divide between the eastern and western parts of the empire, Byzantium and Rome, and between Latin and Greek Christianity, further inflected East-West differences. The Crusades, ostensibly aimed at the Muslim world, eventually succeeded in weakening Byzantium. East-West rivalries *within* the empire were a subtext of the Crusades.

Early globalization may be dated, following Hobson (2004), from 500–1000 CE, using the camel caravan trade, and centered on the Middle East with Mecca, Baghdad, and Damascus as hubs in long-distance trade. Muslim traders migrating eastward and stimulating commerce as far as China contributed to recentering economic forces. During the second phase of oriental globalization, starting ca. 1100 CE (Hobson) or 1400 (according to Frank 1998, Pomeranz 2000), China and India assumed key roles as propelling forces in the world economy, leading in productivity, innovation, and trade. Goods, technologies, and cultural influences traveled along the Silk Routes overland and by sea, carrying silk, muslin, cotton, spices, paper, gunpowder, and the compass.

The impact on Europe was tremendous. The arrival of gunpowder in fifteenth-century Europe essentially ended feudalism and the castle system, and power gradually shifted to the towns, so oriental influences are at the root of the development of free towns and the rise of Europe's bourgeoisie. Among the first "free towns" in Europe were Italian ports that bought their freedom thanks to the Levant trade. The Levant trade brought prosperity to Livorno, Pisa, Levanto, Venice, and other port cities which, in turn, spurred the prosperity of the hinterland. The ports of Livorno and Pisa were the original foundation of the wealth of Florence and the Medici. There are many links between "eastern civilization" and the "rise of the West," between the Orient and the Italian Renaissance. The oriental styles of medieval and Renaissance churches and buildings in Tuscany and Umbria are lasting testimony to these connections. Beginning in the 1300s and 1400s, luxury goods from Islamic and Asian countries brought to Europe in huge quantities on Italian merchant ships inspired Italian craftsmen in textiles, ceramics, glass, bookbinding, and metalwork, and their craftsmanship gradually began to compete with the imports. Italian painting reflected trans-Mediterranean trade and travel with representations of carpets and ceramics from the East, as well as textiles with bands of writing replicating or suggesting Arabic script. Thus Islamic and Asian motifs were absorbed into Christian contexts (Mack 2002).

Venice's rise as the "bazaar of Europe" and its oriental character are well on record. The crafts of the Mamluk, Ottoman, and Safavid empires in inlaid metalwork, ceramics, lacquer ware, gilded and enameled glass, textiles, and carpets found echoes in the Serenissima Republic. Venice was Europe's gateway for Islamic art and Persian and Ottoman miniatures (Carboni 2007, Gombrich 1984).

Eventually East-West differences went into the demarcation and identity of "Europe," again, of course, as a tenuous boundary. Thus Zeus in the form of a bull abducted Europa, daughter of Agenor, king of Tyre in what we now call Lebanon, and brought her to Europe.[2]

ISLAM-WEST

The cultural friction between the West and Islam seems one of the most contrived and exaggerated cultural divides ever. What is striking, first, is that it is a *recent* cleavage which follows centuries and millennia of intermixture. What is often overlooked, too, is that the Islamic world is profoundly mixed, a middleman world that straddles geographic and civilizational spheres and combines, among others, Mesopotamian, Sumerian, Acadian, Nabatean, Arab, Bedouin, Persian, Hebrew, Phoenician, African, and Hellenic influences. The prophet most often mentioned in the Koran is Moses. Of course Islam is steeped in the Hebrew and Christian traditions, and of course Islam comes in many varieties— rural and folk, Sufi and scriptural, urban and clerical, Arab, Persian, Turkish, Berber, Indian, Malay, Chinese, African, European, and American.

The Hellenic world—itself a composite incorporating many oriental influences—exercised a major influence on the Arab and Islamic world (Amin 1978). When the cosmopolitan worlds of Sanskrit and Latin receded and gave way to vernacular cultures (Pollock 1996, 2000), Arabic and the world of Islam succeeded in their place and, in time, extended beyond their reaches. The world of Islam became a cosmopolitanism that bridged the ancients and the moderns and reached most continents (Nederveen Pieterse 2007, Kamali 2006).

During Europe's Middle Ages, when the Mediterranean became, in the words of Henri Pirenne, "a Muslim lake," the East acquired yet another connotation. Much of the recent East-West divide and, of course, much of Orientalism is owed to this friction, which is both recent and concerns neighboring cultures and civilizations.

European influence was felt in other continents particularly after 1500, after the journeys of reconnaissance, the ventures of the chartered companies, and later the triangular trade. In the third major phase of globalization, European chartered companies traded directly with the Orient, cut out middlemen, and brought spices from the Southeast Asian islands and tea, silk, and porcelain from China. Sprinkled along the routes of the Dutch East India Company (VOC), for instance, in Cape Town (now in the National Museum), are remnants of Chinese porcelain, followed by Chinese ceramics commissioned by the VOC and adorned with VOC emblems and, in turn, blue ware made in Delft, mixing Dutch and Chinese motifs. From the Indies the Dutch brought batik techniques and introduced them in West Africa on the route of the returning ships, as in Elmina Castle on the Gold Coast. This laid the foundation for African wax prints and the central role, up to now, of Dutch production of African wax prints by companies like Vlisco. Thus, ironically, genuine "African wax prints" neither originated in Africa nor, until recently, were produced in Africa.

Mughal miniature painting has exercised a vast influence on visual styles in South Asia and beyond. Mughal miniatures influenced the seventeenth-century Dutch masters: "Rembrandt loved the East. He did not hesitate to use turbans, jewelry and various other accessories in order to re-create a faraway exoticism. He actually took interest in Indian Mughal miniatures and the copies he made of them are considered among the most stunning drawings of his work" (Bach and Bressan 1995: 94). Rembrandt's students, such as Aert de Gelder and Willem Schellinks, shared this interest and did several Mughal-inspired paintings, for instance, of Shah Jahan and his sons. Because of the Dutch East India Company's presence in Surat, the miniatures were also referred to as "Surats." This early lineage of Orientalism in painting is interesting too if we consider that Mughal painting combined many strands of influence: "a contribution coming from the 'Indian' cultural environment, the great Persian tradition, the Central-Asian heritage, Chinese influence and the new contacts with Europe" (Bressan 1995: 37).

Since the Portuguese occupied the island of Goa from 1510, Jesuits established a mission there and European merchants visited Goa. Emperor Akbar came in contact with the Portuguese when he spent time in Gujarat and Surat. He invited Jesuit missions to visit his court in 1580, 1591, and 1595 and, knowing his love of paintings, they presented him with paintings and engravings—a beautifully illustrated edition of Plantyn's Polyglot Bible in eight volumes with engravings by Flemish artists, a copy of the Borghese Madonna, a copy of the Madonna del Popolo, and other religious pictures. The gifts continued with Jahangir and Shah Jahan. Mughal artists made copies or adaptations of these pictures. "The introduction of Christian religious subject matter to the Mughal artists and to the Mughal school of painting" gave rise to a genre of "Mughal-Christian miniatures" with, for instance, miniatures of Jahangir with the Madonna, Jahangir next to Christ and the cross, Jahangir and Akbar seated on cushions with Christian cherubs hovering overhead, a Sufi saint with depictions of Christ going to Calvary in the background, and so forth. It led to Christian motifs appearing in Mughal miniatures, such as the use of the golden halo in representations of the emperors, depictions of the peaceful company of a lion and a lamb, cow, or ox, and the subtle influence of Renaissance painterly techniques such as foreground, background, shadows, chiaroscuro, the appearance of clouds in the sky, and a new realism in depicting human anatomies and landscapes (Ahmed 1995: 22–27; Bressan 1995). Thus Italian Renaissance artists such as Raphael, Flemish painters, and painters such as Albrecht Dürer found followers in Mughal India. The adoption of Mughal motifs in seventeenth-century European painting, then, also echoes European influences in Mughal miniatures and is thus an interlacing of cultural influences—i.e., interculturalism moving in circles.

Arts and crafts have been sites of mixing throughout time (Cisler 2005). Art is often a display window of political power, but of course that doesn't exclude mixing across boundaries, as in Mughal painting. Besides, mixing in arts and crafts often unfolds far removed from the frontiers of the usual identity battles. At any rate, many of these battles date from the nineteenth and twentieth centuries, the heyday of national, racial, and civilizational identity politics. But indeed, even as imperialism and nationalism set the tone politically and ideologically, hybrid motions in arts and crafts continued and in fact intensified. This is partly so because they concern the emotive, subliminal, and subconscious realms of appeal and attraction—the night world rather than the work day. As street wisdom has it, "music and fashion are the keys to integration," and the reason why this is so is probably that they represent the flow and the whisper of libido—of the pleasure principle rather than the reality principle. As Rudolf Wittkower shows in his compelling accounts of the East-West movements of art and the travel of symbols (1977, 1989), the imagination spills over ideological and political boundaries. Freud in his interpretation of dreams and Carl Jung in his understandings of symbols and the collective unconscious also found that in dream worlds there are no boundaries. On Freud's desk in his study in Vienna were statues from ancient Egypt, Greco-Roman gods, and African figurines, an imaginary that crossed cultural boundaries and that displays a pagan Freud (Barker 1996). Cross-cultural influences have been part of the foundations of modern art and modernism. Boundary crossing is a defining feature of avant-garde art from Dada to Dalí and surrealism.[3]

Layered and circular East-West and West-East movements and influences are spectacularly on display in Istanbul. The capital of the Ottoman Empire was a "second Byzantium," and architecture and arts display a merry-go-round of influences, with basilicas modeled after ancient temples, mosques modeled after basilicas, and churches modeled after mosques (Findley 2005). The Hagia Sophia, the world's largest cathedral for a thousand years after it was built in 532–537 CE, followed the cupola design of the Pantheon in Rome, and was redecorated and used as a mosque in Ottoman times. The Ottoman architect Koca Mimar Sinan was born a Christian and became a Janissary. His great

Süleymaniye Mosque in Istanbul and the Selimiye Mosque in Edirne paraphrased the structural scheme of the St. Sophia.

Sultan Mehmed II, the conqueror of Constantinople, "whom Christian propaganda of the age characterized as the 'Grand Turk,' the most feared and wicked man of the time, was himself a lover of the classical literature of ancient Greece and Rome. . . . Mehmed styled himself not on Islamic predecessors but on the Roman emperors he had read about and, above all, on that great stylist of the self and Renaissance idol, Alexander the Great" (Inglis and Robertson 2006: 98–99). The name of the city remained officially Constantinople (Konstantiniyye, according to the Ottomans) and was not renamed Istanbul until the end of the empire. Mehmed's ambition was to be emperor of Rome. He had money coined with the inscription "Basileus Romeon" (King/Emperor of Romans). Keen to turn the city into a magnificent capital, Mehmed II turned to Italian architects.

> Leon Battista Alberti was highly popular among Italian rulers for his brand of grandiose imperial architecture, so much so that it rapidly became an "internationally" recognised style. Eyeing with some envy the designs Alberti had constructed for his Italian peers, Mehmed II hired a number of Alberti's pupils, such as de Pasti, Michelozzo and Filarete to work on the new Topkapi palace, a situation that resulted in its mixed Islamic, Italian, Greek and Roman influences. Filarete's international career is attested by his next project, the new Kremlin palace built for the Tsar of Russia. It was not only the Sultan who copied the Italians; the Italians also copied the Sultan. For example, Federico, ruler of the principality of Urbino, tasked his architects to ape the style of the Topkapi palace; and Justus of Ghent, another international artistic "name" of the time, was hired by Federico to paint representations of such Renaissance heroes as Plato and Aristotle. The style he used to carry out his commission was remarkably "Ottoman" in nature. (Inglis and Robertson 2006: 100–101)

As Inglis and Robertson observe: "cultural production and innovation in the period were marked strongly by east-west, trans-European, and cross-Mediterranean currents and flows" (2006: 101). The Sheesh Mahal, or Hall of Mirrors, in Lahore Fort, constructed under Mughal Emperor Shah Jahan in 1631–1632, prefigures the Hall of Mirrors at Versailles that opened in 1682, but I don't know if there is an actual relationship.

Mark LeVine's book *Heavy Metal Islam* (2008) discusses Muslim punk, gothic Islamic rock, and other subcultures in the Muslim world. They are strong examples of cultural cross flow. But they are not new and the picture changes further if we take into account the influence music from the Muslim world exercised on the West all along.

The Ottoman Mehter bands, founded in the thirteenth century, became the model for the world's marching bands. Accompanying Ottoman ambassadors to Europe, Mehter bands fascinated westerners with their fiery red robes, pulsating rhythms, giant war drums, and the clash of cymbals, drums, and bells. When Vienna developed into a cultural center in the eighteenth century, the fascination with Turkish culture worked its way into plays and operas, as noted by Edward Hines, an American composer who studied Ottoman music in Istanbul. Haydn's Military Symphony and Mozart's piano sonata "Rondo alla Turca" were composed under the influence of this music. Mozart used Turkish motifs in operas such as *The Abduction from the Seraglio*. Beethoven used Mehter-style big drums in his Ninth Symphony. Even today the percussion sections of orchestras are occasionally called the "Turkish section" (Associated Press 2002).

Other accounts reflect on the African Muslim lineages of American blues. Vocal styles such as melisma (stretching a syllable by using many notes), wavy intonation, and the "bending of notes" refer to styles common in Muslim parts of West Africa, as do stringed instruments and solo performances (Kubik 1999). The guitar derives from the Arab oud.

Muslim soldiers introduced the *haik*—an outer garment consisting of a large piece of white cloth, worn by men and women in northern Africa—in Spain, and Spanish rule in the sixteenth century introduced this dress in the Low Countries. The black habit of nuns resembles the *haik*, as does the Persian chador. There are striking similarities, too, between the dress styles and shawls of Frisian women and oriental styles worn by women in Yemen and North Africa. The word shawl goes back to Persian. The use of oriental textiles such as silk and muslin goes back to Egypt and Rome. In the seventeenth century silk, muslin, brocade fabrics, and Indian cotton became more widely available. Persian and Turkish carpets adorn the paintings of the Dutch old masters. Because cashmere shawls were popular but expensive, Paisley, in Scotland, manufactured cheaper versions, as did Lyon. Renamed as paisley fabrics and motifs they later became part of the Liberty style, so faux Indian became British chic.

Léon Bakst's designs for the *Ballets Russes* in Paris in the early 1900s were spectacularly transcultural in imagination, reflecting the fin de siècle cultural mélange (Bakst 1913). The Japanese kimono inspired painters such as Klimt, Mucha, and Toulouse-Lautrec. In the 1920s Paul Poiret was inspired by "Arab" harem trousers, and in the 1930s pseudo-sarongs were à la mode (Martin and Koda 1995). Gianni Versace's designs of the late 1980s were inspired by "royal Africa and Morocco" along with batik patches on denim, Arabic prints, and iridescent Nehru jackets. Valentino used "ethnic embroideries." Jean Paul Gaultier designed jewelry inspired by the Masai "combined with Jeanne d'Arc." Giorgio Armani brought the inspiration for bracelets decorated with silver beads and spirals from Tunisia. Donna Karan used rippled tissue after the ancient methods of African peoples. A circle is rounded when a Chinese designer, Ma Ke, makes her debut in twenty-first-century Paris, not with ready-to-wear but with haute couture, launching "Oriental haute couture" (Leong 2008).

The Muslim world is both deeply integrated in western capitalism and stands apart. Deeply integrated because of the long presence of European powers, because of the oil majors, the postwar alliance of oil exporting countries with the United States, the investment of oil gains in western ventures, and support for American policies, and yet apart because of religious commitments, profound differences with regard to Israel and the Palestinians, critique of western double standards in the Middle East, oligarchic political institutions, and the political economy of the "resource curse." The Middle East is deeply and yet unevenly modern. The Muslim world is economically integrated into western capitalism and yet alienated from its geopolitics. For all these reasons the Muslim world is a fertile area of hybridization under headings such as "western science, Islamic values," a world that combines American capitalism and Islamic economics, American consumerism, along with Muslim preferences and restrictions. High energy prices—especially since 2003—have highlighted some of these features.

Ben Barber draws a contrast, *Jihad vs. McWorld*, but the bricolage of McDonaldization *and* Jihad, the interlacing of western capitalism and consumerism and Islamic values and institutions, is much closer to the mark. "Islamic modern" is an increasingly familiar trope (Peletz

2002, Kamali 2006), as is "Islamic postmodern" (Ahmed 1992). Islamic "fundamentalism" itself is deeply modern as a perspective and practice. Timothy Mitchell captured this as "McJihad," which refers not to occasional bricolage but rather to a long-term and strategic pattern of collaboration of the Saudi royal family, Big Oil, the US government, American arms suppliers, and conservative Wahhabi clerics (2002). In short, Big Oil and the United States have long been funding and sponsoring Islamic conservatism. Steve Coll's book *The Bin Ladens* (2008) chronicles the contradictions of this collaboration in the setting of a family clan "torn between moderate Islam and radical jihadism."

Burger King, KFC, and McDonald's restaurants line the streets that lead to Mecca's holy Ka'aba square. This is another side of the Mecca Cola trend that many have noted, extending in many different spheres (Samman 2007, Ram 2007). During the holy month of Ramadan in Indonesia KFC doubles its sales: "In the world's largest Muslim nation there is no month more lucrative for KFC than Ramadan." This may be at odds with Indonesian attitudes to the US government; fast food outlets such as KFC and McDonald's remain powerful symbols of western affluence in Indonesia and Malaysia (Donnan 2003). In France the *Beurger King Muslim* chain adheres strictly to Muslim dietary laws and serves halal food to five million Muslims ("beur" is a play on words on the nickname for North Africans in France; C. Smith 2005).

The Fulla doll, who wears either a black abaya or a white headscarf, is a popular alternative to Barbie in the Middle East. In the United States a new ritual is "the all-girl Muslim Prom." "It is perhaps a new version of having it all: embracing the American prom culture of high heels, mascara, and adrenaline while being true to a Muslim identity" (Brown 2003). Bikinis and burkas are both part of this cultural scene. As a Saudi woman remarked, "What do you think the 'black ghosts' wear underneath their abayas?" (Kristof 2002b).

Arab women, especially in conservative societies like Saudi Arabia, have come to like dubbed television soap operas from Turkey, such as *Noor*, that show a romance and passion missing in their lives. According to a Lebanese viewer, "*Noor*'s secret is that it's about people who live western lives but they're easterners, they're easy to relate to" (Khalaf 2008).

Such bricolage is commonplace the world over; in the Islamic world it seems striking because of Muslim boundary marking, conflicts in the Middle East, and the prevalence of totalizing paradigms such as the "clash of civilizations." These exercises in reproducing Orientalism are politically motivated and, to put it euphemistically, short on sociology and ethnography.

The Gestalt approach to cultures—the idea that cultures are wholes that can only be understood in their entire configuration—was formulated in anthropology by Ruth Benedict (1935) and enshrined essentialism in thinking about cultures (it did not introduce it because essentialism was much older). The Gestalt approach matches authoritarian and centrist perspectives; in this view, there is no place for margins, subcultures, or countercurrents. Her main case was Japan. "Benedict took the ideology of a class for the culture of a people, a state of acute dislocation for the normal condition" and her approach had pernicious implications for the way Americans understood and dealt with Japan (Lummis 2007: 3). Increasing migration, travel, communication, cross-border media and marketing, multiculturalism, and so forth have made dents in this homogenizing view.

Spaces of hybridization are not necessarily smooth spaces—to address another extreme view—but are more frequently edgy with sharp and jagged edges, as the entire history of colonialism and imperialism testifies. Thus the Dutch-Indonesian relationship is one of hundreds of years of mingling and mixing—for instance, in *tempo doeloe* or "sweet time," the culture of the settled, acculturated Dutch in the East Indies—and yet one that is marked by wars and frictions such as the Aceh War. Unfolding over centuries, the Dutch-Indonesian relationship left its traces on both sides of the equator in literature, architecture, arts, and music (Wolters 1995). Yet as Jeroen Dewulf (2006) notes, the Dutch also displayed "mixophobia" and bequeathed "apartheid" to the global vocabulary.

In Turkey the hybrid combinations of "Muslim modernity" have been extensively discussed (e.g., Göle 2000). Turkish nationalism and Kemalism competing with Islam yields other terrains of friction (Cinar 2005). One of the ironies of the resolute Turkification of names and places is that the name Istanbul derives from a Greek name, Stanbolin. The interlacing of Greek and Turkish culture is a large chapter in itself (e.g., Volkan and Itzkowitz 1994).

EASTERNIZATION, WESTERNIZATION,
AND BACK AGAIN

Millennia of East-West osmosis have produced intercontinental cross flow, and European and western culture is part of this global mélange. For a long time Europe was on the receiving end of influences from the Orient and, according to recent assessments, the dominance of the West dates mainly from 1800 onward. China's and India's lead in world production lasted well into the nineteenth century. Agricultural technologies from China played a major part in modernizing agriculture in Britain, and cotton and cotton manufacturing techniques from India exercised a major influence on British manufacturing (Pomeranz 2000, Washbrook 1997). Thousands of years during which the currents of influence ran predominantly (though rarely exclusively) in an East-West direction overlap with approximately two hundred years of predominantly West-East influence (much shorter in duration than is usually argued). By the late twentieth century, the currents of influence again turned in an East to West direction, though now at a much higher overall level of economic interdependence and integration.

Europe's influence became dominant on a global scale only after 1800, through industrialism and commerce, improvements in shipping and growing military reach, colonialism, and imperialism. The European impact includes science, nationalism, and state institutions such as modern bureaucracies and constitutions. Attempts at industrialization in Egypt and Persia, the Tanzimat reforms in the Ottoman Empire, the Meiji restoration in Japan, and in the early 1900s, the Young Turks and Young Persians reflect the impact of Europe. In time, Siam renamed itself Thailand, and Japan and Indonesia modeled their armies, constitutions, and bureaucracies after the German model.

In the course of the nineteenth century, the East-West rift was reinterpreted as "occidental liberty" and "oriental despotism." This followed many centuries of viewing the Orient as a place of civilizational accomplishment, enlightenment, and enlightened despotism, notably China during the eighteenth century. The Chinese designs and motifs in the British royal family's summer palace in Brighton exemplify the admiration for China. Occidental liberty, a nineteenth-century theme with romantic and Euro-chauvinist overtones, played a part in philhellenism and British support for the Greek national liberation struggle against the Ottoman Empire.

In the twentieth century, Oswald Spengler, reflecting on Europe, coined the phrase "Caesaro-papism." Not long after, Karl Wittfogel developed the idea of oriental despotism according to which "hydraulic societies," in which organizing irrigation requires major public works, foster authoritarian rule. The Cold War revived the trope of occidental liberty (the "free world" vs. communism). After the "end of history" and the waning of the Cold War, it was brought back to life in yet another guise, in Bernard Lewis and Samuel Huntington's "clash of civilizations." This was taken up by the neoconservative international and by the George W. Bush administration as "the ideological battle of our generation" and the great war of the twenty-first century—with spectacularly disastrous consequences over time.

In the course of the twentieth century, the "orientalization of the world" and easternization, in contrast to westernization, resumed with the growing influence of Japan. Japan's "Toyotism," or lean production, has become a world standard (and Toyota the world's leading auto-maker), and Japanese management techniques such as quality control circles have been widely adopted. This was followed by the rise of the Asian Tiger economies and Southeast Asia, which spawned the (contro-versial) idea of an "Asian model" and of the twenty-first century as an "Asian century." With the rise of China and India has come the idea of a "Beijing consensus" as an alternative and challenge to the Washing-ton consensus (Nederveen Pieterse 2008a). Table 6.2 gives a précis of trends in twentieth- and twenty-first-century globalization.

A defining feature of recent history has been the interdependence of the United States and East Asia. This began with the United States relying on East Asian countries for war supplies during the Korean and Vietnam wars; and with the United States treating East Asian countries as front lines in the Cold War and as showcases of capitalist development. It continued with the United States promoting economic liberalization and export-led development in East Asia, American firms relocating production plants to Asia, and American firms importing products from Asia on a massive scale. East and Southeast Asia took off in offshore production and South Asia in offshore software and back-office services. Over time this division of labor created growing im-balances. American corporations moving production overseas turned *economies*

American exports into imports. Thus, in the twenty-first century, in Paul Krugman's words, "we became a nation in which people make a living by selling one another houses, and they pay for the houses with money borrowed from China" (2006). American-Asian interdependence now takes the form of Asian vendor financing of American consumption. The 2007 subprime mortgage crisis and the ensuing financial crisis, volatility of the US dollar, and weakness of Wall Street financial powerhouses suggest that a new global balance is in the making (Nederveen Pieterse 2008b).

The Pacific Rim economy is as defining a feature of contemporary globalization as the Atlantic, Mediterranean, and Silk Routes economies were during previous eras. Each came with characteristic patterns of intercultural braiding. Each represents a phase and pattern of global mélange. The headings under which hybridity is acknowledged—such as creolization, mestizaje, crossover, fusion, orientalization—reflect the diverse vantage points from which global mélange is experienced over time. Different epochs correspond to different eras and styles of industrialization. Asia and the Middle East paved the way with crafts and artisanal manufactures, Europe led in craft industrialism, the United States in mass production (Taylorism), and Japan in flexible production ("just in time" production). Each built on previous acumen. European craftsmen adopted Asian skills in porcelain and fabrics. British producers copied Indian textile-making techniques. Japanese and Korean producers innovated on the basis of European and American techniques.

Thus, examining East-West relations over time shows that globalization is braided and influence is interlaced: East-West, West-East, East-West, and so on. Jack Goody refers to this process as "alternation" (2010: 96–97). Globalization goes in circles and eventually the lines of influence arrive back where they came from. This exercise also implies a deconstruction of the terms in which it is constructed; the very terms East and West unravel in the process of use. The analysis subverts the terms of analysis and several counterpoints follow. First, "East-West" reflects a segmented, binary division of the world. What matters, in the end, is not binary history but parallel history, as mentioned before. Second, East-West is only part of the global field. Flows are not two-way but multidirectional and multipolar. East-East and South-South flows and other permutations are as important as East-West flows. Third, the

critique of East-West divides reproduces and privileges these divides in the process. Fourth, these divides and their critiques presume geographical or civilizational units. Contemporary trends in globalization involve firms as the units of competition (and cooperation), rather than or at least as much as countries or regions. Thus in human resource management the search for talent is global and involves fashioning "project teams" that combine skills across multiple and diverse terrains. According to current management thinking, "the dynamic reconfiguration of talent" involves Velcro organizations and—wouldn't it be nice—Velcro employees (Prahalad and Krishnan 2008). Fifth, global interplay becomes increasingly multidimensional over time, and if economic considerations define the phases of globalization because they mark stages in the density and nature of accumulation trends, they are of course not the only ones that count. Finally, hybridities are braided and interlaced, layer upon layer, to the point that it may be difficult to decide which is which.

Is then the relationship between East and West as in Rudyard Kipling's *Ballad of East and West*: "Oh East is East and West is West and never the twain shall meet"? Or is it rather like that described in Goethe's collection of lyrical poems, the *West-Östlicher Divan*, early in the nineteenth century (1819):

> Wer sich selbst und Andre kennt
> Wird auch hier erkennen:
> Orient und Okzident
> Sind nicht mehr zu trennen

> [Who knows oneself and other
> will here also know
> Orient and Occident
> can no longer be divided]

Goethe's poems were dedicated to the Persian poet Hafiz of Shiraz. Indeed, the consciousness of romantic inspiration is profoundly different from the relationship of power and domination. Globalization's braids show that the East is in the West as the West is in the East (as in Goody 2006). New braids keep on being woven.

CHAPTER 7

HYBRID CHINA

The movie *Transformers: Age of Extinction*, released in summer 2014, was a greater box office success in China than in the US. "It is the first time that a Hollywood blockbuster had a larger box office in China than in its home market of North America" (Lixin 2014). The filmmakers adopted a hybrid strategy. The film "features several Chinese actors, such as Li Bingbing; was shot in Hong Kong and in cities on the mainland [Beijing, Tianjin, Chongqing]; and includes a number of product placements for Chinese brands" (Lixin 2014).

The *Wall Street Journal* headline read, "'Transformers' Script: Lights! Cameras! China!" "In the run-up to the movie's release, the studio directed much of its global marketing firepower at China, where it has struck numerous promotional partnerships with companies" (Schwartzel and Burkitt 2014). The paper's review section describes the film as an "Advanced Case of Metal Fatigue" (J. Anderson 2014).

The film review aggregator Rotten Tomatoes gave the movie an overall rating of 17 percent, the worst rating of the franchise.

China is the world's fastest growing film market. In 2013 China "eclipsed Japan to become the number two film market in the world. This year, box office rose 39 per cent in the first quarter to $1.13bn" (Shone 2014). "Many Hollywood blockbusters have Chinese advertising sponsors, including *Iron Man* and *The Avengers*, as well as the popular television show *Big Bang Theory*" (Yang 2014). Chinese sponsors give Hollywood access to the marketing channels of Chinese brands, and for the brands it opens up entertainment marketing. This follows several forms of Chinese cooperation with Hollywood, against the background of "the State's encouragement of 'going out' and 'culture export.' . . . Investments from China into Hollywood started in earnest in 2012 when the Dalian Wanda Group, the largest property developer and cultural enterprise in China, acquired an 80 percent stake in AMC, the US-based global movie theater chain, for $2.6 billion. The deal made Wanda the biggest cinema operator in the world" (Yang 2014).

For Hollywood this development is not merely an opportunity, it's a necessity. According to an American box office analyst, "In order to be the biggest movie of the summer you now have to spend $400m. In order to make that back, you've got to be making as much in China as you do in the US, so somebody has to figure out how to appeal to both of those markets, without offending either of them" (quoted in Shone 2014).

According to film historian Neal Gabler, "The overseas market has changed the DNA of American movies. . . . The bigger-faster-louder aesthetic is very deeply embedded in the American psyche. . . . The things that make our movies so popular overseas are now larger than the American market can support by itself. The giganticism must be subsidized" (quoted in Shone 2014: 2). *Iron Man 3* took in $121 million in China but was bifurcated into two movies, a Chinese version and an American version. *Transformers IV* did achieve the coveted "co-production" status, required to penetrate China's quota system that limits the number of foreign films shown. *Variety* magazine notes that *Transformers* is "a very patriotic film. It's just Chinese patriotism on the screen, not American" (D. Cohen 2014). "Those worried about Hollywood's possible evolution into China's entertainer-in-chief have missed the boat—it *has* already evolved into that role. . . . Hollywood

. . . now finds itself in the role of global jukebox, with other countries piling in the quarters" (Shone 2014).

This development—widely covered in Chinese as well as American and British newspapers—exemplifies several ongoing trends: the growing size and importance of China's market, and western companies adjusting to China, at times bending over backward, in the process transforming the character and culture of production. The flip side of this cooperation is that Chinese firms sponsor the dumbest side of Hollywood and the hyperviolence of macho-adolescent fantasies. This, however, reflects the general trend of the cinema-going audience becoming younger and thus more thrill seeking (so much so that creativity has shifted to television productions). In time, Chinese filmmakers may use co-productions to contribute new, creative narratives.

Hollywood cooperation with Chinese firms follows cooperation with Bollywood studios in Mumbai. Film is just one example of sprawling cooperation with China. Luxury products, advertising, cosmetics and chocolate companies, wine merchants, diamond traders, architects, art dealers, law firms, banks, and MBAs have all been going east for some time. This trend is reinforced as new prosperity in East Asia and China comes at a time of economic slowdown in advanced economies. Consider a sampling of recent newspaper headlines:

"Why Brands Now Rise in the East"
"Consumption Starts to Shift to China, India and Brazil"
"Architecture Firms Go East for Work"
"Bankers Sense Shift in Capital Flows"
"Benchmark Expert Watches Market Weight Shift Eastwards"
"U.S. Cities Seek to Woo Chinese Investment"
"Chinese Investment Keeps Greece, Iceland and Others Afloat"
"The Deal Makers Who Matter Are Rising in the East"[1]

As chapter 5 argues, hybridity is important as a counterpoint to essentialism and stereotypes. The "China threat" is a familiar trope—China as cutthroat competitor and manipulator of its currency, causing job loss in the US and elsewhere, a cherished theme in American media and Congress. Variations on the theme are the "China Price" (Harney 2009)—now outdated because Chinese manufacturing wages have risen and China is no longer just a low-cost producer—"China

Inc." (Fishman 2005), "Death by China" (the title of a documentary film and book, Navarro and Autry 2011), and more generally "China effects"—the worldwide ramifications of Chinese growth. Such stereotypes are examples of Orientalism applied to China (Vukovich 2012). Some are variations on the trope of the "Yellow Peril." Faced with such representations, unbundling China and showing its hybrid character makes sense. Hybridity—China as a postrevolutionary hybrid formation navigating the paradoxes of globalization—has also been a theme in Chinese debates since the 1990s (Liu Kang 2004).

It is worth zeroing in on China for other reasons as well. China represents a fifth of humanity, so it is important per se. Like no other society, it has been growing rapidly in scale and influence and is now the world's second largest economy, probably soon to be the first. As a powerhouse of accelerated globalization, China exemplifies contemporary trends that are also unfolding in Brazil, Mexico, Turkey, South Korea, Indonesia, and other emerging economies, but because of China's size and scope, these take on a more momentous character.

There is also a historical dimension to this. For many centuries, China has been a major force in oriental globalization, the predecessor of occidental globalization. In effect, twenty-first-century globalization is resuming earlier historical trends of globalization. Hybrid China in a historical and contemporary sense contrasts with several perceptions and representations of China, both domestic and international. Emerging economies, with China in the lead, are changing the power balance in global political economy and in contemporary hybridization processes, and alter the terms of mixture. According to Axford (2013: 105) and many others, "the major failing of research on cultural hybridity has been its neglect of power and inequality." The case of China, however, sheds light on the role of agency and power in hybridity, which is discussed below as "smart borrowing" and which is relevant way beyond China.

This chapter first takes up historical strands of China's globalization with a focus on the Silk Roads—continuing the discussion of East-West and West-East flows of chapter 6. The chapter then turns to different faces of China's globalization—China globalized and globalizing and examples of hybridity with Chinese characteristics, which show how processes of and perspectives on hybridity are changing. To profile the agency of Chinese actors in international cooperation and hybrid combinations, this chapter spells out some of the scale and scope of developments in China. The China files, of course, are very large, complexity is spilling over in all directions, and this can only be a limited discussion.

There is an impression, also in China, of globalization as a juggernaut that steamrolls countries—as in the influence of American popular culture, American movies and TV, consumerism, lifestyle images, the American lead in spheres such as data banks, geopolitics, the "Asia pivot" (repositioning US military forces from the Middle East to Asia), and so forth. According to Yu Keping, "Chinese intellectuals are thus loudly proclaiming that 'globalization is Americanization'" (Keping 2003: 139). He also observes many countervoices, such as the 1996 book *China Can Say "No"* and conservative Confucians according to whom "Chinese civilization can overcome the shortcomings of Western civilization and the twenty-first century will be a century of Chinese civilization" (141). This is part of wide-ranging debates on globalization in China (e.g., Garrett 2001, Liu Kang 2004, Yan 2008). This chapter argues that processes of hybridization have been changing over time, from China *being hybridized* (notably during the Tang dynasty, the Opium Wars, and the nineteenth and early twentieth centuries) to China *hybridizing*—in other words, exercising agency and selectivity in processes of mixing (notably during the Ming dynasty and from the mid-twentieth century onward).

SILK ROADS

For historians of ancient Rome, the leading paradigm has long been *Romanization*, a perspective that looks from Rome outward and focuses on how Rome has affected the world. A recent successor paradigm is globalization (Pitts and Versluys 2015), which means, among other things, decentering Rome (Nederveen Pieterse 2015). Similarly, a leading paradigm in Chinese studies has been *Sinification*, or the influence of China on the surrounding world over time (e.g., Katzenstein 2012). China's influence has radiated outward through trade, the influence of Confucianism, Chinese diasporas, and conquest (during the period of Mongol rule).

Sinification also carries other meanings. It refers to the ways Han civilization assimilated outside influences and conquerors such as the

Yuan dynasty and the Manchus. It refers to Han chauvinism as the cultural and political hegemony (with 92 percent of the population) and minority nationalities and influences as peripheral, as in the settlement of Han Chinese in Tibet and Xinjiang, "autonomous regions" without autonomy (in Xinjiang, the Han Chinese are now over 40 percent of the population and Uighurs face job discrimination; Kaltman 2007). And it refers to viewing and representing China's culture as homogeneous—in other words, the Sinification of China.

If for China we would replace Sinification with globalization, it would likewise mean to decenter China. This is an easier task than decentering Rome because "China" has changed places many times—different states, different regions, different combinations of peoples, different dynasties, different names, different capitals (Hsienyang, Chang'an/Xian, Kaifeng, Luoyang, Hangzhou, Nanjing, Beijing), and so forth. Sinification has no fixed meaning, for *which China* does it refer to? When Mandarin was established as the national language in 1909, this late exercise of Sinicizing China was done according to a northern China standard—and was contested, then as now, as "an alien tongue spoken by a non-Han minority, 'a northern Chinese dialect heavily influenced by non-Han Chinese'" (Hau 2012: 196).

The notion of *Zhongguo*, the "Middle Kingdom" dates from around 1000 BCE when it designated the Chou Empire situated on the North China Plain, in the belief that their empire occupied the middle of the earth, surrounded by barbarian peoples. During the period of the Warring States (475–221 BCE), it referred to the valley of the Yellow River. During the Han dynasty, *Zhongguo* variously meant the capital, the center of civilization, the central states, and a name for "China." By the nineteenth century, the term emerged as a common name for the whole country, which was often referred to as Great Qing but increasingly as *Zhongguo* (Haw 1990).

As has often been noted, the Roman Empire was contemporaneous with the Han dynasty (206 BCE–220 CE). But there are profound differences between the two:

> Rome was the outgrowth of a city state; the Han empire the amalgamation of ancient kingdoms, already a great area. There was a unity of speech, custom and ethnic character in China far greater than that of the Roman world. The Han empire was a land mass to which maritime

communications were of secondary importance. The theory of society, the enlarged family with joint responsibility, the emperor as head of the human race in a paternal as well as a political sense, the secondary importance of his military role and the primary importance of his religious function, are all features of Chinese society which are sharply different from those of the classical West. (Fitzgerald 1973: 114–15)

As I noted elsewhere,

China is widely viewed, in some ways like Japan, as a society that has been continuous over a long stretch of time and that has been relatively homogeneous, clustered around the Han Chinese with ethnic groups at the margins, such as Mongolians, Uighurs, and minorities in Yunnan and the south. In fact, this matches the self-image of fifteenth-century Ming China. After the Chinese state expansion to Inner Asia in the seventeenth and eighteenth centuries under Manchu rule, China redefined itself as a multiethnic state (Zhao 2006). Indeed, China has been ruled by non-Han rulers and dynasties more often, longer, and during more significant periods than by Han. Major dynasties have come from China's margins of Turkic-speaking peoples, Mongolians (Yuan dynasty), Manchurians (Qing), and other Northerners (Liao). China's centers of power shifted repeatedly in all directions, as did the size of the state. The "Han" are an ethno-linguistic category rather than an ethnic group, an ethnic canopy whose origins are lost in time. During several periods China consisted of multiple states. Through much of Chinese history what mattered was whether power centers, such as Chang'an, controlled the trade and caravan routes of Central Asia. . . . Chinese culture evolved as a composite shaped by the general Asian confluence of cultures with major influences from India (including Buddhism and spices), Central Asia (trade links, music), Southeast Asia (spices), Persia, Turkic-speaking peoples and Mongolians. China coheres on cultural grounds, not on the basis of an ethnic definition. Confucianism emerged as the umbrella under which outlying groups were integrated. What mattered in relation to minorities, for instance, in Hainan, was whether they adopted Chinese cultural attributes in clothing, hair style, and language (Csete 2001, Dikötter 1992, Blue 1999). Thus it is appropriate to view China, like Japan, as a rainbow culture ethnically and culturally. (Nederveen Pieterse 2007: 12–13)

Han Chinese is a cultural category that springs from many processes of ethnic amalgamation, with northern nomadic tribes (Mei 2004: 4) and peoples in the south and southwest such as the Wu and Chu states. The waning and end of feudalism (see Cotterell 1981) meant there was no elite independent of the state. In China's civilization-state, the Confucian bureaucracy played a key part from early on. Will Hutton observes,

> Competitive written examinations were the key to entry. These were first established in the second century BC, and they were open to all, even the lowliest peasant. In Europe the first comparable written examinations began in 1702; in the United States they began in 1883 and were opposed for some years as a Chinese import and therefore un-American. By the time of the Northern Song dynasty (960–1127 AD) the system had become as fair as possible. Examination papers were kept secret, locked in safe rooms; essays were read by at least two independent examiners only after they had been transcribed to identical calligraphy to avoid bias. . . . As far as can be established, the Chinese mandarinate drew its members from across Chinese society. One study found that 83 per cent of those who came out on top in the intensely competitive exams, so-called champions, were from lower-class families, with the rest from the upper class, almost exactly mirroring China's social structure. . . . Far from being a closed caste, Confucian bureaucracy was organised as the world's first genuine meritocracy. (Hutton 2007: 48, 49)

Trade and migration—and conflict and conquest—are cornerstones of globalization. They are also fundamental processes of hybridization, and China is a formidable case study of globalization—a society profoundly globalized and profoundly globalizing.

Phases of China's involvement in the world economy range from early Eurasian trade, the early and later Silk Roads, and involvement with Europe and the West from the Opium Wars (1840) onward. With the Bronze Age that unfolded across Eurasia came plow agriculture and the use of animal traction, an urban revolution, and the ongoing existence of urban cultures (Goody 2010). Besides silk and cotton from China, early trade in Eurasia included lapis lazuli, turquoise, agate, and beads. One of China's ancient trade routes is the Jade Road to Central Asia, which dates back to 3000 BCE. The Hellenic-Roman world emerged as a western extension of Bronze Age culture.

The early Silk Road, extending from Chang'an to the Mediterranean, goes back to 800 BCE (Mair 1998). It was part of a "commercial revolution" that unfolded from 1000 BCE:

> a web of direct commercial ties that linked a very large portion of the world, with active points in the eastern Mediterranean, south China, and India, and with connections to Europe, West Africa, East Africa, Indonesia, Central Asia, the north Pacific and the western Pacific. The main elements of this new system of commerce and its changes from earlier systems of exchange included: an expanded set of commodities; the use of widely recognized systems of money; the development of new technology of shipping, accounting, and merchandising; the establishment of well-traveled commercial routes, with ports and caravanserai; the creation of social institutions of commerce such as trade diasporas; and the development of ideas and philosophies to address the problems of commerce. (Manning 2005: 87)

The overland routes went into decline after the fall of the Roman Empire, while in the East the Han empire disintegrated (Yiping 2005: 65). But maritime commerce continued. As Jack Goody (1996) notes, India established maritime relations with China from the third century BCE, and Chinese goods came to the Ganges Valley by sea. Close relations existed with the port of Guangzhou (Canton) from the seventh century. "It was only after the third century that the Chinese engaged in long-distance voyages, which achieved their zenith in the thirteenth century. They reached Penang in Malaya about 350 CE, Sri Lanka towards the end of that century and probably the mouth of Euphrates and Aden by the following one" (Goody 1996: 260).

Much Silk Roads history, in view of its heading and Chinese silk as the most valuable commodity, focuses on the *East-West* movement of trade and culture. This downplays the *West-East* movements from the Middle East toward Asia that preceded and accompanied the East-West movements as part of a long history of osmosis in both directions. Part of this history is Muslim traders, Arab and Persian, going east as far as China and Korea. "The first Muslim embassy reached China in 651 and a century later in 758 their presence was powerful enough to lead to the burning and looting of Canton. In the following century they established 'factories' in areas of Guangdong where they had been preceded by Syrians and Graeco-Egyptians as long ago as the third century" (Goody 1996: 260). Ninth-century postmasters in Persia and the Arab world kept detailed records of Asian routes as far as Korea (Hoerder 2002). Muslim merchants reconnected China and East Asia with the world economy, which at the time was centered in Baghdad, Basra, and Mecca—reconnected because earlier trade links and overland silk routes between East Asia and the Greco-Roman world had declined after the fall of the Roman Empire (Abu-Lughod 1989: 256; Teggart 1939).

Muslim Afro-Eurasia was a vast intercultural expanse in which merchants and scholars traveled, the world of Ibn Battuta, Ibn Khaldun, Ibn Rushd, Maimonides, a world in which Chinese, Indian, Persian, Turkic, Central Asian, African, Muslim, Arabic, Mongol, Jewish, and Berber cultures mingled. The *Dâr al-Islâm*, the "abode of Islam," was not the world's earliest cosmopolitanism but one that stretched further and endured longer than any other (Hodgson 1974, Nederveen Pieterse 2007). It gave rise to the encounter of the trading religions Buddhism and Islam (Elverskog 2006).

The rise of Islam was contemporaneous with the Tang dynasty (618–907) in China. The largest Muslim populations in China are in the southwest and northwest. Jack Goody notes, "In the ninth century there were said to be over 100,000 Muslim merchants in Canton" (2010: 254). Admiral Zheng He, the fifteenth-century Chinese mariner and predecessor of Columbus, was a Hui-Muslim, also known as Ma Sanbao and Hajji Mahmud Shamsuddin. A quarter of the merchants in tenth-century Baghdad were Chinese (Goody 2013: 60).

In a speech in June 2014 to Kazakh students visiting Beijing, Xi Jinping said, "If you are to understand the China of 3,000 years of history, you should visit Xian. If you are to understand the China of 1,000 years of history, you should visit Beijing, and if you are to understand the China with 100 years of history, you should visit Shanghai" (Jiao 2014). Xian, the eastern terminal of the Silk Road, was the capital of the Tang dynasty, then named Chang'an. The Tang dynasty was an "open empire," and

Chang'an was a truly cosmopolitan city with only one close rival, Byzantium. . . . Moslem traders from the Red Sea, Persian merchants, Turk cavalry officers, Indian scholars, Japanese religious pilgrims, Byzantine agents, Islamic teachers, Zoroastrian masters, Manichean and Nestorian priests, and ships from the Mediterranean, Zanzibar, Ceylon, and Sumatra—all came freely to T'ai-tsung's empire. The influx introduced everything from practical techniques for growing and grinding sugar cane to new Buddhist thought. (Harrison 1972: 218–19)

Chinese decorative arts show links with Polynesia and Melanesia (Williams 1974: xxiv); other early imports into China include spices from the Malay world and India and horses from the Ferghana Valley. But the Tang era saw "the crystallization of Sino-foreign cultural flavors": stone lions and ostrich eggs from Parthia (Persia), Indian peacocks, crystal plates from Qiantu, alfalfa and grapes from Dawan, glue from Rome, the Hufu from India and Persia, hair styles from West Asia, singing and dancing from Central Asia, rugs and musical instruments from India and Persia, polo from Persia (Yiping 2005, Mei 2004). The symbol of the lion as protector of the sacred probably hails from Buddhism (Williams 1974: 253–54), and the stone lion—which is now ubiquitous in front of Chinese temples, palaces, banks, department stores, and major hotels—probably derived from Parthia (Yiping 2005: 49). Buddhism merged with Taoism and Chinese folk culture. The Tang maintained friendly relations with over seventy countries and allowed foreigners to take written exams for the selection of government officials (Mei 2004: 29).

Goody observes, "The imperial library in China in 978 CE consisted of 80,000 books, the library of al-Hakam in Cordoba in the tenth century had 400,000 'books'—whereas the largest library in northern Europe at that time, at the monastery of St Gall in Switzerland, had some 800 volumes. The difference is staggering" (2010: 91). Frank's *ReOrient* (1998) and historians of Asia and the Indian Ocean view Asia from 1000 or 1100 CE, particularly Song China and India, as driving forces of the world economy, which they remained until at least 1800 (Pomeranz 2000).

NEW SILK ROADS

The ancient Silk Roads may represent civilizational romance, but now they have gathered dust and the caravanserais have long been in quiet decay. Yet in China the Silk Roads are now in the news literally every day, especially since Xi Jinping gave a speech in Kazakhstan in fall 2013 about establishing a Silk Road Economic Belt. In October 2013 he gave a speech in Indonesia about reviving the ancient route that linked the Pacific and Indian Oceans in a "Maritime Silk Road of the Twenty-First Century."

China has begun studying a 1,800-kilometer high-speed rail link (200 kph) to Gwadar Port in Pakistan, passing through Islamabad and Karachi. China gained control of Gwadar Port in spring 2013, so it now runs a port just opposite the Gulf of Oman, a major route of oil tankers. China's government has decided to develop three main economic corridors through southern, central, and northern Xinjiang, which connect China with Russia, Europe, and Pakistan. A northern corridor line runs from Beijing via Moscow on to Helsinki, with a branch splitting off to Berlin and Rotterdam. The central corridor would run from Shanghai and Xian via Kashgar, Tashkent, and Tehran to Paris and Calais. The southern corridor runs from Guangzhou via Hotan and Kashgar to Gwadar Port in Pakistan (Jia 2014). This Silk Road revival project "could involve more than 40 Asian and European countries and regions with a combined population of 3 billion" (Tao and Chongfang 2014).

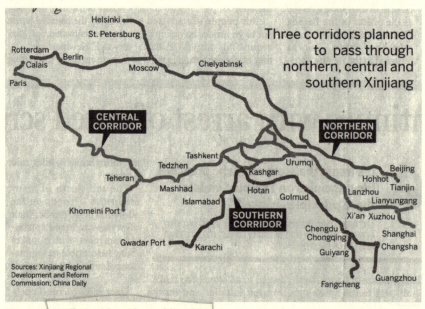

Map 7.1.   Rail Corridors Planned by China
Source: Jia 2014

Another high-speed rail line is being planned from Kunming, Yunnan Province, via Laos, Thailand, and Malaysia to Singapore, as part of building the twenty-first-century maritime Silk Road. Guangzhou, the capital of Guangdong Province, is to develop an industrial alliance with port cities along the ancient maritime trade route, with production centers and e-commerce services extending to Southeast Asia, South Asia, and Africa, resuming the city's history as the starting point of the maritime Silk Road 2,200 years ago (Quanlin 2014). It comes with an application to UNESCO for World Heritage status for the ancient maritime Silk Road, a status already granted in 2013 to the overland Silk Road, with Xian and Gansu Province as starting points (Yuanqing 2014). The dynamism is huge and action is fast (for instance, by comparison to the United States, where talk about high-speed trains has gone on for decades).

This is one of several Silk Road projects. In 2011 the US State Department developed a "New Silk Road" initiative to integrate Afghanistan in Central and South Asia with an electricity grid (CASA-1000) and road construction. This has been in a fledgling state following political volatility in the region and the imminent departure of American forces. In Russia the Putin government has been seeking to rebuild its past sphere of influence in a Eurasian Union. The Chinese view is that Russian and American projects were aimed at political integration rather than promoting regional economic cooperation, while China adheres to the principle of separating political and economic issues. "The economic integration promoted by China will cover 10 to 15 times the population and market of the Eurasian Union being promoted by Russia. . . . China welcomes Russia participating in the construction of the Silk Road economic belt." An accord has been achieved on connecting Russia's Trans-Eurasia railway with the Silk Road economic belt and the maritime Silk Road (Qiang 2014).

HYBRIDITY WITH CHINESE CHARACTERISTICS

The migration of Chinese overseas has been a major force of China globalizing. As Chan (2011) notes, Chinese diasporas should be in the plural because there have been many. Chinese migration in Asia goes back many centuries (Seagrave 1996). Overseas Chinese now number forty-eight million.

Cross-cultural braiding, discussed in chapter 6, continues its weaves. I will discuss one particular instance of Chinese migrants in Prato, Italy. The original foundation of Tuscan cloth manufacture was the medieval wool industry of Florence. It was located in places where water and other necessities for producing cloth were available, such as Prato and Lucca, a little north of Florence. Cloth from the Orient and silk from China, arriving in the ports of the Levant trade, spurred the development of weaving techniques in the Tuscan hinterland. By the end of the 1700s, the production of fezzes or "Levantine berets" was a mainstay of the region. This specialization contributed to the growing skill of Italian textile production, which has set world standards of quality and refinement. Tailors from Britain to Japan use Italian fabrics.

Prato is one of Europe's foremost centers of textile manufacture with a textile industry that comprises approximately nine thousand small and medium-size companies in an area of about seven hundred square kilometers, operating in all sectors of the textile industry. In the 1980s Prato began to attract Chinese entrepreneurs and labor, particularly from Wenzhou, a mountainous, land-poor region south of Shanghai with a reputation for commercial prowess (Wenzhou people are colloquially nicknamed "Jews of China"). Migrants from Wenzhou are prominent among the Chinese in Europe, notably in Paris and Barcelona.

Prato is Italy's oldest garment production center, a city of 191,000 that now holds Europe's largest Chinese community of up to 30,000 (16,000 of which are legal), all employed in textile production (Johanson and Denison 2008, Johanson and Smyth 2008). Chinese companies now own nearly 45 percent of the city's manufacturing business, with some 8,200 factories in textile and garment manufacture (Povoledo 2013). In turn, the chain migration to Prato has increased prosperity in Wenzhou.

In 2009 a center-right city government was elected in Prato that stepped up controls and crackdowns on Chinese immigrants and enterprises. In 2013 a deadly fire in one of the establishments where Chinese workers worked and lived claimed seven victims. Italian responses in Prato were mixed. Sympathy for the victims ("Sorrow has no color") mixed with anger. Chinese businesses "have flourished while Italian companies have failed because the Chinese ones depend on poorly paid labor and have ignored workplace safety standards in the name of cut-

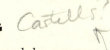

ting costs" (Povoledo 2013). Yet the Chinese companies also provide revenue for the local economy, such as rental income from properties and warehouses. Unlike many Italian companies, they have been able to withstand the economic crisis, and "Italian companies use Chinese-run factories to reduce their cost" (Povoledo 2013). Thus another twist in globalization's long braids has taken shape, a Chinese-Italian-Chinese-Italian combination.

GLOBALIZED, GLOBALIZING

Much discussion of globalization has been dominated by western power—European colonialism, the American century, neoliberalism and the Washington consensus. Globalization, in overdrive since the 1980s and especially in the wake of 1989, with multinational corporations, ICT, international banks, and international financial institutions in league with Washington, was the manifestation and exercise of this hegemony. This reverberates in concepts such as global capitalism, global crisis, global neoliberalism, "neoliberalism everywhere." In this overall imaginary, hybridity is real but marginal and mostly determined by *global* (American, western) influences shaping and penetrating *local* institutions and practices. No wonder questions of power and asymmetry keep popping up in the discussion—as discussed in several chapters above. The overriding, overwhelming character of North-South power relations cannot but shape the terms of cultural mixture. In the twenty-first century, however, the overall balance has been changing markedly in favor of emerging economies, with Northeast Asia and China in the lead (Nederveen Pieterse 2011, 2012a).

In this context, hybridity takes on a significantly different character; the issue is no longer how China is *being hybridized*—which after all it has been throughout its history—but how it is *hybridizing*, and the agency and choice of Chinese actors (across the spectrum of government, firms, entrepreneurs, consumers, migrants, tourists) move to the foreground as key variables.

Such agency, of course, is by no means new. Many countries have practiced "smart borrowing," borrowing technologies and institutions to help them achieve development. Examples are the American Republic selectively borrowing from the British Empire (Alexander Hamilton, posted in the British West Indies, saw up close the efficacy of tariff protection), Germany borrowing from the American Republic (Friedrich List was secretary of Alexander Hamilton), Japan borrowing especially from German examples (Okuda 2001), South Korea and Taiwan selectively and critically borrowing from Japanese examples, and so forth (see Studwell 2013). Latecomers to industrialization undergo a phase of *being hybridized*, being exposed to and imbibing outside influences, followed by a phase of *actively hybridizing*, selectively and critically seeking out best practices, technologies, and institutions from elsewhere, copying and reverse engineering them, and in the process catching up. Such has been the career of all late (and late-late) industrializers, a process also known as "modernization."

For some time, emerging economies have not only entered the phase of active, critical hybridization but have acquired leverage in the process—leverage because of a growing middle class, because of industrialization and participation in global value networks, because of scale, because of technological upgrading, because of high commodity and energy prices (especially during 2003–2008), because of slowdowns in advanced economies, because of capable policies, and so forth.

Hybridity in China displays many strands. It has proliferated, of course, since Deng Xiao Ping's "four modernizations" in 1981 (J. Wang 1996). It accompanies China's joining the WTO (2001) and intertwining with global value networks and economies the world over, such as the American economy (nicknamed "Chamerica") and those of India ("Chindia"), the Middle East ("Chime": China, India, Middle East), Latin America, and Africa.

Chinese debates on globalization have gone through several cycles. Debates in the 1990s focused on Deng Theory and developmentalism, on neoliberalism and consumerism (J. Wang 1996, Xin 2003). Part of the debate was the legacy of Mao (Wang Hui 2003, 2009). Magazines devoted polls and articles to the question whether Mao was 70 percent right, 30 percent wrong, as Deng Xiao Ping claimed, or the other way round.

In the 1990s the Jiang Zemin government followed the "Singapore model" of fast-lane growth led by foreign direct investment. Ethnic Chinese tycoons from Southeast Asia investing in special economic zones played a major role in this stage. This growth model produced sharp imbalances between coastal and inland development and between economic growth and development. The New Left criticized growing consumerism, materialism, and neoliberalism. Beginning in 2003, the

Hu Jintao and Wen Jiabao government initiated "harmonious society" and the "scientific outlook on development" as policy frameworks. In 2007 Premier Wen Jiabao warned that while the Chinese economy looked strong on the surface, in terms of GDP and employment growth, it was increasingly "unbalanced, unstable, uncoordinated, and unsustainable," an assessment that became known as the "four uns." Unbalanced—in terms of urban-rural and east-west disparities; unstable—with overheated investment, excess liquidity, and large current-account surplus; uncoordinated—with regional fragmentation, excess manufacturing and an undeveloped services sector, excess investment and lagging consumption; unsustainable—in view of environmental degradation, excess resource use, and persistent tensions in income distribution (Roach 2009).

These considerations set the stage for the twelfth five-year plan (2011–2015), which aims at building broad social safety, reducing the need for household savings, urbanization to bridge urban-rural income gaps, thus boosting domestic consumption, and reorienting the economy away from export dependence. China has moved on from its growth and survival stage to its transformation stage (see Fulin 2010). At issue is "shifting the development model." Implementing this may slow growth rates and runs counter to powerful elite interests, so it is a long and winding road.

Accordingly, the agenda has moved on from China globalized to China globalizing; I will briefly review trends under this heading. They mostly unfold in economic and development policies, rather than in cultural trends and "soft power," in which China, like other emerging societies, still experiences a "trade deficit." They concern reflexivity and development as a collective learning process (discussed in Nederveen Pieterse 2010a), an outlook that started with Deng's "crossing the river by feeling the stones."

The Chinese might as well consume what they produce, so it's no wonder that on Chinese high streets western brands predominate, the usual fast fashion of H&M, Zara, Gap, and Calvin Klein, along with Asian brands, Japanese (Uniqlo), Hong Kong (Giordano), Malaysian (Parkson), and Chinese stores, some with faux English names (such as Youngor, Soso).

The preference of Chinese consumers for well-known brands is a matter of instant globalization. As newcomers to global consumption,

Chinese consumers lack the savvy of knowing quality independent of brands and go for established brands as a guarantee of quality and as markers of status. Brands are a shortcut to quality and status. In Chengdu, the capital of Sichuan Province, West China's major transport hub and an upcoming city that grew from eleven million in 2005 to fourteen million in 2010, the vast new shopping streets make Shanghai's Nanjing Road look like kid stuff. Chengdu alone has no less than seven Louis Vuitton stores. One sees more Louis Vuitton bags on China's high streets—whether real or fake, who knows—than in Europe or the US, where such display may be viewed as ostentatious and gauche. Meanwhile, on Chengdu's central square, in front of the Science and Technology Museum, a giant white marble statue of Mao stretches its right arm forward pointing west toward Renmin Road.

From early on, China has been a tough negotiator in foreign direct investment, insisting on early technology transfer, which in view of its scale, the country is in a stronger position to achieve than other developing countries. Local content clauses prompt foreign companies to invest in China. China has become increasingly strategic in relation to joint ventures and foreign direct investment. Developments in 2014 include government probes in foreign companies with corruption (GlaxoSmithKline) and antitrust and competition investigations (e.g., Microsoft, Qualcomm, Daimler-Benz, Audi, and BMW are charged with overcharging for spare parts).

Chinese companies listed in the top ten of the Fortune 500 are China Petrochemical Corporation (ranked three), China National Petroleum Corporation (four), and State Grid Corporation of China, and further down the list are the Industrial and Commercial Bank of China, China Construction Bank, Agricultural Bank of China, China State Construction Engineering Corporation, China Mobile Communications Corporation, Bank of China, Pacific Construction Group (166), and Huawei (285) (Tian 2014). These are mostly state-owned enterprises (SOE) and reflect the investment-led character of China's growth path.

Government and corporate investment has increasingly turned to research and development and innovation. China's fifteen-year Plan for Science and Technology, adopted in 2005, set the target "to transform the country into an innovative society by 2020 and a world leader in science and technology by 2050" (Moody 2014). The objective is to move from "made in China" to "created in China." The twelfth five-year plan emphasizes breakthroughs in areas such as integrated circuits, nanotechnology, and space research. Strategies to achieve these aims include major investments in science and industrial parks, firms acquiring technology through acquisitions (notably in Germany and the US), and industrial upgrading ("Chinnovation"; Tan 2011). Lenovo bought IBM's laptop division and more recently Google's Motorola handset division. Chinese firms such as Alibaba, Baidu, and Tencent invest in Silicon Valley startups. Multinational corporations also locate R&D centers in China, such as Bell Labs of Alcatel-Lucent (Moody 2014).

Government investment in science and industrial parks has been major and long-term. The Suzhou Industrial and Science Park, established in 2002, now has a GDP of $30 billion (2013) and aspires to become "a world standard for high-tech industrial parks and a modern and eco-balanced new type of city. . . . The park has been very selective in introducing new companies." Criteria for admission are that they are eco-friendly and value-added industries (Hayan et al. 2014). The Xian High-Tech Zone, started in 2012, hosts more than eighteen thousand enterprises, including Samsung Electronics, with an investment of seven billion dollars in memory chip manufacturing.

China is in the process of achieving industry leadership in high-speed trains and aerospace. The length of China's high-speed railway network, which is now over eleven thousand kilometers long, is expected to reach twenty-one thousand kilometers by 2020. China's fast-train technology is inexpensive, at a cost two-thirds of that in the rest of the world (Hayan 2014). Huawei is now the world's second largest telecom gear maker. In 2013 China became the largest robotics market ("with a total of 27,000 industrial robots being sold by overseas companies . . . up 20 percent year-on-year"). Local governments follow this trend. "Zhejiang province, which is known for exports largely dependent on low-cost labor, announced that 36,000 local companies will be replacing human workers with machines by 2017" (Jing 2014).

China's new airports, railway stations, metros, and other facilities are often more tech advanced than in the older modernities of the US and Europe. In China, traffic lights are digital. In South Korea, taxis are equipped with GPS that gives traffic densities and weather reports. This is the principle of the "retarding lead." Every observer is struck by the vast scale of construction and the tempo of development in China.

at a cost.

Logistics centers such as the new center in Xian extend for miles. Forests of high-rises of thirty-three floors encircle cities. China is building for the future; malls are built with a view to five years from now, with mega urbanization of hundreds of millions along with roads, shops, services, malls, and so on. Consider this: "in just two years—2011 and 2012—China produced more cement than the US did in the whole of the 20th century" (Anderlini 2014). The whole country is a vast long-term development project.

China, like India, has kept a close guard on its financial autonomy, has been circumspect with external borrowing, and has kept its distance from Washington financial institutions. China was unaffected by the 1997 Asian crisis. From Japan, China learned the lesson of not devaluing its currency under outside pressure (as Japan did in the 1985 Plaza Accord). China's central bank and sovereign wealth fund have followed prudent courses. Since the 2008 crash, the tables have turned, with overt criticism of American policies. In 2009 Premier Wen Jiabao urged the US to take measures to guarantee its "good credit," expressing concern about the safety of China's huge holdings of US government debt. About two-thirds of China's $3.2 trillion currency reserves are invested in US dollar denominated assets. As the largest holder of American government and corporate debt, China has a major stake in prudent American policies. According to China's central bank governor, "the US must behave more responsibly to consider not just the US economy but the global economy" (Browne 2012). Chinese officials have criticized American Federal Reserve policies of "quantitative easing" for its effects on the status of the dollar: "We hope the US government will earnestly adopt responsible policies to strengthen international market confidence, and to respect and protect the interests of investors" (Rabinovitch 2011). Part of China's globalizing agenda in finance is establishing the renminbi as an internationally traded currency, which over time may erode the role of the US dollar as world reserve currency.

China plays a leading role in the BRICS. The BRICS development bank, established in 2014 with an initial capital of $50 billion, will fund infrastructure projects. It will first be based in Shanghai. The BRICS accord includes an emergency financing arrangement of $100 billion, a swap line to help developing countries and emerging markets cope with external shocks. China also pushes the idea of an Asian infrastructure investment bank. These initiatives nibble away at the role of the IMF, World Bank, and Asian Development Bank and introduce a welcome element of competition. The same applies to China's role as lender to developing countries (its loans now exceed those of the World Bank) and to its role as investor worldwide. As investors, Chinese companies need not only "going out," but also need rules and guidelines for "going in" and reckoning with the development objectives of host countries and the interests of stakeholders. In the region, China has a free trade agreement with ASEAN, is establishing access to ports in Myanmar (via the Mandalay Road) and Pakistan (Gwadar), and is expanding its influence in the South China Sea.

Different strands of thought are viewing China as the new face of globalization, as an alternative force in a multipolar world order, as development partner, as economic competitor, and as colonizer (Alden 2007). China also views itself, in Hu Jintao's words, as "the biggest developing country." China is also the sole Asian permanent member of the UN Security Council and a player in a wide range of multilateral coalitions and negotiations.

With Xi Jinping's "Chinese dream" and his campaign against corruption and excess government spending, the country enters another phase of reform. The so-called China model and Beijing consensus are metamorphosing in the process (Ferchen 2013). In large infrastructure projects in Africa, China proposes cooperation with the US, which triggers doubt and ambivalence in Washington (Dyer 2014).

Obviously, as much as agency matters, it doesn't necessarily stack up to success. Investment and infrastructure still lead as a share of China's GDP. Inequality continues to grow. Consumption still lags behind (at 35 percent of GDP). The increase of the vote quota of developing countries in the IMF to a meager 6 percent (an increase of only 2.6 percent) has been blocked by the American Congress. China's claims in the South China Sea spark clashes with Japan, Vietnam, and the Philippines. Reporting on China remains a roller coaster from euphoria to alarm, casting China as the engine of the world economy or, alternatively, as reeling from mounting risks, including pollution, ballooning debt in the property sector, overcapacity, shadow banking, inefficient SOEs, local government corruption, and the need for democratic reform (e.g., Shirk 2008). Urbanization is now being reframed as sustainable urbanization, but investment-led growth and increasing private consumption do not necessarily go well with China's ecological rebalancing.

In closing, this chapter addresses a key point of hybridity—whether mixing occurs in the passive tense (being mixed) or in the active (hybridizing). According to Chan Kwok-bun's book on hybridity in Asia, "Hotchpotch, a bit of this and a bit of that, change-by-fusion, change-by-conjoining is how newness enters the world" (2011: 92), which is true, but of course newness enters in many fashions, including deliberate ones. Chan also refers to hybridization as selective adaptation (2011: 149) and cites Berger, for whom hybridization is "the deliberate effort to synthesize foreign and native cultural traits." An example is "the case of software engineers in Bangalore who garland their computers in Hindu ceremonies" (Berger 2002: 10–11; Chan 2011: 92). Hybridization also means tweaking and repurposing. China adopted the Holiday Inn hotel chain franchise in 1984, but in China, Holiday Inn hotels are business hotels, while in the US they are leisure hotels, as the name indicates. The English name matters more than what it actually means.

Why is agency and power so often being missed in literature on hybridity? The first problem is the failure to see the full spectrum of hybridity and to adequately distinguish types of hybridity. If hybridity is defined as hotchpotch (Chan 2011: 92), agency is, per definition, ruled out, or is marginal at most. The spectrum of hybridity is discussed below. The second limitation is that most literature focuses on culture, so changing power balances in political economy fall outside the frame. More precisely, the way culture is understood is often narrow and overlooks dimensions such as the cultural economy (Amin and Thrift 2004; discussed in chapter 8). Third, much globalization literature remains under the shadow cast by the 1990s. And because much literature is concerned with western countries and cultures, nonwestern developments are missed.

Hybridity refers to a wide range of practices. Combinations and mixtures that come about haphazardly and ad hoc, as in potpourri, hotchpotch, bric-à-brac, don't involve agency. At the other end of the continuum are selective and controlled combinations, as in horticulture, plant and animal breeding, grafting, crossbreeding, and cross-fertilization. This is where the idea of hybridity originally stems from. Here hybridization can be highly, meticulously controlled, down to molecular or genetic levels. In business, hybridity invariably refers to controlled combinations. Thus the hybridized supply chain refers to combinations of far-flung and local components. In cuisine, fusion refers to controlled combinations. Gilroy's view that "cultural production is not like mixing cocktails" (quoted in Axford 2013: 105) is right in that cultural production doesn't follow set recipes, yet production per definition involves agency and control. In music, cut and mix is controlled. In art, collages and installations are controlled combinations. Mixing diverse elements in film, fashion, design, and architecture is likewise controlled. In between the extremes of haphazard and controlled mixtures are gray scales such as bricolage and jam sessions (improvisation leads but within a particular genre of jazz). Tutti-frutti doesn't literally mean all fruits and flavors, but a selection.

The point is that where mixing is willed, the selection of components and the process of mixing are also willed and controlled. It is therefore odd and misleading that so many accounts of cultural hybridity would represent it as simply haphazard and only focus on one end of the spectrum of hybridity. For obvious reasons, smart borrowing has a wide and deep history.

CHAPTER 8

GLOBAL MÉLANGE

Globalization and culture is not an innocent theme. The intervening variable in most accounts is modernity. Three vectors—globalization, modernity, culture—come together in a package with modernization as the deciding variable. Consider the subtitle of Bernard Lewis' book, *The Clash between Islam and Modernity in the Middle East* (2002). Modernity is the subtext of the alleged clash of civilizations. Modernity is also a polite, sociological way of saying capitalism. The sociologists Axford (1995) and Tomlinson (1999), among others, struggle with this question and in the end tiptoe over to the side of modernity (read the logics of western modernization) shaping cultural dynamics. It's difficult to argue with the combined power of modernity and capitalism, with technology and economics on their side, and therefore, it seems, global (read western culture) wins out from local culture. Yet one wonders whether these accounts are actually about culture or about power.

My reading of trends past and current runs quite differently. First, the conventional account that "the rise of the West" spawned an integrated world economy, modernity, and capitalism has been refuted by radically different accounts. An integrated world economy—it may be termed an Afro-Eurasian economy—predates the rise of the West by many centuries (Abu-Lughod 1989, Frank 1998, Hobson 2004). At the core of this world economy were China and India, with Europe at the outer rim. In the core regions, sprawling outward to West Asia, the Ottoman Empire, and Persia, rates of population growth, urbanization, industrial and agricultural productivity, infrastructures, and institutions of commerce, all outstripped those that existed in Europe at the time, and continued to do so until the early nineteenth century. Accordingly, the groundwork for modernity and capitalism lies in these regions, not in Europe. Anthony King (1995) argues, with ample irony, that in colonial cities postmodern identities *preceded* the development of modernity in Europe. We can add that modern conditions prevailed in the urban centers of India and China before they emerged in Europe. This makes dead wood of the usual occidental stories of Marx (Asian mode of production), Weber (Protestant ethic), and Wallerstein (modern world-system). As a latecomer Europe was an importer of cultural and other goods, which shows in the mélange character of early European culture.

Second, both "modernity" and "capitalism" are lumping concepts that need to be unpacked. Modern sociology is gradually giving way to sociology of modernity and to anthropology of modernity. In the process, modernity yields to *modernities* and by the same token, anthropological angles on modernization come into their own in interpreting local changes. "Modernity viewed through the prism of the local" (Miller 1995) yields unexpected outcomes. Development as modernization = westernization is a passed station. Now countries with a decade and more of growth rates higher than in the West have been spawning new modernities. What is the character and outlook of these new, mélange modernities? Globalization, increased communication, and mobility generally create opportunities for new combinations between "traditional" and "modern" practices, for instance, novel forms of cooperation between local and international NGOs and "traditional" organizations. Likewise capitalism yields unexpected faces when viewed through an ethnographic lens (Miller 1997). It's not just that capitalism shapes culture but capitalism is embedded in culture: capitalism is a cultural rendezvous. *Capitalisms* plural, for various reasons, then, is a more productive angle than capitalism singular. It is against this backdrop that hybridity has gradually become an increasingly prominent narrative and a new convention in interpreting local changes, past and present (as in Siebers 1996, Matsuda 2001, Silva 2002, Whatmore 2002).

As Walter Anderson notes, "Symbols of all kinds have detached themselves from their original roots and float freely, like dandelion seeds, around the world" (2001: 89). And so the list of hybridities goes on and on: "klezmer flamenco, Japanese salsa, French bluegrass," German Indians (W. Anderson 2001: 90). This book makes additional points: bricolage doesn't just apply to symbols but also to structures and institutions; and while mixing has accelerated in recent times it is as old as the hills, so the roots themselves are mixed. Cultural mélange and cosmopolitanism, then, is not merely a precious elite experience but a collective condition and experience. Global mélange does not merely follow but also *precedes* nations. We live lives of everyday cosmopolitanism already. The Latino writer Richard Rodriguez takes this a little forward: "We're looking at Evangelicals coming up from Latin America to convert the US at the same time that LA movie stars are taking up Indian pantheism. We're looking at such enormous complexity and variety that it makes a mockery of 'celebrating diversity.' . . . Diversity is going to be a fundamental part of our lives. That's what it's going to mean to be modern" (London 1997).

In the shantytowns of Khartoum, hybridity means that sweeping social engineering such as the imposition of Islamic Sharia law does not work (Simone 1994: 224). This doesn't mean that border zones are typically pleasant meadows of métissage. They can be bulwarks of conservatism, ramparts of resistance, precisely because they are borders. In Andalusia in Spain, the last of the Reconquista territories, Catholicism, reaffirmed during the grim Franco years, has taken hold as the dominant, deeply conservative identity (Dietz 2001, González Alcantud 1993). The region offers a warmer welcome to tourists who come to gape at the splendor of the Alhambra than to the Moroccan migrants whose ancestors built it. La Mezquita, the Grand Mosque in Córdoba, the dean of mosques in Spain and the most accomplished monument of the Umayyad dynasty of Córdoba, has been occupied by Cordóba's Roman Catholic diocese and has not been allowed to reopen as a mosque.

What does hybridity mean in settings of polarization and conflict? Niru Ratnam asks, "Can hybridity even begin to deal with issues such as the Lawrence murder?" and observes, "Hybridity is simply not the language of Eltham, South London" (1999: 156, 158). Does this mean, on the other hand, that one should gloss over the increasingly complex meanings of what it means to be British (Parekh 2002) or ignore the growing number of mixed marriages in England and the complex biographies that this gives rise to (Phillips 2001, Alibhai-Brown 2001, Twine 2011)?

Polarization means the suppression of the middle ground, but does suppression mean that the middle ground does not exist? What of hybridity amid the world's most chronic conflict zone, the borderlands of Israel and Palestine? Does recognizing this conflict dragging on and on mean ignoring multiple identities on either side, the complex identity of Israeli Arabs and the backdrop of the Levant on *both* sides of the border (Alcalay 1993)?

The nation state bonds that have exerted such great influence grew out of sedentary experiences, agriculture, urbanism, and then industry as anchors of the national economy. The nation state inherited older territorial imperatives, and "national interest" translated them into geopolitical and geostrategic niches and projects. Together they make up a real estate vision of history. Deleuze and Guattari (1984) distinguish between sedentarism and nomadism as paradigms of perception. The moment we shift lenses from sedentary to *mobile* categories the whole environment and the horizon change: hunting, nomadic pastoralism, fishing, trade, transnational enterprise, and hyperspace all have deterritorialization built in. Why should identity be centered on sedentary rather than mobile categories if mobility defines the species as much as settlement does? Why should analysis privilege real estate rather than mobility? Over time, in view of changing technologies, we may expect mobility to become as salient as or more salient than sedentarism. Crossborder activities are on the rise; border conflicts will remain, but will they be the overall, defining dynamic?

Futures also belong to the *longue durée*, so evolutionary perspectives on world history and politics are relevant (W. Thompson 2001). But futures are mortgaged. The Mexican philosopher José Vasconcelos anticipated a future planetary human blend, a *Cosmic Race* (1948), but in doing so reproduced the old preoccupation with "race." Likewise

Richard Rodriguez (2002) by using the color brown to open up present times stays with tones of skin color.

Another misperception that I have sought to avoid or dispel in this account is that "culture" is a rarefied, separate domain, somewhere on the soft side of the hard realities of economics and politics. Culture is not just an afternoon spent in the Louvre or a night at La Scala in Milan or the Hard Rock Café, but is also an afternoon patrolling Hebron. Culture is general human software—and none of the world's hard enterprises functions without software. Desires and goals, and methods and expectations in achieving goals, are all of a cultural nature. Power itself is a cultural dream. "Of the infinite desires of man," notes the philosopher Bertrand Russell, "the chief are the desires for power and glory" (1938: 11).

With constructivism in social science comes the awareness that social realities and boundaries are socially constructed. Discourse analysis makes the same point. This places "culture" in the center of social science. It is by virtue of particular cultural understandings of nationhood (or ethnicity, religion, identity, national security, national interest) that boundaries end up where they do. Powerful interests are invested in boundaries and borders, affecting the fate of classes, ethnic groups, elites; while borders and boundaries are a function of differentials of power, they are social constructions that are embedded and encoded in cultural claims. The distinction, then, does not run between conflict and culture, for conflict itself is a cultural exercise. Domestic politics is conducted through politics of cultural differences (Leege et al. 2002) and so is international politics (Nederveen Pieterse 2004). This is what is at stake in discussions of culture. Since culture is a battleground, hybridity is a matter of mapping no-man's-land. Hybridity does not preclude struggle but yields a multifocal view on struggle and, by showing multiple identity on both sides, transcends the "us versus them" dualism that prevails in cultural and political arenas.

NOTES

CHAPTER 2 GLOBALIZATION
AND HUMAN INTEGRATION

1. Sources include Neville-Sington and Sington 1993, Grosso 1995, D. Thompson 1996. Cohn 1993, among others, discusses the dark, apocalyptic side of utopias.

2. On Mughal cultural influence, see Ahmed 1995, which discusses the mutual influence of Mughal miniatures and European painting. This is discussed in chapter 6.

3. Discussed in Skolimowski 1994 and Nederveen Pieterse 2010a, chapter 9.

4. Social capital, ethnicity, and multiculturalism are discussed at length in Nederveen Pieterse 2007.

5. See Castles 1998. Only a few economists are consistent in that they advocate free trade *and* open migration policies, or managed migration (Bhagwati 1997, 2003).

CHAPTER 3   GLOBALIZATION AND CULTURE

1. That an open definition of culture is relevant also in international relations is apparent in a collection that adopts a working definition of culture as "any interpersonal shared system of meanings, perceptions and values" (Jacquin et al. 1993: 376).

2. The theme of capitalisms is developed in Nederveen Pieterse 2004, 2014.

3. See, for example, Wilson and Dissanayake 1996, Jameson and Miyoshi 1998, Appadurai 2001, Comaroff and Comaroff 2001.

4. This example illustrates the political inconclusiveness of hybridity, which is taken up in the next chapters while chapter 7 offers an alternative perspective.

5. On McDonald's decline see, e.g., J. Ghazvinian and K. L. Miller, "Hold the Fries," *Newsweek*, 30 December–6 January, 2002–2003: 17–19. On the McDonaldization paradigm, see Taylor and Lyon 1995 and chapter 3 below. On variations on McDonaldization see, e.g., Drane 2002, Ritzer 2002, Bryman 2004.

CHAPTER 4   GLOBALIZATION AS HYBRIDIZATION

1. An equivalent view in international relations is Morse 1976. After arguing for globalizations in the plural, I will continue to use globalization singular because it matches conventional usage and there is no need to hammer the point by way of inelegant grammar.

2. The mélange element comes across, for instance, in the definition of semiperiphery of Chase-Dunn and Hall (1993: 865–66): "(1) a semiperipheral region may be one that mixes both core and peripheral forms of organization; (2) a semiperipheral region may be spatially located between core and peripheral regions; (3) mediating activities between core and peripheral regions may be carried out in semiperipheral regions; (4) a semiperipheral area may be one in which institutional features are in some ways intermediate between those forms found in core and periphery." Interestingly, Chase-Dunn and Hall also destabilize the notions of core and periphery, pointing to situations "in which the 'periphery' systematically exploits the 'core'" (1993: 864). I am indebted to an anonymous reviewer of *International Sociology* for alerting me to this source and the relevance of semiperiphery in this context.

3. I argue this case in Nederveen Pieterse 1994 and 1989: chapter 15.

4. As against *peninsulares*, born in the Iberian Peninsula, *indigenes*, or Native Americans, and *ladinos* and *cholos*, straddled betwixt those of European and Native American descent.

5. In *Pour Rushdie*, a collection of essays by Arab and Islamic intellectuals in support of freedom of expression, Paris is referred to as a "capitale Arabe." This evokes another notion of hybridity, one that claims a collective ground based on multiple subjectivities in the name of a universal value.

6. I use critical globalism as an approach to current configurations. This discussion of imperialism versus globalization is dated since in the wake of 9/11 has come a new imperial turn, which is taken up in *Globalization or Empire?* (Nederveen Pieterse 2004).

7. Some of the "primitive isolates," the traditional study objects of anthropology, might be exceptions, although even this may be questioned in the long stretch of time.

8. See Pickering 1995. I owe these points to Jong-Young Kim.

9. Sources include Florida 2008, Zachary 2000, Cowen 2002, Sirkin et al. 2008, and Prahalad and Krishnan 2008. Zachary and Cowen, in particular, highlight hybridity as a force in economic dynamism.

CHAPTER 5   HYBRIDITY, SO WHAT?

1. For example, in the work of Hall, Bhabha, Gilroy, Hannerz, Hebdige, Appadurai, Rushdie, Canclini.

2. An interesting discussion of this period is Hughes 1958. On the layered nature of Freud's sensibilities, combining pagan, classical, Hebrew, and positivist strands, see Loewenberg 1996.

3. "In Latin *hybrida* originally meant the offspring of a tame sow and a wild boar" (Cashmore 1996: 165).

4. Criticisms along these lines include Shohat and Stam 1994, Fusco 1995, Young 1995, McLaren 1997, McLaren and Farahmandpur 2000, Brah and Coombes 2000. McLaren reviews objections to hybridity thinking (1997: 10–11) and then gives a different take on "critical reflexivity and posthybridity as narrative engagement" (76–114). Friedman (1990) refers to creolization in an earlier discussion.

5. Benita Parry (1987) argues against the hybridity view as privileging discourse and ignoring the material realities of colonialism, a view that is taken further by Ahmad (1992). Bauman (1998: 3) also views hybridity as a matter of "top culture." Other sources are Žižek 1997, Nanda 2001.

6. I argue that this pathos only dates from after 1800 (Nederveen Pieterse 1994).

7. Hybridity and multiple identities among second- and third-generation immigrants have been extensively discussed. On Asian Americans see Lowe 1991, Liu 1998, Tamayo Lott 1997, Yang et al. 1997, and on Korean

Americans, Hyun 1995. Japanese influence in the United States (Conor 1991, Feinberg 1993) and, vice versa, changes in Japan (Kosuka 1989, Matsuda 2001) are widely discussed.

8. This kind of angle is apparent in Friedman's work and in Žižek 1997. McLaren's work shows that Marxism and aversion to multiculturalism need not coincide.

9. Besides confirming the evolutionary out-of-Africa thesis Cavalli-Sforza (2000) documents a tree of human evolution: a branching diagram of relations among different populations. He shows that the European population is the most genetically mixed up on earth, quite contrary to Comte de Gobineau who ascribed European genius to their being the most genetically pure and the least "weakened" by racial mixture. This matches the findings of human genome research: there is but one race—the human race; 99.9 percent of the human genome is the same in everyone. So-called racial differences are literally only skin deep (Angier 2000).

10. Since all forms of regulation (in the sense of the French régulation school) are historically developed and consist of political compromises, there are no "pure" forms of regulation.

11. Now cities are generally characterized as hybrid: "Cities are essentially culturally hybrid" (Amin et al. 2000: vi). Cf. King 1996, AlSayyad 2001.

12. A theme in French anthropology is la *pensée métisse*, in response to Lévi-Strauss' *Pensée sauvage*; see Amselle 1990, Horton 1990, Gruzinski 1999.

13. Fusco 1995 quoted in McLaren 1997: 10. Cf. Shohat and Stam 1994, Axford 2013: 105, Nederveen Pieterse 1998b and chapter 4 above.

14. Ayse Caglar (personal communication) notes that cross-class mixtures are rarely referred to as hybrid (cf. the old terminology of mésalliance). It would apply to phenomena such as the newly rich (cf. Robison and Goodman 1996).

15. What is globalization? In answer to this question a Pakistani colleague recounts: "An English Princess (Princess Diana) with an Egyptian boyfriend, uses a Norwegian mobile telephone, crashes in a French tunnel in a German car with a Dutch engine, driven by a Belgian driver, who was high on Scottish whiskey, followed closely by Italian paparazzi, on Japanese motorcycles, treated by an American doctor, assisted by Filipino para-medical staff, using Brazilian medicines, dies!"

In the Philippines, a new version of this message circulates via e-mail: "And this is sent to you by a Filipino, using Bill Gates' technology, which he stole from the Japanese. You are probably reading this on one of the IBM clones that use Taiwanese-made chips and Korean-made monitors, assembled by Bangladeshi workers in a Singapore plant, transported by lorries driven by Indians, hijacked by Indonesians and finally sold to you by Chinamen!"

16. In anthropology, liminality refers to Arnold van Gennep's rites of passage between different states and Victor Turner's "liminal space" as a space of transformation. In postcolonial studies, Bhabha refers to the liminal as an interstitial passage between fixed identifications. *Limen*, a journal for the theory and practice of liminal phenomena published in Croatia (2001), seeks to address the "liminal generation in-between industrial and post-industrial, socialism and capitalism, etc."

CHAPTER 6   GLOBALIZATION IS BRAIDED

1. This is the point of Gamble's book on "the prehistory of global colonization" (1993). Robbie Robertson (2003) also adopts a long-term approach to globalization. Cf. Nederveen Pieterse 2012b.

2. See Dainotto 2007: 18; Hay 1957.

3. Stuart Hughes devoted a study to the role of consciousness and the recovery of the unconscious in European social thought, 1890–1930 (1958). On the origins of avant-garde art see Shattuck's *The Banquet Years* (1967).

CHAPTER 7   HYBRID CHINA

1. In sequence, J. Gapper, *Financial Times*, 23 April 2009; E. Rigby, *Financial Times*, 21 April 2010: 3; M. W. Sadovi, *Wall Street Journal*, 21 October 2008: C8; G. Tett, *Financial Times*, 22 January 2010: 6; M. Mobius, *Financial Times*, 6 November 2009: 24; K. Chen, *Wall Street Journal*, 6 April 2010: A6; Liu Jie, *Shanghai Daily*, 1 July 2010: A6; D. K. Berman, *Wall Street Journal*, 21 September 2010: C1.

BIBLIOGRAPHY

Abdel-Malek, Anouar. *Civilizations and Social Theory*. 2 vols. London: Macmillan, 1981.

Abu-Lughod, Janet L. *Before European Hegemony: The World-System* A.D. *1250–1350*. New York: Oxford University Press, 1989.

Adams, F., S. Dev Gupta, and K. Mengisteab, eds. *Globalization and the Dilemmas of the State in the South*. London: Macmillan, 1999.

Ahmad, Ajjaz. *In Theory: Classes, Nations, Literatures*. London: Verso, 1992.

Ahmed, Akbar S. *Postmodernism and Islam*. London: Routledge, 1992.

Ahmed, Khalid Anis. "History of Mughal Painting: Intercultural and Artistic Influences." Pp. 11–28 in *Intercultural Encounter in Mughal Miniatures*, edited by K. A. Ahmed. Lahore: National College of Arts, 1995a.

———, ed. *Intercultural Encounters in Mughal Miniatures*. Lahore: National College of Arts, 1995b.

Al-Azmeh, Aziz. *Islams and Modernities*. London: Verso, 1993.

Albert, Michel. *Capitalism against Capitalism*. London: Whurr, 1993.

Albrow, Martin. "Introduction." In *Globalization, Knowledge and Society*, edited by M. Albrow and E. King. London: Sage, 1990.

Alcalay, Ammiel. *After Jews and Arabs: Remaking Levantine Culture*. Minneapolis: University of Minnesota Press, 1993.

Alden, Chris. *China in Africa*. London: Zed, 2007.

Alfino, Mark, John S. Caputo, and Robin Wynyard, eds. *McDonaldization Revisited: Critical Essays on Consumer Culture*. Westport, CT: Praeger, 1998.

Alibhai-Brown, Yasmin. *Mixed Feelings: The Complex Lives of Mixed-Race Britons*. London: Women's Press, 2001.

AlSayyad, Nezar, ed. *Hybrid Urbanism*. Westport, CT: Praeger, 2001.

Ambrose, Stephen E. *Rise to Globalism: American Foreign Policy since 1938*. London: Lane, 1971.

Amin, Ash, Doreen Massey, and Nigel Thrift. *Cities for the Many, Not the Few*. Bristol: Policy Press, 2000.

Amin, Ash, and Nigel Thrift, eds. *The Cultural Economy Reader*. Oxford: Blackwell, 2004.

Amin, Samir. *The Arab Nation*. London: Zed, 1978.

———. *Delinking: Towards a Polycentric World*. London: Zed, 1990.

———. *Capitalism in the Age of Globalization*. London: Zed, 1997.

Amselle, Jean-Loup. *Logiques Métisses: Anthropologie de l'identité en Afrique et Ailleurs*. Paris: Payot, 1990. [*Mestizo Logics: Anthropology of Identity in Africa and Elsewhere*. Stanford, CA: Stanford University Press, 1998.]

Anderlini, Jamil. "Property Bubble Is 'Major Risk to China.'" *Financial Times*, 25 August 2014.

Anderson, Benedict. "The New World Disorder." *New Left Review* 190 (1992): 3–14.

Anderson, J. "'Transformers': Advanced Case of Metal Fatigue." *Wall Street Journal*, 27 June 2014: D3.

Angier, N. "Do Races Differ? Not Really, Genes Show." *New York Times*, 22 August 2000.

Anzaldúa, Gloria. *Borderland/La Frontera*. San Francisco: Spinsters/Ann Lute, 1987.

Appadurai, Arjun. "Disjuncture and Difference in the Global Political Economy." Pp. 295–310 in *Global Culture*, edited by Mike Featherstone. London: Sage, 1990.

———, ed. *Globalization*. Durham, NC: Duke University Press, 2001.

Appiah, Kwame Anthony. *In My Father's House: Africa in the Philosophy of Culture*. Oxford: Oxford University Press, 1992.

Araeen, Rasheed. "A New Beginning: Beyond Postcolonial Cultural Theory and Identity Politics." *Third Text*, no. 50 (2000): 3–20.

Arjomand, Said Amir, and Elisa Reis, eds. *Worlds of Difference*. London: Sage, 2013.

Arnason, Johann P. "Nationalism, Globalization and Modernity." Pp. 207–36 in *Global Culture*, edited by Mike Featherstone. London: Sage, 1990.

Associated Press. "Invading Turks' Music Marked West." *International Herald Tribune*, 10 March 2002.

Aurobindo, Sri. *The Ideal of Human Unity* [1st ed. 1915]. In *The Penguin Aurobindo Reader*, edited by M. Paranjape. New Delhi: Penguin, 1999.

Avneri, Uri. *My Friend the Enemy*. London: Zed, 1986.

Axford, Barrie. *The Global System: Economics, Politics and Culture*. Cambridge: Polity, 1995.

———. *Theories of Globalization*. Cambridge: Polity, 2013.

Bach, P. "European Painting and Mughal Miniatures." Pp. 29–36 in *Intercultural Encounter in Mughal Miniatures*, edited by K. A. Ahmed. Lahore: National College of Arts, 1995.

Bach, P., and L. Bressan. "Mughal Influences on European Painting of the 17th Century." Pp. 93–102 in *Intercultural Encounter in Mughal Miniatures*, edited by K. A. Ahmed. Lahore: National College of Arts, 1995.

Bakhtin, Mikhail. *Rabelais and His World*. Cambridge: MIT Press, 1968.

Bakst, Léon. *The Decorative Art of Léon Bakst*. London: Fine Art Society, 1913.

Banuri, Tariq. "Modernization and Its Discontents: A Cultural Perspective on Theories of Development." Pp. 73–101 in *Dominating Knowledge*, edited by F. Appfel-Marglin and S. A. Marglin. Oxford: Clarendon Press, 1990.

Barber, Benjamin R. *Jihad vs. McWorld*. New York: Times Books, 1995.

Barker, Stephen, ed. *Excavations and Their Objects: Freud's Collection of Antiquity*. Albany: State University of New York Press, 1996.

Barrow, T. "Introduction to the New Edition." Pp. xvii–xxiv in C. A. S. Williams, *Outlines of Chinese Symbolism and Art Motives*, 3rd ed. Rutland, VT: Charles E. Tuttle, 1974.

Bastide, Roger. "Mémoire collective et sociologie du Bricolage." *L'Année Sociologique* 211 (1970).

Bateson, Gregory. *Steps to an Ecology of Mind*. San Francisco: Chandler, 1972.

Baudet, H. *Paradise on Earth: Some Thoughts on European Images of Non-European Man*. New Haven, CT: Yale University Press, 1965.

Bauman, Zygmunt. *Modernity and the Holocaust*. Ithaca, NY: Cornell University Press, 1989.

———. *Globalization: The Human Consequences*. Cambridge: Polity, 1998.

Bayart, François. *L'état en Afrique: La politique du ventre*. Paris: Fayard, 1992.

Bayly, C. A. *The Birth of the Modern World, 1780–1914*. Oxford: Blackwell, 2004.

Beale, D. *Driven by Nissan? A Critical Guide to New Management Techniques*. London: Lawrence and Wishart, 1999.

Beck, Ulrich. *What Is Globalization?* Oxford: Blackwell, 2000.

Bell-Fialkoff, Andrew. "A Brief History of Ethnic Cleansing." *Foreign Affairs* 72, no. 3 (1993): 110–21.

Bello, Walden. *The Future in the Balance: Essays on Globalization and Resistance*, edited by A. Mittal. San Francisco: Food First, 2001.

Belting, Hans. "Contemporary Art as Global Art: A Critical Estimate." Pp. 38–73 in *The Global Art World: Audiences, Markets, and Museums*, edited by H. Belting and A. Buddensieg. Ostfildern, Germany: Hatje Cantz Verlag, 2009.

Benedict, R. *Patterns of Culture*. London: Routledge and Kegan Paul, 1935.

Benn, Denis, and Kenneth Hall, eds. *Globalization: A Calculus of Inequality, Perspectives from the South*. Kingston, Jamaica: Ian Randle, 2000.

Berger, Peter L. "Introduction: The Cultural Dynamics of Globalization." Pp. 1–16 in *Many Globalizations: Cultural Diversity in the Contemporary World*, edited by Peter Berger and S. P. Huntington. Oxford: Oxford University Press, 2002.

Bernal, M. *Black Athena: Afroasiatic Roots of Classical Civilization; The Fabrication of Ancient Greece, 1785–1985*. London: Free Association Press, 1987.

Bérubé, Michael. "Hybridity in the Center: An Interview with Houston A. Baker, Jr." *African American Review* 26, no. 4 (1992): 547–64.

Bestor, T. C. "How Sushi Went Global." *Foreign Policy*, May 2008.

Bhabha, Homi K. "Dissemination: Time, Narrative and the Margins of the Modern Nation." In *Nation and Narration*, edited by Homi K. Bhabha. London: Routledge, 1990.

Bhagwati, Jagdish. *A Stream of Windows: Unsettling Reflections on Trade, Immigration and Democracy*. Cambridge: MIT Press, 1997.

———. "Borders beyond Control." *Foreign Affairs* 82, no. 1 (2003): 98–104.

Bhargava, Rajeev. "Forms of Secularity before Secularism: The Political Morality of Ashoka and Akbar." Pp. 94–120 in *Worlds of Difference*, edited by S. A. Arjomand and E. Reis. London: Sage, 2013.

Bhavnani, Kum Kum. "Rassismen Entgegnen: Querverbindungen und Hybridität." Pp. 186–203 in *Gegen-Rassismen*, edited by B. Kossek. Hamburg: Argument Verlag, 1999.

Billington, James H. *Fire in the Minds of Men: The Origins of the Revolutionary Faith*. New York: Basic Books, 1980.

Bird, Jon, Barry Curtis, Tim Putman, George Robertson, and Lisa Tickner, eds. *Mapping the Futures: Local Cultures, Global Change*. London: Routledge, 1993.

Bista, Dor B. *Fatalism and Development: Nepal's Struggle for Modernization*. Calcutta: Orient Longman, 1994.

Blue, Gregory. "Gobineau on China: Race Theory, the 'Yellow Peril,' and the Critique of Modernity." *Journal of World History* 10, no. 1 (1999): 93–139.

Bor, Joep. "Studying World Music: The Next Phase." Unpublished paper, 1994.

Botev, Nikolai. "Where East Meets West: Ethnic Intermarriage in the Former Yugoslavia, 1962 to 1989." *American Sociological Review* 59 (1994): 461–80.

Boyer, Robert, and Daniel Drache, eds. *States against Markets: The Limits of Globalization*. London: Routledge, 1996.

Brah, Avtah, and Annie Coombes, eds. *Hybridity and Its Discontents*. London: Routledge, 2000.

Brennan, Timothy. *Salman Rushdie and the Third World: Myths of the Nation*. New York: St. Martin's Press, 1989.

Bressan, L. "Mughal-Christian Miniatures." Pp. 37–78 in *Intercultural Encounter in Mughal Miniatures*, edited by K. A. Ahmed. Lahore: National College of Arts, 1995.

Brown, P. L. "At Muslim Prom, It's a Girls-Only Night Out." *New York Times*, 6 September 2003: A1, 20.

Browne, A. "China Bank Chief Cautions the US." *Wall Street Journal*, 4 April 2012: A10.

Bruignac-La Hougue, V. de, et al. *Touches d'exotisme, XIV–XX siècles*. Paris: Union Centrale des Arts Décoratifs, 1998.

Bryman, A. *The Disneyization of Society*. Thousand Oaks, CA: Pine Forge Press, 2004.

Budde, H. "Japanische Farbholzschnitte und Europäische Kunst: Maler und Sammler im 19. Jahrhundert." In *Japan und Europa 1543–1929*, edited by D. Croissant et al. Berlin: Berliner Festspiele/Argon, 1993.

Caine, Barbara, Elisabeth A. Grosz, and Marie De Lepervanche, eds. *Crossing Boundaries: Feminisms and the Critique of Knowledges*. Sydney: Allen and Unwin, 1988.

Calderón, F. "América Latina, Identitad y Tiempos Mixtos, o Cómo Pensar La Modernidad Sin Dejar de Ser Boliviano." Pp. 225–29 in *Imágenes Desconocidas*. Buenos Aires: Ed. CLACSO, 1988.

Camilleri, Joseph A., and Chandra Muzaffar, eds. *Globalization: The Perspectives and Experiences of the Religious Traditions of Asia Pacific*. Petaling Jaya, Malaysia: International Movement for a Just World, 1998.

Canclini, García Nestor. *Hybrid Cultures*. Minneapolis: University of Minnesota Press, 1995.

———. "A Re-imagined Public Art on the Border." In *Intromisiones Compartidas: Arte y Sociedad en la Frontera Mexico/Estados Unidos*, edited by N. G. Canclini and J. M. V. Arce. San Diego, Tijuana: Conaculta, Fonca, 2000.

Canevacci, Massimo. "Image Accumulation and Cultural Syncretism." *Theory, Culture and Society* 9, no. 3 (1992): 95–110.

———. "Fragmented Identity, Governmental Policy and Cultural Syncretism." Unpublished paper, 1993.

Carboni, Stefano. *Venice and the Islamic World, 828–1797*. New Haven, CT: Yale University Press, 2007.

Cashmore, Ellis. *Dictionary of Race and Ethnic Relations*. 4th ed. London: Routledge, 1996.

———. "The Impure Strikes Back." *British Journal of Sociology* 54, no. 3 (2003): 407–14.

Castles, Stephen. "Globalization and Migration: Some Pressing Contradictions." *International Social Science Journal* 50, no. 2 (1998): 179–86.

Cavalli-Sforza, L. L. *Genes, Peoples, and Languages*. New York: Farrar, Straus & Giroux, 2000.

Cerny, Philip G. *The Changing Architecture of Politics: Structure, Agency and the Future of the State.* London: Sage, 1990.

Chan Kwok-bun, ed. *East-West Identities: Globalization, Localization, and Hybridization.* Leiden: Brill, 2007.

———. *Hybridity: Promises and Limits.* Whitby, ON: De Sitter, 2011.

Chase-Dunn, Christopher, and Thomas D. Hall. "Comparing World-Systems: Concepts and Working Hypotheses." *Social Forces* 72, no. 1 (1993): 851–86.

Chideya, Farai. *The Color of Our Future: Race for the 21st Century.* New York: Quill, 1999.

Cinar, Alev. *Modernity, Secularism, and Islam in Turkey: Bodies, Places, and Time.* Minneapolis: University of Minnesota Press, 2005.

Cisler, Steve. "Arts, Crafts, and Globalization." *Switch,* 2005.

Clark, Robert P. *The Global Imperative: An Interpretive History of the Spread of Humankind.* Boulder, CO: Westview Press, 1997.

Clarke, John J. *Oriental Enlightenment: The Encounter between Asian and Western Thought.* London: Routledge, 1997.

Clifford, James. "Mixed Feelings." Pp. 362–70 in *Cosmopolitics,* edited by P. Cheah and B. Robbins. Minneapolis: University of Minnesota Press, 1998.

Cohen, David. "Bay, Spielberg and Paramount Kowtow for Cash." *Variety,* 3 July 2014.

Cohen, Warren I. *East Asia at the Center: Four Thousand Years of Engagement with the World.* New York: Columbia University Press, 2000.

Cohn, Norman. *Cosmos, Chaos, and the World to Come: The Ancient Roots of Apocalyptic Faith.* New Haven, CT: Yale University Press, 1993.

Coll, Steve. *The Bin Ladens: An Arabian Family in the American Century.* New York: Penguin, 2008.

Comaroff, Jean, and John L. Comaroff, eds. *Millennial Capitalism and the Culture of Neoliberalism.* Durham, NC: Duke University Press, 2001.

Connell, Raewyn. "The Shores of the Southern Ocean: Steps toward a World Sociology of Modernity, with Australian Examples." Pp. 58–72 in *Worlds of Difference,* edited by S. A. Arjomand and E. Reis. London: Sage, 2013.

Connolly, William E. *Identity/Difference: Democratic Negotiations of Political Paradox.* Ithaca, NY: Cornell University Press, 1991.

Connors, Michael. *The Race to the Intelligent State: Charting the Global Information Economy in the 21st Century.* Oxford: Capstone, 1997.

Conor, Bernard E. *Japan's New Colony: America.* Greenwich, CT: Perkins Press, 1991.

Cooperrider, David L., and Jane E. Dutton, eds. *Organizational Dimensions of Global Change: No Limits to Cooperation.* London: Sage, 1999.

Cotterell, Arthur. *The First Emperor of China.* London: Penguin, 1981.

Cowen, Tyler. *Creative Destruction: How Globalization Is Changing the World's Cultures.* Princeton, NJ: Princeton University Press, 2002.

Cox, Robert W. "Global Perestroika." Pp. 26–43 in *New World Order? Socialist Register 1992*, edited by Ralph Miliband and Leo Panitch. London: Merlin Press, 1992.

Crothers, Lane. *Globalization and American Popular Culture*. 2nd ed. Lanham, MD: Rowman & Littlefield, 2010.

Csete, Anne. "China's Ethnicities: State Ideology and Policy in Historical Perspective." Pp. 287–308 in *Global Multiculturalism: Comparative Perspectives on Ethnicity, Race, and Nation*, edited by G. H. Cornwell and E. W. Stoddard. Lanham, MD: Rowman & Littlefield, 2001.

Cullen, Lisa Takeuchi. "When Eat Meets West." *Time*, 28 January 2008: 44–46.

Curtin, Philip D. *Cross-Cultural Trade in World History*. Cambridge: Cambridge University Press, 1984.

Dahrendorf, Ralf. *Pfade Aus Utopia*. München: Piper, 1967.

Dainotto, R. M. *Europe (In Theory)*. Durham, NC: Duke University Press, 2007.

Dallmayr, Fred R. *Achieving Our World: Toward a Global and Plural Democracy*. Lanham, MD: Rowman & Littlefield, 2001.

Dathorne, O. R. *Asian Voyages: Two Thousand Years of Constructing the Other*. Westport, CT: Bergin and Harvey, 1996.

Deacon, Bob, M. Hulse, and P. Stubbs. *Global Social Policy*. London: Sage, 1998.

Delanty, G., ed. *Europe and Asia beyond East and West: Towards a New Cosmopolitanism*. London: Routledge, 2006.

Deleuze, George, and Felix Guattari. *Anti-Oedipus: Capitalism and Schizophrenia*. New York: Viking Press, 1984.

Denitch, Bogdan. *Ethnic Nationalism: The Tragic Death of Yugoslavia*. Minneapolis: University of Minnesota Press, 1994.

Dewulf, Jeroen. "From the Polders to the Mangroves: A Polycentric View on Dutch Language and Culture." *Interdisciplinary Journal for Germanic Linguistics and Semiotic Analysis* 11, no. 1 (2006): 19–34.

———. "As a Tupi-Indian, Playing the Lute: Hybridity as Anthropophagy." Pp. 81–97 in *Reconstructing Hybridity: Post-Colonial Studies in Transition*, edited by J. Kuortti and J. Nyman. Amsterdam: Rodopi, 2007.

Dietz, Gunther. "Frontier Hybridization or Culture Clash? Transnational Migrant Communities and Sub-national Identity Politics in Andalusia, Spain." Working Paper 35. La Jolla: University of California at San Diego, Center for Comparative Immigration Studies, 2001.

Dikötter, Frank. *The Discourse of Race in Modern China*. Stanford, CA: Stanford University Press, 1992.

Dirlik, Arif. "The Postcolonial Aura: Third World Criticism in the Age of Global Capitalism." *Critical Inquiry* (Winter 1992): 328–56.

Dirlik, Arif, Vinay Bahl, and Peter Gran, eds. *History after the Three Worlds: Post-Eurocentric Historiographies*. Lanham, MD: Rowman & Littlefield, 2000.

Dobbin, Christine. *Asian Entrepreneurial Minorities: Conjoint Communities in the Making of the World-Economy, 1570–1940*. Richmond, UK: Curzon Press, 1996.

Donnan, Shaw. "Ramadan Sees Finger-Licking Sales at Outlets for Fast Foods." *Financial Times*, 13 November 2003: 6.

Dower, J. *Japan in War and Peace: Essays on History, Race and Culture*. London: HarperCollins, 1995.

Doyle, Michael W. *Empires*. Ithaca, NY: Cornell University Press, 1986.

Drane, J. W., ed. *The McDonaldization of the Church: Consumer Culture and the Church's Future*. London: Smyth & Helwys, 2002.

Dyer, G. "Washington Split over Working with Beijing on Infrastructure." *Financial Times*, 6 August 2014: 3.

Eisenstadt, Shmuel N., ed. *Multiple Modernities*. New Brunswick, NJ: Transaction Books, 2002.

Elverskog, Johan. *Our Great Qing: The Mongols, Buddhism, and the State in Late Imperial China*. Honolulu: University of Hawaii Press, 2006.

Enloe, Cynthia. *Bananas, Beaches, and Bases: Making Feminist Sense of International Politics*. Berkeley: University of California Press, 1989.

Etzioni, Amitai. "Other Americans Help Break Down Racial Barriers." *International Herald Tribune*, 10 May 1997.

Falk, Richard. *On Humane Governance: Towards a New Global Politics*. Cambridge: Polity, 1994.

Fanon, Franz. *The Wretched of the Earth*. Harmondsworth, UK: Penguin, 1967.

Fears, D. "Racial Label Surprises Latino Immigrants." *Guardian Weekly*, 9–15 January 2003: 29.

Featherstone, Mike, ed. *Global Culture: Nationalism, Globalization and Modernity*. London: Sage, 1990.

Featherstone, Mike, Scott Lash, and Roland Robertson, eds. *Global Modernities*. London: Sage, 1995.

Februari, Vernon A. *Mind Your Colour: The "Coloured" Stereotype in South African Literature*. London: Kegan Paul International, 1981.

Feddema, R. "Op Weg tussen Hoop en Vrees: De levensoriëntatie van jonge Turken en Marokkanen in Nederland." Utrecht University, Ph.D. diss., 1992.

Feinberg, W. *Japan and the Pursuit of a New American Identity: Work and Education in a Multicultural Age*. New York: Routledge, 1993.

Ferchen, Matt. "Whose China Model Is It Anyway? The Contentious Search for Consensus." *Review of International Political Economy* 20, no. 2 (2013): 390–420.

Findley, C. V. *The Turks in World History*. London: Oxford University Press, 2005.

Fischer, M. M. J. "Orientalizing America: Beginnings and Middle Passages." *Middle East Report* 22, no. 5 (1992): 32–37.

Fishman, Ted C. *China, Inc.* New York: Scribner, 2005.

Fitzgerald, C. P. "The History of China to 1840." Pp. 103–46 in *China's Three Thousand Years*, edited by L. Heren et al. New York: Collier, 1973.

Fletcher, M. A. "Tiger Woods and the Melting Pot: New Categories Break the Mold." *International Herald Tribune*, 24 April 1997.

Florida, Richard. *Who's Your City?* New York: Basic Books, 2008.

Foster-Carter, Aidan. "The Modes of Production Controversy." *New Left Review* 107 (1978): 47–77.

Frank, Andre Gunder. *Re-Orient: Global Economy in the Asian Age.* Berkeley: University of California Press, 1998.

French, Howard W. *China's Second Continent: How a Million Migrants Are Building a New Empire in Africa.* New York: Alfred A. Knopf, 2014.

Friedman, Jonathan. "Being in the World: Globalization and Localization." Pp. 311–28 in *Global Culture*, edited by Mike Featherstone. London: Sage, 1990.

——. *Cultural Identity and Global Process.* London: Sage, 1994.

——. "Global Crises, the Struggle for Cultural Identity and Intellectual Pork-barrelling: Cosmopolitans versus Locals, Ethnics and Nationals in an Era of De-Hegemonisation." Pp. 70–89 in *Debating Cultural Hybridity*, edited by Pnina Werbner and Tariq Modood. London: Zed, 1997.

——. "The Hybridization of Roots and the Abhorrence of the Bush." Pp. 230–55 in *Spaces of Culture: City–Nation–World*, edited by Mike Featherstone and Scott Lash. London: Sage, 1999.

Frow, John. "The Concept of the Popular." *New Formations* 18 (1992): 25–38.

Fulin, Chi, ed. *Change of China's Development Models at the Crossroads.* Beijing: China Intercontinental Press, 2010.

Fusco, C. *English Is Broken Here: Notes on Cultural Fusion on the Americas.* New York: New Press, 1995.

Galtung, Johan. "Structure, Culture and Intellectual Style." *Social Science Information* 206, no. 6 (1981): 816–56.

Gamble, C. *Timewalkers: The Prehistory of Global Colonization.* London: Penguin, 1993.

Gaonkar, Dilip P., ed. *Alternative Modernities.* Durham, NC: Duke University Press, 2001.

Garrahan, M., and J. Leahy. "Guru Love: Bollywood Looks to Spielberg to 'Create New Magic.'" *Financial Times*, 21–22 June 2008: 8.

Garrett, B. "China Faces, Debates the Contradictions of Globalization." *Asian Survey* 41, no. 3 (2001): 409–27.

Giddens, Anthony. *The Consequences of Modernity.* Stanford, CA: Stanford University Press, 1990.

Ginneken, Jaap van. *Understanding Global News.* London: Sage, 1998.

Glenny, Misha. *McMafia: A Journey through the Global Criminal Underworld.* New York: Vintage, 2009.

Goethe, J. W. von. *West-Östlicher Divan.* Leipzig: Insel Verlag, 1972.

Göle, Nilufer. "Snapshots of Islamic Modernities." *Daedalus* 129, no. 1 (2000): 91–117.

Gombrich, E. H. *The Sense of Order: A Study in the Psychology of Decorative Art.* Ithaca, NY: Cornell University Press, 1984.

González Alcantud, José A. *Agresión y Rito y Otros Ensayos de Antropología Andaluza*. Granada: Biblioteca de Etnología, 1993.

Goodman, David, and Michael J. Watts, eds. *Globalising Food: Agrarian Questions and Global Restructuring*. London: Routledge, 1997.

Goody, Jack. *The East in the West*. Cambridge: Cambridge University Press, 1996.

———. "Europe and Islam." Pp. 138–47 in *Europe and Asia beyond East and West*, edited by G. Delanty. London: Routledge, 2006.

———. *The Eurasian Miracle*. Cambridge: Polity, 2010.

Goonatilake, Susantha. *The Evolution of Information: Lineages in Gene, Culture and Artifact*. London: Pinter, 1991.

———. *Toward a Global Science*. Bloomington: Indiana University Press, 1999.

Gopal, S. "Images of World Society: A Third World View." *Social Science Information Journal* 24, no. 1 (1998): 375–79.

Gottdiener, Mark, ed. *New Forms of Consumption: Consumers, Culture, and Commodification*. Lanham, MD: Rowman & Littlefield, 2000.

Graham, R., ed. *The Idea of Race in Latin America, 1870–1940*. Austin: University of Texas Press, 1990.

Grandis, Rita de, and Zila Bernd, eds. *Unforeseeable Americas: Questioning Cultural Hybridity in the Americas*. Amsterdam: Rodopi, 2000.

Grant, Jeremy. "Golden Arches Bridge Local Tastes." *Financial Times*, 9 February 2006: 10.

Gray, H. P. "Globalization versus Nationhood." *Development and International Cooperation* 9, no. 16 (1993).

Greenfeld, K. T. *Speed Tribes: Children of the Japanese Bubble*. London: Boxtree, 1994.

Greenfield, L. *Nationalism: Five Roads to Modernity*. Cambridge, MA: Harvard University Press, 1992.

Griffin, Keith. "Culture, Human Development and Economic Growth." Working Paper in Economics 96–17. Riverside: University of California, Riverside, 1996.

———. "Culture and Economic Growth: The State and Globalization." Pp. 189–202 in *Global Futures*, edited by Jan Nederveen Pieterse. London: Zed, 2000.

Griffin, Keith, and A. Rahman Khan. *Globalization and the Developing World*. Geneva: UNRISD, 1992.

Grosso, Michael. *The Millennium Myth: Love and Death and the End of Time*. Wheaton, IL: Quest Books, 1995.

Group of Lisbon. *Limits to Competition*. Cambridge: MIT Press, 1995.

Gruzinski, Serge. *La Pensée Métisse*. Paris: Fayard, 1999. [*The Mestizo Mind: The Intellectual Dynamics of Colonization and Globalization*. New York: Routledge, 2002.]

Gunn, G. C. *First Globalization: The Eurasian Exchange, 1500–1800*. Lanham, MD: Rowman & Littlefield, 2003.

Gurnah, Ahmed. "Elvis in Zanzibar." Pp. 116–41 in *The Limits of Globalization*, edited by A. Scott. London: Routledge, 1997.

Gurtov, M. *Global Politics in the Human Interest*. 3rd ed. Boulder, CO: Lynne Rienner, 1994.

Guthrie, Doug. *China and Globalization: The Social, Economic, and Political Transformation of Chinese Society*. New York: Routledge, 2006.

Hamelink, Cees. *Cultural Autonomy in Global Communications*. New York: Longman, 1983.

Hannerz, Ulf. "The World in Creolisation." *Africa* 57, no. 4 (1987): 546–59.

——. "Culture between Center and Periphery: Toward a Macroanthropology." *Ethnos* 54 (1989): 200–216.

——. *Cultural Complexity*. New York: Columbia University Press, 1992.

Harney, Alexandra. *The China Price*. London: Penguin, 2009.

Harris, Nigel. *National Liberation*. London: I. B. Tauris, 1990.

Harrison, John A. *The Chinese Empire*. New York: Harcourt Brace Jovanovich, 1972.

Harrison, Lawrence E., and Samuel P. Huntington, eds. *Culture Matters: How Values Shape Human Progress*. New York: Basic Books, 2000.

Harvey, David. *The Condition of Postmodernity*. Oxford: Blackwell, 1989.

Harvey, Penelope. *Hybrids of Modernity: Anthropology, the Nation State and the Universal Exhibition*. London: Routledge, 1996.

Hau, Caroline S. "Becoming 'Chinese' in Southeast Asia." Pp. 175–206 in *Sinicization and the rise of China*, edited by P. J. Katzenstein. New York: Routledge, 2012.

Haw, Stephen. *China: A Cultural History*. London: Batsford, 1990.

Hay, D. *Europe: The Emergence of an Idea*. Edinburgh: Edinburgh University Press, 1957.

Hayan, Hu. "China Fast-Tracking Its Way to Global Railway Success." *Wall Street Journal*, 31 July 2014: A10.

Hayan, Hu, Song Wenwei, and Zhou Furong. "Business Hotspot: Suzhou." *China Daily*, 18–24 July 2014: 16.

Hechter, Michael. *Internal Colonialism: The Celtic Fringe in British National Development, 1536–1966*. London: Routledge and Kegan Paul, 1975.

Held, David. "Democracy: From City-States to a Cosmopolitan Order?" Pp. 13–52 in *Prospects for Democracy*, edited by D. Held. Cambridge: Polity, 1992.

——. *Democracy and Global Order*. Cambridge: Polity, 1995.

——. *Globalization/Anti-Globalization*. Oxford, Blackwell, 2002.

Held, David, Anthony McGrew, David Goldblatt, and J. Perraton. *Global Transformations*. Cambridge: Polity, 1999.

Helly, D. O., and S. M. Reverby, eds. *Gendered Domains: Rethinking Public and Private in Women's History*. Ithaca, NY: Cornell University Press, 1992.

Henderson, J. *The Globalisation of High Technology Production*. London: Routledge, 1993.

Hickman, Jacob. "'Is It the Spirit or the Body?' Syncretism of Health Beliefs among Hmong Immigrants to Alaska." *Anthrosource, NAPA Bulletin*, no. 27 (2007): 176–95.

Hill, John. *Through the Jade Gate to Rome: A Study of the Silk Routes during the Later Han Dynasty*. Charleston, SC: BookSurge, 2011.

Hines, Colin. *Localization: A Global Manifesto*. London: Earthscan, 2001.

Hirsch, H. *Genocide and the Politics of Memory: Studying Death to Preserve Life*. Chapel Hill: University of North Carolina Press, 1995.

Hirst, Paul Q., and Grahame Thompson. *Globalization in Question*. Cambridge: Polity, 1996.

Hitchings, Henry. *The Secret Life of Words: How English Became English*. New York: Farrar, Straus & Giroux, 2008.

Hobson, John M. *The Eastern Origins of Western Civilization*. Cambridge: Cambridge University Press, 2004.

Hodgson, Marshall G. S. *The Venture of Islam: Conscience and History in a World Civilization*. 3 vols. Chicago: University of Chicago Press, 1974.

Hoerder, Dirk. *Cultures in Contact: World Migrations in the Second Millennium*. Durham, NC: Duke University Press, 2002.

Horton, Robin. *La Pensée Métisse: Croyances Africaines et rationalité occidentale en questions*. Paris: Presses Universitaires de France, 1990.

Hösle, V. "The Third World as a Philosophical Problem." *Social Research* 59, no. 2 (1992): 227–62.

Howe, Stephen. *Afrocentrism: Mythical Pasts and Imagined Homes*. London: Verso, 1998.

Huff, Toby E. *The Rise of Early Modern Science: Islam, China and the West*. Cambridge: Cambridge University Press, 2003.

Hughes, H. S. *Consciousness and Society: The Reorientation of European Social Thought, 1890–1913*. New York: Vintage, 1958.

Huntington, Samuel P. *The Third Wave: Democratization in the Late Twentieth Century*. Norman: Oklahoma University Press, 1991.

———. "The Clash of Civilizations." *Foreign Affairs* 72, no. 3 (1993): 22–49.

———. *The Clash of Civilizations and the Remaking of World Order*. New York: Simon and Schuster, 1996.

———. "The Lonely Superpower." *Foreign Affairs* 78, no. 2 (1999): 35–49.

Hutton, Will. *China and the West in the 21st Century*. London: Abacus, 2007.

Hyun, Peter. *In the New World: The Making of a Korean American*. Honolulu: University of Hawaii Press, 1995.

Ibrahim, Anwar. *The Asian Renaissance*. Singapore: Times Books, 1996.

Inglis, David, and Roland Robertson. "Discovering the World: Cosmopolitanism and Globality in the 'Eurasian' Renaissance." Pp. 92–106 in *Europe and Asia beyond East and West*, edited by G. Delanty. London: Routledge, 2006.

Iriye, Akira. *Cultural Internationalism and World Order*. Baltimore: Johns Hopkins University Press, 1997.

Issenberg, Sasha. *The Sushi Economy: Globalization and the Making of a Modern Delicacy*. New York: Gotham Books, 2007.

Iyer, Pico. *The Global Soul: Jet Lag, Shopping Malls, and the Search for Home.* New York: Alfred A. Knopf, 2000.

Jacquin, D., A. Oros, and M. Verweij. "Culture in International Relations." *Millennium* 22, no. 3 (1993): 375–77.

Jameson, Frederick. *Postmodernism, or the Cultural Logic of Late Capitalism.* London: Verso, 1991.

Jameson, Frederick, and M. Miyoshi, eds. *The Cultures of Globalization.* Durham, NC: Duke University Press, 1998.

Jewsiewicki, Bogumil. *Cheri Samba: The Hybridity of Art.* Edited by Esther Dagan. Montreal: Galérie Amrad African Art Publications, 1995.

Jia, Cui. "China Studying New Silk Road Rail Link to Pakistan." *China Daily,* 28 June 2014: 6.

Jiao, Wu. "Xi Greets Kazakh Students Studying Silk Road." *China Daily,* 25 June 2014: 2.

Jing, Shi. "Machines Steal the Show at Robotics Expo." *China Daily,* 10 July 2014: 13.

Johanson, Graeme, and Tom Denison. "The Chinese in Prato: Islands in the Stream, Globalization and Community." *Around the Globe* 4, no. 3 (2008): 32–36.

Johanson, Graeme, and Russell Smyth, eds. *Living Outside the Walls: The Chinese in Prato.* Cambridge: Cambridge Scholars Publishing, 2008.

Johnson, Chalmers. *Blowback: The Costs and Consequences of American Empire.* New York: Henry Holt, 2000.

Just World Trust. *Dominance of the West over the Rest.* Penang, Malaysia: JUST, 1995.

Kaltman, Blaine. *Under the Heel of the Dragon: Islam, Racism, Crime, and the Uighur in China.* Athens: Ohio University Press, 2007.

Kamali, Masoud. "Middle Eastern Modernities, Islam and Cosmopolitanism." Pp. 161–77 in *Europe and Asia beyond East and West,* edited by G. Delanty. London: Routledge, 2006.

Kaplan, Robert D. *The Ends of the Earth.* New York: Random House, 1996.

Karl, Terry L. "The Hybrid Regimes of Central America." *Journal of Democracy* 6, no. 3 (1995): 72–86.

Katenstein, Peter J., ed. *Sinicization and the Rise of China: Civilizational Processes beyond East and West.* New York: Routledge, 2012.

Kavolis, V. "Contemporary Moral Cultures and the 'Return of the Sacred.'" *Sociological Analysis* 49, no. 3 (1988): 203–16.

Keping, Yu. "Americanization, Westernization, Sinification: Modernization or Globalization in China." Pp. 134–49 in *Global America? The Cultural Consequences of Globalization,* edited by U. Beck and N. Sznaider. Liverpool: University of Liverpool Press, 2003.

Keys, Donald. *Earth at Omega: Passage to Planetization.* Boston: Branden Press, 1982.

Khalaf, Roula. "Arab Women Fall for Soap's Turkish Delight." *Financial Times*, 30–31 August 2008: 4.

King, Anthony D. *Urbanism, Colonialism, and the World Economy: Cultural and Spatial Foundations of the World Urban System*. London: Routledge, 1990.

———. "Introduction: Spaces of Culture, Spaces of Knowledge." Pp. 1–18 in *Culture, Globalization and the World-System*, edited by Anthony D. King. Basingstoke, UK: Macmillan, 1991a.

———, ed. *Culture, Globalization and the World-System: Contemporary Conditions for the Representation of Identity*. Basingstoke, UK: Macmillan, 1991b.

———. "The Times and Spaces of Modernity (or Who Needs Postmodernism?)." Pp. 108–23 in *Global Modernities*, edited by Featherstone et al. London: Sage, 1995.

———, ed. *Representing the City: Ethnicity, Capital and Culture in the 21st Century Metropolis*. Houndmills, UK: Macmillan, 1996.

Kobrin, Stephen J. "Back to the Future: Neomedievalism and the Postmodern Digital World Economy." *Journal of International Affairs* 51, no. 2 (1998): 361–86.

Kossek, Brigitte, ed. *Gegen-Rassismen*. Hamburg: Argument Verlag, 1999.

Kosuka, Masataka, ed. *Japan's Choice: New Globalism and Cultural Orientation in an Industrial State*. London: Pinter, 1989.

Kothari, Rajni. *Rethinking Development*. Delhi: Ajanta, 1988.

Kotkin, Joel. *Tribes: How Race, Religion, and Identity Determine Success in the New Global Economy*. New York: Random House, 1992.

Kraidy, Marwan M. *Hybridity, or the Cultural Logic of Globalization*. Philadelphia: Temple University Press, 2005.

Kreidt, D. "Kann Uns Zum Vaterland die Fremde Werden? Exotismus im Schauspieltheater." Pp. 248–55 in *Exotische Welten, Europäische Phantasien*. Wurttemberg: Cantz, 1987.

Krishna, Anirudh, and J. Nederveen Pieterse. "Hierarchical Integration: The Dollar Economy and the Rupee Economy." *Development and Change* 39, no. 2 (2008): 219–37.

Kristof, Nicholas D. "Love and Race." *New York Times*, 6 December 2002a: A33.

———. "Saudis in Bikinis." *New York Times*, 25 October 2002b: A35.

Krugman, Paul. "Coming Down to Earth." *New York Times*, 19 May 2006.

Kubik, Gerhard. *Africa and the Blues*. Jackson: University Press of Mississippi, 1999.

Küng, Hans. *Global Ethics for Global Politics and Economics*. Oxford: Oxford University Press, 1997.

La Ferla, Ruth. "Generation E.A.: Ethnically Ambiguous." *New York Times*, 28 December 2003: 9.1–9.

Lavie, Smadar. "Blow-ups in the Borderzones: Third World Israeli Authors' Gropings for Home." *New Formations* 18 (1992): 84–106.

Lee, Jennifer 8. *The Fortune Cookie Chronicles: Adventures in the World of Chinese Food*. New York: Twelve, 2008.

Leege, D. C., K. D. Wald, B. S. Krueger, and P. D. Mueller. *The Politics of Cultural Differences: Social Change and Voter Mobilization Strategies in the Post–New Deal Period*. Princeton, NJ: Princeton University Press, 2002.

Leong, Karen. "Oriental Haute Couture." *Financial Times*, 9–10 August 2008: 6.

LeVine, Mark. *Heavy Metal Islam: Rock, Resistance, and the Struggle for the Soul of Islam*. New York: Three Rivers Press, 2008.

Lewis, Bernard. *What Went Wrong? The Clash between Islam and Modernity in the Middle East*. New York: Oxford University Press, 2002.

Li, Liu. "Theoretical Theses on 'Social Modernization.'" *International Sociology* 4, no. 4 (1989): 365–78.

Lieberman, Victor, ed. *Beyond Binary Histories: Re-imagining Eurasia to c. 1830*. Ann Arbor: University of Michigan Press, 1999.

Light, Ivan, and S. Karageorgis. "The Ethnic Economy." Pp. 647–71 in *The Handbook of Economic Sociology*, edited by N. J. Smelser and R. Swedberg. Princeton, NJ: Princeton University Press, 1994.

Linke, Uli. *Blood and Nation: The European Aesthetics of Race*. Philadelphia: University of Pennsylvania Press, 1999.

Lipschutz, Ronald D. "Reconstructing World Politics: The Emergence of Global Civil Society." *Millennium* 21, no. 3 (1992): 389–420.

Lipset, Seymour Martin. *American Exceptionalism: A Double-Edged Sword*. New York: Norton, 1996.

Liu, Hong. "Old Linkages, New Networks: The Globalization of Overseas Chinese Voluntary Associations and Its Implications." *China Quarterly* 155 (1998): 582–609.

Liu Kang. *Globalization and Cultural Trends in China*. Honolulu: University of Hawaii Press, 2004.

Lixin, Xiao. "*Transformers* Highest-Grossing Film in China." *China Daily*, 9 July 2014: 3.

Loewenberg, Peter. "The Pagan Freud." Pp. 13–32 in *Excavations and Their Objects: Freud's Collection of Antiquity*, edited by S. Barker. Albany: State University of New York Press, 1996.

London, S. "Crossing Borders: An Interview with Richard Rodriguez." *Sun*, August 1997.

Longworth, Richard. *Caught in the Middle: America's Heartland in the Age of Globalism*. New York: Bloomsbury, 2008.

Lowe, Lisa. "Heterogeneity, Hybridity, Multiplicity: Marking Asian American Differences." *Diaspora* 1, no. 1 (1991): 24–44.

Lowe, Lisa, and David Lloyd, eds. *The Politics of Culture in the Shadow of Capital*. Durham, NC: Duke University Press, 1997a.

———. "Introduction." Pp. 1–32 in *Politics of Culture*, edited by Lisa Lowe and David Lloyd. Durham, NC: Duke University Press, 1997b.

Lummis, Douglas C. "Ruth Benedict's Obituary for Japanese Culture." *Japan Focus*, 23 July 2007, www.japanfocus.org.

MacDougall, H. A. *Racial Myth in English History: Trojans, Teutons and Anglo-Saxons*. Montreal: Harvest House, 1982.

Mack, Rosamond E. *Bazaar to Piazza: Islamic Trade and Italian Art, 1300–1600*. Berkeley: University of California Press, 2002.

Mackenzie, J. *Orientalism: History, Theory and the Arts*. Manchester: Manchester University Press, 1995.

Mahathir, Mohamad, and S. Ishihara. *The Voice of Asia*. Tokyo: Kodansha International, 1995.

Mahtani, Minelle. "What's in a Name? Exploring the Employment of 'Mixed Race' as a Category." *Ethnicities* 2, no. 4 (2002): 469–90.

Mair, Victor H. *The Bronze Age and Early Iron Age Peoples of Eastern Central Asia*. Washington, DC: Institute for the Study of Man, 1998.

Malkani, Gautam. *Londonstani*. London: Penguin, 2006.

Malkki, Liisa. "National Geographic: The Rooting of Peoples and the Territorialization of National Identity among Scholars and Refugees." *Cultural Anthropology* 7, no. 1 (1992): 24–44.

———. "Citizens of Humanity: Internationalism and the Imagined Community of Nations." *Diaspora* 3, no. 1 (1994): 41–68.

Mallory, J. P. *In Search of the Indo-Europeans: Language, Archaeology and Myth*. London: Thames and Hudson, 1991.

Mander, Jerry, and Edward Goldsmith, eds. *The Case against the Global Economy and for a Turn toward the Local*. San Francisco: Sierra Club, 1996.

Mann, Michael. *The Sources of Social Power*. Cambridge: Cambridge University Press, 1986.

———. "Has Globalization Ended the Rise and Rise of the Nation State?" *Review of International Political Economy* 4, no. 3 (1997): 472–96.

Manning, Patrick. *Migration in World History*. London: Routledge, 2005.

Martin, Richard, and Harold Koda. *Orientalism: Visions of the East in Western Dress*. New York: Harry N. Abrams, 1995.

Massey, Doreen. "A Global Sense of Place." Pp. 232–40 in *Studying Culture*, edited by A. Gray and J. McGuigan. London: Edward Arnold, 1993.

Matsuda, Takeshi, ed. *The Age of Creolization in the Pacific: In Search of Emerging Cultures and Shared Values in the Japan-America Borderlands*. Hiroshima: Keisuisha, 2001.

Mazlish, Bruce, and Ralph Buultjens, eds. *Conceptualizing Global History*. Boulder, CO: Westview Press, 1993.

McGrew, Anthony G., and P. G. Lewis, eds. *Global Politics*. Cambridge: Polity, 1992.

McLaren, Peter. *Revolutionary Multiculturalism: Pedagogies of Dissent for the New Millennium*. Boulder, CO: Westview Press, 1997.

McLaren, Peter, and R. Farahmandpur. "Reconsidering Marx in Post-Marxist Times: A Requiem for Postmodernism?" *Educational Researcher* (2000): 25–33.

McMichael, Philip. *Development and Social Change: A Global Perspective*. Thousand Oaks, CA: Pine Forge Press, 1996.

McNeill, Desmond. "On Interdisciplinary Research: With Particular Reference to the Field of Environment and Development." *Higher Education Quarterly* 53, no. 4 (1999): 312–32.

McNeill, William. *Plagues and Peoples*. Oxford: Blackwell, 1977.

——. *The Pursuit of Power*. Chicago: University of Chicago Press, 1982.

Mei, Hua. *Chinese Clothing*. Beijing: China Intercontinental Press, 2004.

Melucci, Alberto. *Nomads of the Present*. London: Hutchinson Radius, 1989.

Miliband, Ralph, and Leo Panitch, eds. *New World Order? Socialist Register 1992*. London: Merlin Press, 1992.

Miller, Daniel. "A Theory of Christmas." Pp. 3–37 in *Unwrapping Christmas*, edited by D. Miller. Oxford: Oxford University Press, 1993.

——, ed. *Worlds Apart: Modernity through the Prism of the Local*. London: Routledge, 1995a.

——. "Introduction: Anthropology, Modernity and Consumption." Pp. 1–22 in *Worlds Apart*, edited by Daniel Miller. London: Routledge, 1995b.

——. *Capitalism: An Ethnographic Approach*. Oxford: Berg, 1997.

Milner, Helen. "International Political Economy: Beyond Hegemonic Stability." *Foreign Policy* 110 (1998): 112–23.

Mitchell, T. "McJihad: Islam in the US Global Order." *Social Text* 20, no. 4 (2002): 1–18.

Moody, A. "Unleashing the Power of Innovation." *China Daily*, 7 July 2014: 13.

Moore, M., and A. Buchanan, eds. *States, Nations and Borders: The Ethics of Making Boundaries*. Cambridge: Cambridge University Press, 2003.

Morley, David. "Postmodernism: The Highest Stage of Cultural Imperialism?" Pp. 133–57 in *Altered States: Postmodernism, Politics, Culture*, edited by M. Perryman. London: Lawrence and Wishart, 1994.

Morrison, A. J., D. A. Ricks, and K. Roth. "Globalization versus Regionalization: Which Way for the Multinational?" *Organizational Dynamics* (1991): 17–29.

Morse, E. L. *Modernization and the Transformation of International Relations*. New York: Free Press, 1976.

Moynihan, Daniel P. *Pandaemonium: Ethnicity in International Politics*. New York: Random House, 1993.

Nanda, Meera. "We Are All Hybrids Now: The Dangerous Epistemology of Post-Colonial Populism." *Journal of Peasant Studies* 282 (2001): 162–87.

Nandy, Ashis. *The Intimate Enemy: Loss and Recovery of Self under Colonialism*. New Delhi: Oxford University Press, 1983.

Navarro, Peter, and Greg Autry. *Death by China: Confronting the Dragon—A Global Call to Action*. Upper Saddle River, NJ: Pearson Prentice Hall, 2011.

Nederveen Pieterse, J. *Empire and Emancipation: Power and Liberation on a World Scale*. New York: Praeger, 1989.

——. *White on Black: Images of Africa and Blacks in Western Popular Culture.* New Haven, CT: Yale University Press, 1992.

——. "Unpacking the West: How European Is Europe?" Pp. 129–49 in *Racism, Modernity, Identity,* edited by A. Rattansi and S. Westwood. Cambridge: Polity, 1994.

——. "Globalization as Hybridization." Pp. 45–68 in *Global Modernities,* edited by Mike Featherstone et al. London: Sage, 1995.

——. "Globalization and Emancipation: From Local Empowerment to Global Reform." *New Political Economy* 2, no. 1 (1997): 79–92.

——. "Hybrid Modernities: Mélange Modernities in Asia." *Sociological Analysis* 1, no. 3 (1998a): 75–86.

——. "Sociology of Humanitarian Intervention: Bosnia, Rwanda and Somalia Compared." Pp. 230–65 in *Humanitarian Intervention and Beyond: World Orders in the Making,* edited by J. Nederveen Pieterse. London: Macmillan, 1998b.

——, ed. *Global Futures: Shaping Globalization.* London: Zed, 2000.

——. "Collective Action and Globalization." Pp. 21–40 in *Globalization and Social Movements,* edited by P. Hamel et al. London: Palgrave, 2001.

——. "Fault Lines of Transnationalism: Borders Matter." *Bulletin of the Royal Institute of Inter-faith Studies* 4, no. 2 (2002).

——. *Globalization or Empire?* New York: Routledge, 2004.

——. "The Long Nineteenth Century Is Too Short." *Victorian Studies* (Autumn 2005): 113–25.

——. "Oriental Globalization: Past and Present." Pp. 61–73 in *Europe and Asia beyond East and West,* edited by G. Delanty. London: Routledge, 2006.

——. *Ethnicities and Global Multiculture: Pants for an Octopus.* Lanham, MD: Rowman & Littlefield, 2007.

——. "Globalization the Next Round: Sociological Perspectives." *Futures* 40, no. 8 (2008a): 707–20.

——. *Is There Hope for Uncle Sam? Beyond the American Bubble.* London: Zed, 2008b.

——. "Multipolarity Means Thinking Plural: Modernities." *Protosociology* 26 (2009): 19–35.

——. *Development Theory: Deconstructions/Reconstructions.* London: Sage, 2010a.

——. "New Modernities: What's New?" Pp. 85–102 in *Decolonizing European Sociology: Transdisciplinary Approaches,* edited by M. Boatca et al. Aldershot, UK: Ashgate, 2010b.

——. "Global Rebalancing: Crisis and the East-South Turn." *Development and Change* 42, no. 1 (2011): 22–48.

——. "Twenty-First-Century Globalization: A New Development Era." *Forum for Development Studies* 39, no. 1 (2012a): 1–19.

——. "Periodizing Globalization: Histories of Globalization." *New Global Studies* 6, no. 2 (2012b): 1–25.

———. "Rethinking Modernity and Capitalism: Add Context and Stir." *Sociopedia Colloquium* (2014).

———. "Ancient Rome and Globalization: Decentring Rome." In *Globalisation and the Roman World*, edited by M. Pitts and M. J. Versluys. London: Cambridge University Press, 2015.

Nederveen Pieterse, J., and Bhikhu Parekh, eds. *The Decolonization of Imagination.* London: Zed, 1995.

Nederveen Pieterse, J., and B. Rehbein, eds. *Globalization and Emerging Societies: Development and Inequality.* London: Palgrave Macmillan, 2009.

Nelson, Benjamin. *On the Roads to Modernity.* Edited by T. E. Huff. Totowa, NJ: Rowman & Littlefield, 1981.

Neville-Sington, P., and D. Sington. *Paradise Dreamed.* London: Bloomsbury, 1993.

Obama, Barack. *Dreams from My Father: A Story of Race and Inheritance.* New York: Three Rivers Press, 1995.

O'Brien, Robert, A. M. Goetz, J. A. Scholte, and M. Williams. *Contesting Global Governance: Multilateral Economic Institutions and Global Social Movements.* Cambridge: Cambridge University Press, 2000.

O'Hearn, Denis. *Inside the Celtic Tiger: The Irish Economy and the Asian Model.* London: Pluto, 1998.

Ohmae, Kenichi. *The Borderless World: Power and Strategy in the Global Marketplace.* London: HarperCollins, 1992.

———. *The End of the Nation State: The Rise of Regional Economies.* New York: Free Press, 1995.

Okuda, Kazuhiko. "Transnationalism and the Meiji State: The Question of Cultural Borrowing." *Bulletin of the Royal Institute of Inter-faith Studies* 3, no. 2 (2001): 25–40.

Oliver, A., and K. Montgomery. "Creating a Hybrid Organizational Form from Parental Blueprints: The Emergence and Evolution of Knowledge Firms." *Human Relations* 53, no. 1 (2000).

Oman, Charles. *Globalisation and Regionalisation: The Challenge for Developing Countries.* Paris: OECD, 1994.

Orlean, Susan. "The Congo Sound: How a Record Store in Paris Became a Center of African Music." *New Yorker*, 14–21 October 2002: 114–20.

Ortiz, Renato. "From Incomplete Modernity to World Modernity." *Daedalus* 129, no. 1 (2000): 249–59.

Overholser, Greta. "Look at Tiger Woods and See the Face of America's Future." *International Herald Tribune*, 22 June 2000: 9.

Oza, Rupal. *The Making of Neoliberal India: Nationalism, Gender, and the Paradoxes of Globalization.* New Delhi: Women Unlimited, 2006.

Palan, Ronen, ed. *Global Political Economy: Contemporary Theories.* London: Routledge, 2000.

Pang, Laikwan. *Cultural Control and Globalization in Asia: Copyright, Piracy, and Cinema.* London: Routledge, 2006.

Papastergiadis, Nikos. "Tracing Hybridity in Theory." Pp. 257–81 in *Debating Cultural Hybridity*, edited by Pnina Werbner and Tariq Modood. London: Zed, 1997.

Parekh, Bhikhu. "The Cultural Particularity of Liberal Democracy." Pp. 156–75 in *Prospects for Democracy*, edited by D. Held. Cambridge: Polity, 1992.

———. "Being British." *Government and Opposition* 37, no. 3 (2002): 301–15.

Park, Sung-Jo, ed. *The 21st Century: The Asian Century?* Berlin: EXpress Edition, 1985.

Parry, Benita. "Problems in Current Theories of Colonial Discourse." *Oxford Literary Review* 9 (1987).

Paz, Octavio. *The Labyrinth of Solitude*. London: Allen Lane, 1967.

Peletz, M. *Islamic Modern: Religious Courts and Cultural Politics in Malaysia*. Princeton, NJ: Princeton University Press, 2002.

Peters Talbott, Shannon. "Analysis of Corporate Culture in the Global Marketplace: Case Study of McDonald's in Moscow." Paper presented at International Institute of Sociology Conference, Trieste, 1995.

Phillips, Mike. *London Crossings: A Biography of Black Britain*. London: Continuum, 2001.

Pickering, Andrew. *The Mangle of Practice: Time, Agency, and Science*. Chicago: University of Chicago Press, 1995.

Pitts, M., and M. J. Versluys, eds. *Globalisation and the Roman World: World History, Connectivity and Material Culture*. London: Cambridge University Press, 2015.

Pogge, Thomas. *World Poverty and Human Rights*. Oxford: Blackwell, 2002.

Pollock, Sheldon. "The Sanskrit Cosmopolis, 300–1300 CE: Transculturalization, Vernacularization, and the Question of Ideology." Pp. 197–248 in *Ideology and Status of Sanskrit*, edited by Jan E. M. Houben. Leiden: Brill, 1996.

———. "Cosmopolitan and Vernacular in History." *Public Culture* 12, no. 3 (2000): 591–626.

Pomeranz, Kenneth. *The Great Divergence: China, Europe, and the Making of the Modern World Economy*. Princeton, NJ: Princeton University Press, 2000.

Popper, Karl R. *The Open Society and Its Enemies*. 2 vols. Rev. ed. London: Routledge and Kegan Paul, 1966.

Portes, Alejandro, ed. *The Economic Sociology of Immigration*. New York: Russell Sage Foundation, 1995.

Pour Rushdie. Paris: Ed. La Découverte/Carrefour des Littératures/Colibri, 1993.

Povoledo, E. "Deadly Factory Fire Bares Racial Tensions in Italy." *New York Times International*, 8 December 2013.

Prahalad, C. K., and M. S. Krishnan. *The New Age of Innovation*. New York: McGraw-Hill, 2008.

Pratt, Mary Louise. "Where To? What Next?" Pp. 430–36 in *Cultures of Politics, Politics of Cultures: Re-visioning Latin American Social Movements*, edited by S. E. Alvarez et al. Boulder, CO: Westview Press, 1998.

Pred, Alan, and Michael J. Watts. *Reworking Modernity: Capitalisms and Symbolic Discontent*. New Brunswick, NJ: Rutgers University Press, 1992.

Qiang, Liang. "Geo-economic Strategy for Eurasia." *China Daily*, 19 June 2014.

Qingxin, Li. *Maritime Silk Road*. Beijing: China Intercontinental Press, 2006.

Quanlin, Qiu. "New Maritime Silk Road Supported." *China Daily*, 19 June 2014: 16.

Rabinovitch, S. "China Calls for 'Responsible' US." *Financial Times*, 12 July 2011: 2.

Radhakrishnan, R. *Diasporic Mediations*. Minneapolis: University of Minnesota Press, 1996.

Raghavan, Sudarsan. "Rocking the Subcontinent." *Newsweek*, 14 November 1994: 54–55.

Ram, Uri. "Liquid Identities: Mecca Cola versus Coca-Cola." *European Journal of Cultural Studies* 10, no. 4 (2007): 465–84.

Rao, Shakuntala. "The Globalization of Bollywood: An Ethnography of Non-elite Audiences in India." *Communication Review* 10, no. 1 (2007).

Rashid, Salim, ed. *"The Clash of Civilizations?" Asian Responses*. Karachi: Oxford University Press, 1997.

Räthzel, Nora. "Hybridität Ist Die Antwort, Aber Was War Noch Mal Die Frage?" Pp. 204–19 in *Gegen-Rassismen*, edited by Brigitte Kossek. Hamburg: Argument Verlag, 1999.

Ratnam, Niru. "Chris Ofili and the Limits of Hybridity." *New Left Review* 224 (1999): 153–59.

Ray, Larry. *Globalization and Everyday Life*. London: Routledge, 2007.

Reid, Anthony. *Southeast Asia and the Age of Commerce*. 2 vols. New Haven, CT: Yale University Press, 1993.

Richards, Paul. "Agrarian Creolization: The Ethnobiology, History, Culture and Politics of West African Rice." Pp. 291–318 in *Redefining Nature: Ecology, Culture and Domestication*, edited by R. Ellen and K. Fukui. Oxford: Berg, 1996.

Ritzer, George. *The McDonaldization of Society*. London: Sage, 1993.

———, ed. *McDonaldization: The Reader*. Thousand Oaks, CA: Pine Forge Press, 2002.

Roach, Stephen S. *The Next Asia: Opportunities and Challenges for a New Globalization*. Hoboken, NJ: John Wiley, 2009.

Roberts, B. *Cities of Peasants: The Political Economy of Urbanization in the Third World*. London: Edward Arnold, 1978.

Robertson, Robbie. *The Three Waves of Globalization: A History of a Developing Global Consciousness*. London: Zed, 2003.

Robertson, Roland. *Globalization: Social Theory and Global Culture*. London: Sage, 1992.

———. "Glocalization: Space, Time and Social Theory." *Journal of International Communication* 1, no. 1 (1994).

Robison, Richard, and David S. G. Goodman. *The New Rich in Asia*. London: Routledge, 1996.

Rockwell, John. "Keeping the National in International." *New York Times*, 19 January 2003: AR32.

Rodriguez, Richard. *Brown: The Last Discovery of America*. New York: Viking, 2002.

Rosenau, James N. *Turbulence in World Politics*. Brighton: Harvester, 1990.

Rosenau, James N., and E. O. Czempiel. *Governance without Government*. Cambridge: Cambridge University Press, 1992.

Rowe, William, and Vivian Schelling. *Memory and Modernity: Popular Culture in Latin America*. London: Verso, 1991.

Ruigrok, W., and R. van Tulder. *The Logic of International Restructuring*. London: Routledge, 1995.

Ruijter, Arie de. *Hybridization and Governance*. The Hague: Institute of Social Studies, 1996.

Russell, Bertrand. *Power: A New Social Analysis*. New York: Norton, 1938.

Sachs, Jeffrey. "International Economics: Unlocking the Mysteries of Globalization." *Foreign Policy* 110 (1998): 97–111.

Said, Edward W. *Culture and Imperialism*. New York: Alfred A. Knopf, 1993.

Samman, Khaldoun. *Cities of God and Nationalism: Mecca, Jerusalem, and Rome as Contested World Cities*. Boulder, CO: Paradigm, 2007.

Sardar, Zia, and B. van Loon. *Cultural Studies for Beginners*. Duxford, UK: Icon Books, 1997.

Sassen, Saskia. *The Global City: New York, London, Tokyo*. Princeton, NJ: Princeton University Press, 1991.

Schech, Susanne, and Jane Haggis. *Culture and Development: A Critical Introduction*. Oxford: Blackwell, 2000.

Schiller, Herbert I. *Culture Inc*. New York: Oxford University Press, 1989.

Schirmer, Dominique, Gernot Saalmann, and Christl Kessler, eds. *Hybridising East and West*. Muenster: LIT Verlag, 2006.

Schlosser, Eric. *Fast Food Nation: The Dark Side of the All-American Meal*. New York: HarperPerennial, 2002.

Scholte, Jan Aart. *Globalization: A Critical Introduction*. London: Macmillan, 2000.

Schwartzel, E., and L. Burkitt. "'Transformers' Script: Lights! Cameras! China!" *Wall Street Journal*, 27 June 2014: D1.

Seagrave, S. *Lords of the Rim*. London: Corgi Books, 1996.

Shahanan, S. "Different Standards and Standard Differences: Contemporary Citizenship and Immigration Debates." *Theory and Society* 26 (1997): 421–48.

Sharabi, Hisham. *Neopatriarchy: A Theory of Distorted Change in Arab Society*. New York: Oxford University Press, 1988.

Shattuck, R. *The Banquet Years: The Origins of the Avant-Garde in France*. Rev. ed. New York: Vintage, 1967.

Shaw, Martin. "Global Society and Global Responsibility: The Theoretical, Historical and Political Limits of 'International Society.'" *Millennium* 21, no. 3 (1992): 421–34.

Shaw, Timothy. "Ethnicity as the Resilient Paradigm for Africa: From the 1960s to the 1980s." *Development and Change* 17, no. 4 (1986): 587–606.

Shirk, Susan L. *China: Fragile Superpower*. New York: Oxford University Press, 2008.

Shohat, Ella. "Notes on the 'Post-Colonial.'" *Social Text* 31/32 (1992): 99–113.

Shohat, Ella, and Robert Stam. *Unthinking Eurocentrism: Multiculturalism and the Media*. New York: Routledge, 1994.

Shone, Tom. "Hollywood Transformed." *Financial Times*, 26–27 July 2014: 1–2.

Siebers, Hans. "Creolization and Modernization at the Periphery: The Case of the Q'Eqchi'es of Guatemala." Catholic University Nijmegen, Ph.D. diss., 1996.

Silva, Neluka, ed. *The Hybrid Island: Culture Crossings and the Invention of Identity in Sri Lanka*. London: Zed, 2002.

Simone, T. Abdou Maliqalim. *In Whose Image: Political Islam and Urban Practices in Sudan*. Chicago: University of Chicago Press, 1994.

Singh, Yogendra. *Essays on Modernization in India*. New Delhi: Manohar, 1989.

Sirkin, Harold L., James W. Hemerling, and A. K. Bhattacharya. *Globality: Competing with Everyone from Everywhere for Everything*. New York: Business Plus, 2008.

Sivanandan, A. "Globalism and the Left." *Race and Class* 40, nos. 2/3 (1998): 5–18.

Skolimowski, Henrik. *The Participatory Mind*. London: Penguin/Arkana, 1994.

Smart, Barry, ed. *Resisting McDonaldization*. London: Sage, 1999.

Smith, Anthony D. "Towards a Global Culture?" Pp. 171–92 in *Global Culture*, edited by Mike Featherstone. London: Sage, 1990.

Smith, Craig S. "The Market McDonald's Missed: The Muslim Burger." *New York Times*, 16 September 2005.

Sonoda, S. "Modernization of Asian Countries as a Process of 'Overcoming Their Backwardness': The Case of Modernization in China." Paper presented at the Twelfth World Congress of the International Sociological Association, Madrid, 1990.

Soros, George. *The Crisis of Global Capitalism*. New York: PublicAffairs, 1998.

———. *On Globalization*. New York: PublicAffairs, 2002.

Sowell, Thomas. *Migrations and Culture*. New York: Basic Books, 1996.

Stallings, Barbara, ed. *Global Change, Regional Response: The New International Context of Development*. Cambridge: Cambridge University Press, 1995.

Steger, Manfred B. *Globalism: The New Market Ideology*. Lanham, MD: Rowman & Littlefield, 2002.

———. *Globalization: A Very Short Introduction*. Oxford: Oxford University Press, 2003.

Stein, Joel. "The Hungry American." *Time*, 9 April 2007: 116.

Stevens, Harm. *De VOC in bedrijf, 1602–1799*. Amsterdam: Walburg Pers, 1998.

Stojkovic, Stan, John Klofas, and David B. Kalinich, eds. *The Administration and Management of Criminal Justice Organizations: A Book of Readings*. 3rd ed. Prospect Heights, IL: Waveland Press, 1999.

Storper, Michael. "Lived Effects of the Contemporary Economy: Globalization, Inequality and Consumer Society." Pp. 88–124 in *Millennial Capitalism*, edited by J. Comaroff and J. L. Comaroff. Durham, NC: Duke University Press, 2001.

Strange, Susan. *The Retreat of the State*. Cambridge: Cambridge University Press, 1996.

Studwell, Joe. *How Asia Works*. London: Profile, 2013.

Subrahmanyam, Sanjay. "Connected Histories: Notes towards a Reconfiguration of Early Modern Eurasia." *Modern Asian Studies* 31, no. 3 (1997): 735–62.

———. "Hearing Voices: Vignettes of Early Modernity in South Asia, 1400–1750." *Daedalus* 127, no. 3 (1998): 75–104.

Subramanyan, K. G. *The Living Tradition: Perspectives on Modern Indian Art*. Calcutta: Seagull, 1987.

Sugiyama, Jiro. "From Chang'an to Rome: Transformation of Buddhist Culture." Pp. 55–60 in *The Significance of the Silk Roads in the History of Human Civilizations*. Osaka: National Museum of Ethnology, 1992.

Sutcliffe, Bob. *100 Ways of Seeing an Unequal World*. London: Zed, 2001.

Taguieff, P.-A. *La force du préjugé: Essai sur le racisme et ses doubles*. Paris: 1987.

Tam, Pui-Wing. "Mandarin Pop Swings into U.S." *Wall Street Journal Europe*, 3 April 2000: 31.

Tamayo Lott, J. *Asian Americans: From Racial Category to Multiple Identities*. London: Sage and Altamira Press, 1997.

Tan, Yinglan. *Chinnovation: How Chinese Innovators Are Changing the World*. Hoboken, NJ: Wiley, 2011.

Tao, Gui, and Zhang Chongfang. "Opportunities Bloom on New Silk Road." *China Daily*, 2 July 2014: 7.

Taylor, Jean G. *The Social World of Batavia: European and Eurasian Dutch in Asia*. Madison: University of Wisconsin Press, 1983.

Taylor, S., and P. Lyon. "Paradigm Lost: The Rise and Fall of McDonaldization." *International Journal of Contemporary Hospitality Management* 7, nos. 2–3 (1995): 64–68.

Teggart, F. *Rome and China: A Study of Correlations in Historical Events*. Berkeley: University of California Press, 1939.

Terhal, P. H. J. J. *World Inequality and Evolutionary Convergence*. Delft: Eburon, 1987.

Therborn, Göran. "Routes to/through Modernity." Pp. 125–39 in *Global Modernities*, edited by Mike Featherstone et al. London: Sage, 1995.

Thompson, Damian. *The End of Time: Faith and Fear in the Shadow of the Millennium*. London: Sinclair-Stevenson, 1996.

Thompson, Denise P. "Skin Deep: Citizenship, Inclusion and Entitlements for the 'Dark'-Skinned Woman in Jamaica." Institute of Social Studies, The Hague, MA thesis, 1999.

Thompson, Robert Faris. *Flash of the Spirit: African and Afro-American Art and Philosophy*. New York: Vintage, 1984.

Thompson, William R., ed. *Evolutionary Interpretations of World Politics*. New York: Routledge, 2001.

Tian, Wei. "Firms Moving up Fortune's Ladder." *China Daily*, 9 July 2014: 13.

Tiryakian, Edward A. "Modernization: Exhumetur in Pace." *International Sociology* 6, no. 2 (1991): 165–80.

———. "Three Metacultures of Modernity: Christian, Gnostic, Chthonic." *Theory, Culture and Society* 13, no. 1 (1996): 99–118.

Tominaga, K. "A Theory of Modernization of Non-Western Societies: Toward a Generalization from Historical Experiences of Japan." Paper presented at the Twelfth World Congress of the International Sociological Association, Madrid, 1990.

Tomlinson, John. *Cultural Imperialism*. Baltimore: Johns Hopkins University Press, 1991.

———. *Globalization and Culture*. Chicago: University of Chicago Press, 1999.

Torpey, John. *The Invention of the Passport: Surveillance, Citizenship and the State*. Cambridge: Cambridge University Press, 2000.

Toulmin, Stephen. "The Ambiguities of Globalization." *Futures* 31, nos. 9/10 (1999): 905–12.

Twine, France Winddance. *A White Side of Black Britain: Interracial Intimacy and Racial Literacy*. Durham, NC: Duke University Press, 2011.

Tyrrell, Heather. "Bollywood versus Hollywood: Battle of the Dream Factories." Pp. 327–34 in *Globalization Reader*, edited by F. L. Lechner and J. Boli. Malden, MA: Blackwell, 2008.

UNDP. *Human Development Report*. New York: Oxford University Press, 1999.

Uzzi, Brian. "The Sources and Consequences of Embeddedness for the Economic Performance of Organizations: The Network Effect." *American Sociological Review* 61 (1996): 674–98.

Van Hear, Nicholas. *New Diasporas*. Seattle: University of Washington Press, 1998.

Vargas, Virginia. "The Feminist Movement in Latin America: Between Hope and Disenchantment." Pp. 195–214 in *Emancipations, Modern and Postmodern*, edited by J. Nederveen Pieterse. London: Sage, 1992.

Vasconcelos, José. *La Raza Cosmica*. Mexico: Espasa-Calpe Mexicana, 1948. [Vasconcelos, José, with Didiet Tisde Jaen, *The Cosmic Race*. Baltimore: Johns Hopkins University Press, 1997.]

Vebhiu, Ardian. "Albanian Migration and Media." Amsterdam, unpublished paper, 1999.

Volkan, V. D., and N. Itzkowitz. *Turks and Greeks: Neighbours in Conflict*. Huntingdon, UK: Etheon Press, 1994.

Vukovich, Daniel F. *China and Orientalism: Western Knowledge Production and the P.R.C.* New York: Routledge, 2012.

Wachtel, Howard M. *The Money Mandarins: The Making of a Supranational Economic Order*. Armonk, NY: M. E. Sharpe, 1990.

Wallerstein, Immanuel M. *Geopolitics and Geoculture*. Cambridge: Cambridge University Press, 1991.

Wang, Jing. *High Culture Fever: Politics, Aesthetics, and Ideology in Deng's China*. Berkeley: University of California Press, 1996.

Wang Hui. *China's New Order*. Cambridge, MA: Harvard University Press, 2003.

———. *The End of the Revolution: China and the Limits of Modernity*. London: Verso, 2009.

Warde, A. "Eating Globally: Cultural Flows and the Spread of Ethnic Restaurants." Pp. 299–316 in *The Ends of Globalization: Bringing Society Back In*, edited by D. Kalb et al. Lanham, MD: Rowman & Littlefield, 2000.

Washbrook, David. "From Comparative Sociology to Global History: Britain and India in the Pre-history of Modernity." *Journal of the Economic and Social History of the Orient* 40, no. 4 (1997): 410–43.

Waters, Malcolm. *Globalization*. London: Routledge, 1995.

Waters, R. "Microsoft Unveils Hybrid Computing Platform." *Financial Times*, 23 April 2008: 17.

Watson, James L. *Golden Arches East: McDonald's in East Asia*. Stanford, CA: Stanford University Press, 1997.

Wee, C. W.-L. "Framing the 'New' East Asia: Anti-imperialist Discourse and Global Capitalism." Pp. 75–97 in *"The Clash of Civilizations?"* edited by S. Rashid. Karachi: Oxford University Press, 1997.

Weiss, Linda. *The Myth of the Powerless State*. Ithaca, NY: Cornell University Press, 1998.

Wen Jiabao. "How China Plans to Reinforce the Global Recovery." *Financial Times*, 24 June 2011: 9.

Werbner, Pnina. "Introduction: The Dialectics of Cultural Hybridity." Pp. 1–26 in *Debating Cultural Hybridity*, edited by Pnina Werbner and Tariq Modood. London: Zed, 1997.

Werbner, Pnina, and Tariq Modood, eds. *Debating Cultural Hybridity*. London: Zed, 1997.

Whatmore, Sarah. *Hybrid Geographies: Natures, Cultures, Spaces*. London: Sage, 2002.

Whitten, N. E., Jr., and A. Torres. "Blackness in the Americas." *Report on the Americas* 25, no. 4 (1992): 16–22.

Wildt, M. "Prosecco Tries to Catch the Champagne Wave." *International Herald Tribune*, 23 July 2008: 9.

Will, George. "Race, Now an Anachronism." *San Francisco Chronicle*, 5 May 2003.

Williams, C. A. S. *Outlines of Chinese Symbolism and Art Motives*. 3rd ed. Rutland, VT: Charles E. Tuttle, 1974.

Williams, P., and D. Vlassis. *Migrations and Transnational Organized Crime*. London: Sage, 1997.

Willis, David Blake. "Creole Times: Notes on Understanding Creolization for Transnational Japan-America." Pp. 3–40 in *The Age of Creolization in the Pacific*, edited by Takeshi Matsuda. Hiroshima: Keisuisha, 2001a.

——. "Pacific Creoles: The Power of Hybridity in Japanese-American Relations." Pp. 169–214 in *The Age of Creolization in the Pacific*, edited by Takeshi Matsuda. Hiroshima: Keisuisha, 2001b.

Willis, David B., and Stephen Murphy-Shigematsu, eds. *Transcultural Japan: At the Borderlands of Race, Gender, and Identity*. New York: Routledge, 2008.

Wilson, Fiona. "Indians and Mestizos: Identity and Urban Popular Culture in Andean Peru." *Journal of Southern African Studies* 26, no. 2 (2000): 239–53.

Wilson, Rob, and Wimal Dissanayake, eds. *Global/Local: Cultural Production and the Transnational Imaginary*. Durham, NC: Duke University Press, 1996.

Wittfogel, Karl A. *Oriental Despotism: A Comparative Study of Total Power*. New Haven, CT: Yale University Press, 1957.

Wittkower, Rudolf. *Allegory and the Migration of Symbols*. London: Thames and Hudson, 1977.

——. *The Impact of Non-European Civilizations on the Art of the West*. Edited by D. M. Reynolds. Cambridge: Cambridge University Press, 1989.

Wolters, Hester, ed. *Nederland/Indonesia, 1945–1995. Een culture vervlechting. Suatu Pertalian Budaya*. The Hague: Zoo Produkties, 1995.

Woods, Ngaire, ed. *The Political Economy of Globalization*. New York: St. Martin's Press, 2000.

World Commission on Culture and Development. *Our Creative Diversity*. Paris: UNESCO, 1996.

Xin, Chen. "New Development of Consumerism in Chinese Society in the Late 1990s." Pp. 162–75 in *Asian Exchange: China Reflected*, 18, 2, and 19, 1, edited by Lau Kin Chi and Huang Ping (2003).

Yan, Yunxiang. "Managing Cultural Conflicts: State Power and Alternative Globalization in China." *Art Today* 15 (2008): 131–44.

Yang, Kristine. "Blockbuster Era for Asian Films." *China Daily*, 18 July 2014: 8.

Yang, Jeff, Dina Gan, Terry Hong, and staff of *A. Magazine. Eastern Standard Time: A Guide to Asian Influence on American Culture from Astro Boy to Zen Buddhism*. Boston: Houghton Mifflin, 1997.

Yiping, Zhang. *Story of the Silk Road*. Beijing: China Intercontinental Press, 2005.

Yoo, Jin-Kyung. *Korean Immigrant Entrepreneurs: Network and Ethnic Resources*. New York: Garland, 1998.

Yoshino, Kosaku. *Cultural Nationalism in Contemporary Japan*. London: Routledge, 1995.

Young, Iris Marion. *Justice and the Politics of Difference*. Princeton, NJ: Princeton University Press, 1990.

Young, Robert C. *Colonial Desire: Hybridity in Theory, Culture, and Race*. London: Routledge, 1995.

Yuanqing, Sun. "Standoff in the Sand." *China Daily*, 20 June 2014: 18–19.

Zachary, G. P. *The Global Me*. New York: Barnes and Noble, 2000.

Zakaria, Fareed. *The Post-American World*. New York: Norton, 2008.

Zhang Qizhi, ed. *Traditional Chinese Culture*. Beijing: Foreign Languages Press, 2004.

Zhao, Gang. "Reinventing China: Imperial Qing Ideology and the Rise of Modern Chinese National Identity in the Early Twentieth Century." *Modern China* 32, no 1 (2006): 3–30.

Žižek, Slavoj. "Multiculturalism or the Cultural Logic of Multinational Capitalism." *New Left Review* 225 (1997).

INDEX

ABOUT THE AUTHOR

Jan Nederveen Pieterse is Mellichamp Professor of Global Studies and Sociology at the University of California, Santa Barbara. His research interests include globalization, development studies, and cultural studies. He was previously at Maastricht University; University of Illinois, Urbana-Champaign; Institute of Social Studies, The Hague; University of Cape Coast, Ghana; and University of Amsterdam. He holds the Pok Rafeah research chair at the National University of Malaysia (2014–2015). He has been visiting professor in Argentina, Brazil, China, Germany, France, India, Indonesia, Japan, Pakistan, South Africa, Sri Lanka, Sweden, and Thailand, and has lectured around the world. He is the author or editor of twenty-two books. He is associate editor of the *European Journal of Social Theory*, *Ethnicities*, *Third Text*, *Encounters*, and the *Canadian Journal of Development Studies*. He edits book series with Routledge (Emerging Societies) and Palgrave Macmillan

(Frontiers of Globalization) and has co-organized seven Global Studies conferences. He is a fellow of the World Academy of Art and Science.

* * *

Also by Jan Nederveen Pieterse

*Empire and Emancipation: Power and Liberation on a
World Scale* (1989)
*White on Black: Images of Africa and Blacks in Western
Popular Culture* (1992)
Development Theory: Deconstructions/Reconstructions (2001, 2010)
Globalization or Empire? (2004)
Ethnicities and Global Multiculture (2007)
Is There Hope for Uncle Sam? Beyond the American Bubble (2008)
*Globalization, Development and Emerging Economies: Welcome to the
Multipolar World* (2015)